by
Kathleen M. Harmeyer

AGS®
American Guidance Service, Inc.
Circle Pines, Minnesota 55014-1796

About the Author

Kathleen M. Harmeyer received her B.S. in Mathematics from Towson State University and M.S. in Computer Science from Johns Hopkins University. She has taught mathematics to students in junior and senior high schools as well as to adults. As a mathematics specialist for the Maryland State Department of Education, Ms. Harmeyer assisted in the development of the objectives for the Maryland Functional Mathematics test. Kathleen Harmeyer has taught for the Baltimore County Public Schools, University of Maryland, General Instrument Corporation, and Computer Entry Systems.

As current president of ExperTech, a multimedia training company, Ms. Harmeyer produces educational programs with the application of appropriate technology. In addition to this textbook, she is the author of several journal articles on training.

Consultants

Donald H. Jacobs, M.Ed.
Mathematics Teacher
Baltimore City Public Schools
Baltimore, Maryland

Bert Miller, Ph.D.
Mathematics Teacher, Baltimore County Public Schools, Towson, Maryland
Instructor in Mathematics, Baltimore, Maryland
Essex Community College
Catonsville Community College
Community College of Baltimore

Printed in the United States of America

ISBN 0-88671-507-5 (Previously ISBN 0-7916-0088-2)

Order Number: 80120

A 0 9 8 7 6

CONTENTS

CHAPTER 1

EARNING MONEY

People are paid money for doing work. They may be paid an hourly rate, a piecework rate, or a salary. They may receive overtime pay, tips, or commission. In this chapter you will learn mathematical skills helpful for figuring both gross and net earnings.

WAGES

Many people are paid a certain amount of money for each hour they work. This amount of money is called the *hourly rate*. A regular work week is usually 40 hours. The money received on payday is called *wages*.

Example: Ernie worked 40 hours at an hourly rate of $4.89. What were his wages?

Multiply $4.89 by 40.

$4.89   Hourly rate
x   40   Hours
$195.60   Wages

Exercise A: Find the weekly wages for these people.

Employee	Hourly Rate	Hours Worked
1) Ima Worker	$5.00	40
2) Earl E. Byrd	$4.56	38
3) I. C. Cash	$7.50	40
4) R. U. Paid	$8.95	40
5) I. M. Wealthy	$10.57	37
6) N. E. Bank	$6.13	39
7) Bea Rich	$9.22	40
8) Penny Ernd	$9.56	40
9) Willy Urn	$3.92	35
10) Woody Work	$7.87	40

ANNUAL WAGES

The amount of money earned during a full year is called *annual wages*. To *estimate* an employee's annual wages, first multiply the number of hours worked each week by the number of weeks he or she works in a year. Then multiply the result by the hourly rate.

There are 52 weeks in a year. To allow for unpaid vacations and absences, you can estimate with only 50 weeks. Forty hours multiplied by 50 is 2,000 hours. You multiply the hourly rate by 2,000 hours.

Example: Estimate the annual wages of Lotta Coins. She earns $6.00 an hour.
$6.00 x 2,000 = $12,000.00 estimated annual wages

Exercise A: Estimate the annual wages for these people.

Employee	Hourly Rate	Employee	Hourly Rate
1) Rod Creel	$4.50	2) Jim E. Free	$6.33
3) Leroy King	$7.50	4) Rose Busch	$9.75
5) Tony Legg	$4.15	6) Dusty Golden	$5.25
7) Millard Drake	$8.98	8) Lillie Whyte	$6.75
9) Ann Ewell	$4.15	10) S. Tim Ate	$5.65

TIME WORKED

Employees' wages are based on the time that they spend on the job. In these problems, note that *a.m.* refers to morning; *p.m.* refers to afternoon.

Example: Manny Bucks arrived at work at 9:00 a.m. He went out for lunch at 12:00 noon. He returned at 1:00 and worked until 5:00 p.m. How many hours did Manny work?

Step 1: Find the a.m. time and the p.m. time. Subtract the earlier time from the later time.

12:00	noon (later time)		5:00	p.m. (later time)
- 9:00	a.m. (earlier time)		- 1:00	p.m. (earlier time)
3:00	= 3 hours, 0 minutes		4:00	= 4 hours, 0 minutes

Step 2: Find the total number of hours worked. Add the a.m. time and the p.m. time together.

3 hours and 0 minutes
+ 4 hours and 0 minutes
7 hours and 0 minutes   Manny worked 7 hours.

Exercise A: Find the number of hours worked by each person.

	Employee	a.m.		p.m.	
		In	Out	In	Out
1)	George	7:00	11:00	1:00	4:00
2)	Bertha	9:00	12:00	1:00	5:00
3)	Ann	8:00	12:30	1:00	4:30
4)	Lee	6:00	11:00	2:00	6:00
5)	Kim	10:00	12:00	1:00	5:30
6)	Juan	9:00	12:30	2:00	7:30
7)	Charles	8:30	12:30	1:30	5:30
8)	Richard	7:30	11:30	1:00	6:00

The later time might need to be renamed before you can subtract the earlier time from it. Study the following example of *renaming hours*. Notice the abbreviations of *hr.* for hours and *min.* for minutes.

Example: Grace began work at 8:30 a.m. She went to lunch at 12:00. How many hours did Grace work before lunch?

a.m. — Morning

$$
\begin{array}{rl}
& \quad\quad \overset{11}{\;} \;\; \overset{60}{\;} \\
12:00 & \text{Rename 1 hour} \; \rightarrow \; \cancel{12:00} \\
- 8:30 & \text{to 60 minutes} \quad\quad - 8:30 \\
& \quad\quad\quad\quad\quad\quad\quad 3:30 \; = 3 \text{ hr. } 30 \text{ min.}
\end{array}
$$

After lunch, Grace returned to work at 1:45 and worked until 6:15 p.m. How long did Grace work in the afternoon?

p.m. — Afternoon

$$
\begin{array}{rl}
& \quad\quad\quad \overset{5}{\;} \;\; \overset{75}{\;} \\
6:15 & \text{Rename 1 hour to} \; \rightarrow \; \cancel{6:15} \\
- 1:45 & \text{60 minutes. Add} \quad - 1:45 \\
& \text{those 60 minutes} \quad\; 4:30 \; = 4 \text{ hr. } 30 \text{ min.} \\
& \text{to the 15 minutes.}
\end{array}
$$

Exercise B: For each time below, rename one hour to 60 minutes. Add those 60 minutes to the existing minutes.

2 hours + 60 minutes + 15 minutes

Example: 3:15 = 3̶:̶1̶5̶ = 2 hr. 75 min.

1) 4:10	2) 10:20
3) 11:30	4) 1:30
5) 2:45	6) 12:15
7) 6:40	8) 5:50
9) 2:05	10) 3:35
11) 7:25	12) 9:55

Example: Fred worked from 12:15 p.m. to 5:15 p.m. How many hours did he work?

    5:15   We cannot subtract.

  - 12:15   The 5 must be renamed.

The twelve hours on a clock are used two times during any one 24-hour day. You can add the twelve morning hours to 5:15. (12 + 5:15 = 17:15) Note that 5:15 in the afternoon is the same as 17:15. Now you can subtract.

                      17:15

  5:15   Add 12 hours → ~~5:15~~

- 12:15   - 12:15

                    5:00 = 5 hours and 0 minutes

To find the total hours worked in a day, add the morning hours to the afternoon hours.

Example: Ralph worked 3 hours and 45 minutes in the morning and 4 hours and 30 minutes in the afternoon. How long did he work?

      3 hours and 45 minutes

   + 4 hours and 30 minutes

      7 hours and 75 minutes   (Rename 75 min. to 1 hr., 15 min.)

 or 8 hours and 15 minutes

Exercise C: How long did each person work?

Employee	a.m.	p.m.
1) Thomas	3 hr. 30 min.	4 hr. 30 min.
2) Lucille	4 hr. 15 min.	3 hr. 30 min.
3) Reed	6 hr. 45 min.	1 hr. 30 min.
4) Joan	2 hr. 45 min.	5 hr. 15 min.

Exercise D: Find the number of hours each employee worked each day. Then find the total hours for the week.

1. Bea Busy

Day	a.m. In	a.m. Out	p.m. In	p.m. Out	Daily Hours
Mon.	8:00	11:30	12:30	5:40	8:40
Tues.	7:45	11:45	12:15	4:30	8 15
Wed.	8:00	11:30	12:15	5:30	8 45
Thurs.	7:30	11:00	12:30	4:45	7 45
Fri.	8:30	12:00	1:30	6:00	8

Total Hours for the Week: ___41.25___

2. E. Garbeever

Day	a.m. In	a.m. Out	p.m. In	p.m. Out	Daily Hours
Mon.	7:00	11:30	12:30	5:30	9 30
Tues.	6:45	11:30	12:30	5:15	9 30
Wed.	6:30	11:00	12:00	4:30	9
Thurs.	7:00	11:45	12:45	5:00	9
Fri.	7:15	12:00	1:15	5:30	9

Total Hours for the Week: ___46___

OVERTIME

People paid by the hour are paid extra if they work over 40 hours during a week or if they work on holidays. *Time and a half* means one and one-half, or 1.5, times the regular hourly rate. *Double time* means two times the regular hourly rate. Time and a half is usually paid for overtime on regular work days, Monday through Saturday. Double time is usually paid for working on Sundays and holidays.

Example: Susie earns $6.00 per hour. What are her overtime rates?

Time and a Half	Double Time
$6.00	$6.00
x 1.5	x 2
3000	$12.00
600	
$9.00~~0~~	

Susie's time and a half rate is $9.00. Her double time rate is $12.00.

Exercise A: Complete the chart below. Find the time and a half rate and the double time rate for each hourly rate. Do not round any answers.

	Overtime Rates	
Hourly Rate	Time and a Half	Double Time
1) $4.00	_____	_____
2) $5.00	_____	_____
3) $8.96	_____	_____
4) $10.78	_____	_____
5) $6.50	_____	_____
6) $8.14	_____	_____
7) $9.75	_____	_____
8) $7.25	_____	_____

Exercise B: Time card information for twenty workers is given in the chart below. Add to find each person's total hours. Then find the number of regular hours and overtime hours, if any. Remember that *overtime* hours are those worked beyond a standard day (8 hours) or week (40 hours).

Hours Worked Each Day							Total Hours	Regular Hours	Overtime Hours	
									Time and a Half	Double Time
M	T	W	T	F	S	S	a	b	c	d
1) 8	8	8	9	8	0	0	___	___	___	___
2) 8	8	7	9	8	0	0	___	___	___	___
3) 10	8	9	8	0	0	10	___	___	___	___
4) 8	9	8	8	8	0	3	___	___	___	___
5) 10	9	9	9	9	6	5	___	___	___	___
6) 8	9	8	9	8	0	4	___	___	___	___
7) 8	8	8	8	8	8	8	___	___	___	___
8) 8	9	8	10	0	5	3	___	___	___	___
9) 10	10	10	10	0	10	10	___	___	___	___
10) 8	8	9	6	9	8	8	___	___	___	___

The following people worked on Monday, July 4.
They earned double time for this holiday.

11) 8	8	8	8	8	0	0	___	___	___	___
12) 8	8	9	8	8	2	0	___	___	___	___
13) 10	8	8	8	8	0	0	___	___	___	___
14) 8	9	8	9	8	0	0	___	___	___	___
15) 8	8	8	8	8	8	8	___	___	___	___
16) 8	10	7	8	8	0	0	___	___	___	___
17) 10	8	8	8	8	0	0	___	___	___	___
18) 8	9	8	8	8	5	0	___	___	___	___
19) 8	8	8	8	9	10	5	___	___	___	___
20) 8	8	8	8	8	0	6	___	___	___	___

REGULAR WAGES PLUS OVERTIME

Employees who work both regular hours and overtime may compute their total wages by using subtraction, multiplication, and addition.

Example: Penny worked 43 hours at an hourly rate of $6.24. She was paid time and a half for her overtime. What were her total wages?

Step 1: 43 hours - 40 hours = 3 hours overtime

Step 2:

```
   $6.24     Hourly rate
 x    40     Regular hours
 $249.60     Regular wages
```

Step 3:

```
   $6.24   Hourly rate
 x  1.5    Time and a half
   3120
    624
 $9.36Ø    Overtime rate
```

Step 4:

```
   $9.36    Overtime rate
 x     3    Overtime hours
  $28.08    Overtime wages
```

Step 5:

```
 $249.60   Regular wages
 + 28.08   Overtime wages
 $277.68   Total wages
```

Exercise A: Find total wages. Use time and a half to compute overtime wages.

	Hours Worked	Regular Hours	Overtime Hours	Hourly Rate
1)	42	_____	_____	$4.50
2)	45	_____	_____	$7.80
3)	50	_____	_____	$8.20
4)	31	_____	_____	$6.70
5)	46	_____	_____	$10.00
6)	45	_____	_____	$5.18
7)	48	_____	_____	$9.76
8)	55	_____	_____	$8.94

Exercise B: Compute the total wages for each person described below.

1) Eleanor earns $8.50 per hour. She worked 45 hours from Monday to Friday.

2) Sam earns $6.00 per hour. He worked 40 regular hours and 5 hours on Sunday.

3) Kim earns $9.75 per hour. She worked 32 regular hours and 8 hours on Memorial Day.

4) Keith earns $10.42 per hour. He worked 43 hours from Monday to Friday and 6 hours on Sunday.

5) Bill earns $5 per hour. He worked 40 hours at the regular rate, 2 hours at time and a half, and 3 hours at double time.

6) Roberto earns $6.50 per hour. He worked 32 hours at the regular rate, 8 hours at time and a half, and 8 hours at double time.

7) Larisa earns $4 per hour. She worked 40 hours at the regular rate, 3 hours at time and a half, and 6 hours at double time.

8) Sung Loo worked 54 hours during a special sale at the store. Ten hours were at time and a half, and 4 hours were at double time. Her regular rate was $4.86.

9) After 40 hours of regular time, Rosemary worked 7 hours on a holiday. Her regular rate was $5.98.

10) Ben put in 60 hours at the clock store. The first 40 were paid at $9.55. The remainder was paid at time and a half.

CONSUMER HUMOR

Did you hear that John lost his job at the orange juice plant?

Yes, I understand that he couldn't concentrate.

TIPS

Some workers receive extra money from people who appreciate good service. This money is called a *tip*. Examples of workers who are tipped include waiters, waitresses, cab drivers, porters, and hairdressers.

Example: Alice is a waitress and earns $4.00 an hour. In one week she earned $250 in tips while she worked 40 hours. Find her total income for the week.

$4.00	Hourly rate	$160.00	Regular wages
x 40	Hours	+ 250.00	Tips
$160.00	Regular wages	$410.00	Total income

Alice's total income for the week was $410.00.

Exercise A: Solve these problems.

1) Jon waits on tables and is paid $3.50 an hour. In a 40-hour period, he earned $210.50 in tips. What were his total earnings?

2) Fred, a skycap at the airport, is paid $4.50 per hour. During an 8-hour shift, he averages $40 in tips. About how much does he earn per day?

3) Helene, who drives a cab, is paid $150 per week. She averages $20 per day in tips. About how much does she earn per week?

4) Carla, a hairdresser, received these tips one day: $1.00, $1.50, $2.00, $2.00, $1.50, $1.75, $2.00, $5.00, $1.00, $1.50, $2.00, $1.00, $5.00, and $2.00. What was the total of these tips?

5) Biff is a porter and earns $2.00 an hour. He averages about $6 per hour in tips. About how much does he earn in a 40-hour week?

PIECEWORK

Some people are paid by *piecework;* that is, according to the number of pieces or units of work that they complete. For example, a garment worker may be paid by a rate for the number of collars or cuffs completed in a given day.

Example: Bob Inn works at a garment factory and sews buttons on shirts. For each shirt he completes that passes inspection, he earns $ .24. How much does he earn for 200 good shirts?

$ .24   Piece rate
x 200   Number of shirts
$48.00   Wages

Bob Inn earns $48.00 for 200 good shirts.

Exercise A: Find the wages for each employee.

	Employee	Items Completed	Piece Rate	Wages
1)	A. Brocher	154	$.19	___
2)	B. Verdienen	189	$.09	___
3)	C. Gagner	217	$.08	___
4)	D. Vetements	179	$.12	___
5)	E. Geld	188	$.17	___
6)	F. Shue	305	$.07	___
7)	G. Belt	147	$.26	___
8)	H. Hemm	98	$.37	___
9)	I. Soo	156	$.08	___
10)	J. Blouson	178	$.13	___
11)	K. Vest	197	$.16	___
12)	L. Sox	139	$.21	___
13)	M. Seams	197	$.15	___
14)	N. Snap	204	$.15	___
15)	O. Kay	189	$.27	___

Example: Sue A. Seam stitches complete vests. She made 10 vests on Monday, 12 on Tuesday, 9 on Wednesday, 11 on Thursday, and 15 on Friday. She is paid $5.79 for each completed vest. How much did Sue earn during this week?

Step 1: Add to find the total number of vests.

10	Monday
12	Tuesday
9	Wednesday
11	Thursday
+ 15	Friday
57	Total for week

Step 2: Multiply the piece rate by the total.

	$5.79	Piece rate
x	57	Total vests
	40 53	
	289 5	
	$330.03	Total earnings

Exercise B: Complete the following chart. Find the total items produced and the wages for each employee.

	Employee	\multicolumn{5}{c}{Daily Production}	Weekly Total	Piece Rate	Wages

	Employee	M	T	W	Th	F	Weekly Total	Piece Rate	Wages
1)	A. Chemise	8	9	8	7	10	___	$4.25	___
2)	B. Cravatte	6	9	10	12	9	___	$3.20	___
3)	C. Robe	8	8	8	8	9	___	$6.22	___
4)	D. Nagle	5	6	5	6	7	___	$8.97	___
5)	E. Filetage	10	11	9	8	12	___	$4.87	___
6)	F. Tye	20	20	21	20	23	___	$2.69	___
7)	G. Cote	41	37	48	35	39	___	$ .78	___
8)	H. Sleave	65	71	68	73	70	___	$ .17	___
9)	I. Pokkit	55	57	58	61	63	___	$ .26	___
10)	J. Scarff	95	89	93	87	86	___	$ .24	___

THE KEY TO ROUNDING MONEY

When you multiply or divide amounts of money, the answers may have more than two decimal places. Then you usually round the answer to the nearer cent.

Example: Round $92.0769 to the nearer cent.

Step 1: Locate the digit to which the number is to be rounded. In this case, the *key digit* is 7. The key digit is underlined in the example. $92.0769

Step 2: Check the digit to the right of the key digit. This digit, 6, is boldfaced in the example. $92.0769

Step 3: If that digit is 5 or greater, add 1 to the key digit. 7 + 1 = 8 $92.0869
↕
7 + 1 = 8

Step 4: Drop all the digits to the right of the key digit. $92.0769 rounded to the nearer cent is $92.08. $92.08

Exercise A: Round each amount to the nearer cent.

1) $5.01785	2) $7.8923	3) $10.4856
4) $1.333	5) $29.9987	6) $16.7203
7) $3.7759	8) $2.8135	9) $86.1193
10) $2.065	11) $91.5622	12) $61.825
13) $2.935	14) $9.4862	15) $22.464
16) $1.1966	17) $3.477	18) $1.913
19) $1.2388	20) $67.723	21) $2.0685
22) $9.8716	23) $78.647	24) $1.8946
25) $8.259	26) $8.1672	27) $5.3566
28) $3.204	29) $5.3691	30) $7.345

Amounts of money may also be rounded to the nearest dime or dollar. In some cases, you may replace dropped digits with zeros to hold the places.

Example: Round $7.8923 to the nearer dime.

Step 1:   Locate the key digit. In this case, the key digit is 8. $7.8923

Step 2:   Check the digit to the right of the key digit. This digit, 9, is boldfaced in the example. $7.8923

Step 3:   Because 9 is greater than 5, add 1 to the key digit. 8 + 1 = 9 $7.9923

Step 4:   Drop all of the digits to the right of the key digit. Write a zero in the cents' column to hold the place. $7.8923 rounded to the nearer dime is $7.90. $7.90

$$\updownarrow$$
$$8 + 1 = 9$$

Example: Round $10.48 to the nearer dollar.

Step 1:   Locate the key digit. In this case, the key digit is 0. $10.48

Step 2:   Check the digit to the right of the key digit. This digit, 4, is boldfaced in the example. $10.48

Step 3:   Because 4 is less than 5, do not add to the key digit.

Step 4:   Drop the 4 and the 8. You may replace them with zeros. $10.48 rounded to the nearer dollar is $10.00. $10.00 *or* $10

Exercise B: Round each amount to the nearer cent, dime, and dollar. Write zeros when necessary to hold the places.

	Cent	Dime	Dollar			Cent	Dime	Dollar
1) $64.526	___	___	___	2) $302.1723	___	___	___
3) $404.929	___	___	___	4) $399.802	___	___	___
5) $77.5674	___	___	___	6) $90.1108	___	___	___
7) $5.0178	___	___	___	8) $1.833	___	___	___
9) $29.9987	___	___	___	10) $8.2551	___	___	___

SALARY

Some people are paid a fixed amount of money regularly, no matter how many hours they need to complete their jobs. This money is called a *salary*. *Salaried people* are usually not paid overtime. Professional workers and supervisors in most businesses are among the employees who are paid a salary.

Salaried workers are paid regularly, but the pay periods may differ from job to job; for example, *semimonthly, bimonthly, quarterly,* or *semiannually.*

How often paid	Times per year
Weekly	52 pays per year
Biweekly (every two weeks)	26 pays per year
Semimonthly (twice a month)	24 pays per year
Monthly	12 pays per year
Bimonthly (every two months)	6 pays per year
Quarterly (every three months)	4 pays per year
Semiannually (every six months)	2 pays per year
Annually (every twelve months)	1 pay per year

Exercise A: Find each person's earnings per year.
1) Anita is paid a salary of $250 weekly.
2) Eddie's salary is $1,100 per month.
3) Juan is paid a salary of $625 biweekly.
4) Mr. Lisek's salary is $4,500 quarterly.
5) Dr. Lee receives a salary of $4,792 bimonthly.
6) Glenn earns a salary of $2,376 semimonthly.

JANUARY						
S	M	T	W	T	F	S
					1	2
3	4	5	6	7	8	9
10	11	12	13	14	15	16
17	18	19	20	21	22	23
24	25	26	27	28	29	30
31						

FEBRUARY						
S	M	T	W	T	F	S
	1	2	3	4	5	6
7	8	9	10	11	12	13
14	15	16	17	18	19	20
21	22	23	24	25	26	27
28						

MARCH						
S	M	T	W	T	F	S
	1	2	3	4	5	6
7	8	9	10	11	12	13
14	15	16	17	18	19	20
21	22	23	24	25	26	27
28	29	30	31			

Example: Jay is making a salary of $24,000 per year. He is paid every two weeks, or biweekly. There are 26 pay periods each year. What does Jay earn during each pay period? Round your answer to the nearer cent.

$$\begin{array}{c} \text{rounded to} \\ \underline{\$923.076} \ \approx \$923.08 \\ 26 \,\overline{)\$24,000.000} \end{array}$$

Jay earns a salary of $923.08 each biweekly pay period, or every two weeks.

Exercise B: Complete the following chart. Find the number of times per year that each worker is paid. Then find the amount earned during each pay period.

Worker	Annual Salary	How Often Paid	Times per Year	Amount per Pay Period
1) Pat	$12,000	Weekly	?	?
2) Willie	$18,000	Monthly	?	?
3) Allan	$20,000	Quarterly	?	?
4) David	$16,000	Semimonthly	?	?
5) Steve	$15,000	Bimonthly	?	?
6) Ray	$38,000	Biweekly	?	?
7) Andrew	$32,000	Semiannually	?	?
8) Elmer	$10,000	Semimonthly	?	?
9) Wilda	$13,500	Biweekly	?	?
10) Aaron	$14,750	Weekly	?	?
11) Sarah	$68,580	Monthly	?	?
12) Teresa	$9,500	Weekly	?	?

THE KEY TO PERCENTS AND DECIMALS

Percent compares a number with 100. *Percent* means part "per 100." There are 100 **cents** per dollar. There are 100 years per **century**.

3% means "3 per 100."
3% of these dots are boxed:

75% means "75 per 100."
75% of these squares are shaded:

Did you realize that the % symbol is actually made up of the digits in 100, a 1 and two 0s?

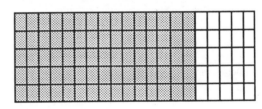

To do a percent problem, you must change the percent to a fraction or to a decimal.

$$3\% = 3 \text{ per } 100 = \tfrac{3}{100} = .03$$

To change any percent to a decimal, locate the decimal point, move it two places to the left, and drop the % sign.

Examples: 4.5% = .045   67% = .67

Exercise A: Change these percents to decimals.

1) 6%	2) 7%	3) 3.5%	4) 9.4%
5) 32%	6) 1%	7) 1.5%	8) 12.5%
9) 10%	10) 50%	11) 66.6%	12) 75%
13) 15%	14) 6.2%	15) 4.02%	16) 23.2%

COMMISSION

Percentage (an amount, not a percent) is calculated by multiplying a percent by a number. Salespeople generally earn a percentage of their total sales. This payment is called a *commission*. The purpose of a commission is to encourage the salesperson to sell more goods or services.

Example: Mr. E. Gar Beaver sold $24,000 worth of computer equipment. His *rate of commission* was 1.3%. What was his commission on that sale?

Commission = Sales x Rate of commission
= $24,000 x 1.3%

Change the percent to a decimal: 1.3% = .013

$24,000   Sales
x   .013   Rate of commission
72000
24000
$312.000   E. Gar's commission was $312.00.

Exercise A: Find the amount of commission earned by each salesperson.

	Salesperson	Amount of Sales	Rate of Commission	Amount of Commission
1)	Vera Good	$3,000	3%	?
2)	I. M. Smooth	$2,478	4%	?
3)	N. A. House	$80,000	1.3%	?
4)	R. U. Slick	$30,000	2.7%	?
5)	Willie Cell	$73,989	5.2%	?
6)	I. Will Bye	$98,605	1.7%	?
7)	Shirley I. Doo	$5,098	6.75%	?
8)	Sue Persales	$6,787	1.9%	?
9)	Andy Didsell	$5,050	2.2%	?
10)	Lotta Charm	$36,999	7.8%	?

SALARY PLUS COMMISSION

Bernice sells shoes in a department store. She earns a weekly salary of $155 plus a commission of 2% on all her sales. Last week her sales were $1,248. How much did she earn?

$1248	Sales	$155.00	Salary
x .02	Rate of commission	+ 24.96	Commission
$24.96	Commission	$179.96	Total earnings

Exercise A: Find the commission and total earnings for the sales listed below.

	Total Sales	Rate of Commission	Salary Earned
1)	$30,000	4%	$500
2)	$120,000	2.5%	$300
3)	$300,000	4.7%	$250
4)	$670,985	6.6%	$150
5)	$90,985	5.4%	$200

COMPUTER APPLICATION

Use this program to check your answers from Exercise A. See the appendix in the back of this text for directions in using computer programs.

```
10    REM SALARY PLUS COMMISSION
20    REM CHAPTER 1
30    PRINT " S A L A R Y  +  C O M M I S S I O N "
40    PRINT "INPUT THE TOTAL SALES (WITHOUT COMMAS)."
50    INPUT S
60    PRINT "INPUT THE RATE OF COMMISSION (WITHOUT % SIGN)."
70    INPUT R
80    PRINT "INPUT THE SALARY EARNED."
90    INPUT E
100   PRINT "TOTAL EARNINGS:  $"; E + S * R/100
110   END
RUN
```

NET PAY

When employees receive their paychecks, they should know that the check does not include their full earnings. Some money has been withheld, or deducted. Employers withhold *deductions* like federal income tax and social security payments. The worker may fill out forms to ask that other deductions be made, such as for health insurance. A worker's full earnings are called *gross pay*. *Take-home pay*, or *net pay*, is the amount the worker receives after all deductions are subtracted from gross pay.

Example: Dee Duction earned $360.56. From her check are deducted federal tax, $64.90; state tax, $5.48; social security tax, $21.09; savings bond contribution, $.85; and dues, $5.00. Find her total deductions and her net pay.

$64.90	Federal		$360.56	Gross pay
5.48	State		- 97.32	Deductions
21.09	Social security		$263.24	Net pay
.85	Savings bond			
+ 5.00	Dues			
$97.32	Total deductions			

Exercise A: The gross pay and deductions are listed below for five workers. Find the total deductions and net pay for each worker.

	Gross Pay	Federal Tax	State Tax	Soc. Sec. Tax	U.S. Bonds	Health Insurance
1)	$600.00	$155.54	$25.00	$37.90	$1.25	$7.56
2)	$500.00	$98.76	$17.98	$29.95	0	$6.23
3)	$403.00	$76.88	$16.88	$23.58	$2.50	$5.67
4)	$76.97	$18.65	$2.34	$4.50	0	0
5)	$120.75	$40.68	$6.77	$7.02	$3.75	$5.42

CHAPTER REVIEW

Solve these problems.

1) Change these percents to decimals.

   43%   13.8%   9%   87.5%

2) Find the wages for a person who earned $8 an hour and worked 45 hours from Monday through Friday.

3) A person came to work at 8:30 a.m., went out at 11:45 a.m., had lunch, came in at 12:30 p.m., and left at 5:15 p.m. How many hours did this person work?

4) A waitress received these tips in a given week. How much were her total tips?

   Monday — $40.50
   Tuesday — $32.95
   Wednesday — $44.78
   Thursday — $56.94
   Friday — $80.42

5) A collar maker earns 27¢ per collar. If he sews 55 good collars, how much will he earn?

6) An apple picker earns 70¢ per basket. If he filled 36 baskets, how much will he earn?

7) What was the monthly income for a person who earned an annual salary of $10,750?

8) What was the weekly income for a person who earned an annual salary of $18,500?

9) A salesperson earned a salary of $12,000 per year plus 5% commission on sales of $100,000. What was his total income?

10) A person has a gross pay of $267.99. Her deductions are $98.65, $14.77, $3.67, $.87, and $2.00. What is her take-home pay?

CHAPTER 2

BUYING FOOD

You will always need food. When you buy food, you have to make decisions. You will have to read and compare prices, compute change, compute unit prices, and use coupons. Some decisions about buying food can be easier to make with the help of mathematics.

EXPRESSING PRICES

Prices may be shown in dollars or in cents. When you compare prices, you must express them the same way. Where is the decimal point in a whole number? You can't see it, but 89 has a decimal point to the right of the 9. 89. The decimal point is not usually written in a whole number, but it is there.

To change cents to dollars: Move the decimal point two places to the left. Remove the ¢ sign and write a $ sign to the left of the price: 49¢ = $ .49

To change dollars to cents: Move the decimal point two places to the right. Remove the $ sign and write a ¢ sign to the right of the price: $1.19 = 119¢

Exercise A: Express these prices as dollars.
1) 45¢   2) 25¢   3) 5¢
4) 25.5¢   5) 139¢   6) 36¢

Exercise B: Express these prices as cents.
1) $ .75   2) $ .80   3) $ .09
4) $3.45   5) $1.299   6) $4.89

READING PRICES

Prices under a dollar can be shown in different ways.
Notice these examples: A. 59¢   B. $ .59   C. .59
Price A has a cent sign. Price B has a dollar sign and a decimal point. Price C uses only a decimal point. These three prices all mean fifty-nine cents.

Exercise A: Copy the three equal prices in each row. Do not copy the price that shows a different value.

1) 17¢	$ .17	.17	$17
2) $ .99	$99.	99¢	.99
3) .68	68¢	6.8¢	$ .68
4) $25.	.25	$ .25	25¢
5) 89¢	8.9¢	.89	$ .89

Prices over a dollar can also can be shown in different ways.
Notice these examples: $2.39   2.39 $2^{39} 2^{39}

Exercise B: Copy the four equal prices in each row. Do not copy the price that shows a different value.

1) $1.09	$109	1.09	1^{09}	$1^{09}
2) 4^{39}	$4.39	$.439	4.39	$4^{39}
3) 3.99	$3^{99}	$39	$3.99	3^{99}
4) $1^{69}	1.69	$1.69	$169.	1^{69}
5) 2^{98}	$2^{98}	$298	2.98	$2.98

ADDING PRICES

Grocery store ads list the prices of foods. Prices may be shown in different ways. Notice the abbreviations *lb.* and *oz.* (for pound and ounce) used in the sample ad shown on the right.

SAVE AT FRIENDLY FOODS!		
Grapes .... lb.	**$1⁴⁹**	
Dill Pickles .... 32-oz. jar	**$4³⁹**	
Corn Flakes ..... 18-oz. pkg.	**$2⁵⁷**	
Rye Bread .... 16-oz. loaf	**$1⁴⁹**	
Boneless Ham .... lb.	**$5⁰⁹**	
Swiss Cheese .... lb.	**$6³⁹**	

Example: Rose wants to buy a pound of Swiss cheese and a loaf of rye bread. How much will these two items cost together?

Step 1: Write a decimal point in each price.
Swiss cheese, $6³⁹ → $6.39   Rye bread, $1⁴⁹ → $1.49

Step 2: Line up the decimal points.
$$\begin{array}{r} \$6.39 \\ 1.49 \end{array}$$

Step 3: Add the two prices.

$6.39	Price of Swiss cheese
+ 1.49	Price of rye bread
$7.88	Total cost

Exercise A: From the ad, find the price for each food item listed below. Then find the total cost of each group of items. *Pkg.* is an abbreviation for package.

1) 1 lb. grapes
    1 lb. ham

2) 1 pkg. corn flakes
    1 jar pickles

3) 1 loaf rye bread
    1 lb. ham
    1 pkg. corn flakes

4) 2 lbs. grapes
    2 jars pickles
    2 lbs. Swiss cheese

COMPUTING CHANGE

Read the following sample ad from a food store.

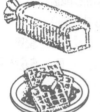

GOOD FOOD STORE   *Specials!*

Cake ....24-oz.	**2^{39}**
White Bread ....16-oz. loaf	**89¢**
English Muffins ....pkg. of 6	**99¢**
	pkg. of 12	**1^{69}**
Waffles ....10-oz. pkg.	**1^{15}**

Eggs ....doz. **1^{39}**	**Mustard** ....6-oz. jar **55¢**
Milk ....gal. **2^{37}**	**Potato Chips** .....16-oz. pkg. **1^{99}**
Lunch Meat ....8-oz. pkg. **3^{79}**	**Bean Soup** ....8 10-oz. cans **4^{49}**
Ravioli ....13-oz. pkg. **2^{49}**	**Apples** ....lb. **1^{79}**

Example #1: John went to the Good Food Store and bought one dozen eggs and one pound of apples. What was the total cost?

Add.
$1.39   Eggs
+ 1.79   Apples
$3.18   Total cost

Example #2: John gave the cashier a $10.00 bill. How much change should the cashier give John?

Subtract.
$10.00   Given to cashier
- 3.18   Cost of groceries
$6.82   Change

Exercise A: Check the correct prices from the ad on page 26. Find the total cost of each list of groceries. Then find the change that each shopper should get from a $20.00 bill. Notice the abbreviations for *gal.* and *doz.* (gallon and dozen) used in these lists.

1) 1 pkg. ravioli
    8 cans soup
    1 lb. apples
    1 loaf bread
    1 doz. eggs

2) 1 jar mustard
    1 pkg. 12 muffins
    1 pkg. lunch meat
    1 gal. milk
    2 doz. eggs

3) 2 gals. milk
    16 cans soup
    2 loaves of bread

4) 2 lbs. apples
    1 gal. milk
    1 cake

5) 2 cakes
    2 gals. milk

6) 1 pkg. 6 muffins
    1 pkg. ravioli
    1 pkg. potato chips

7) 1 pkg. 6 muffins
    2 jars mustard
    1 loaf bread

8) 1 pkg. lunch meat
    1 doz. eggs
    1 lb. apples

9) 16 cans soup
    1 pkg. waffles
    1 gal. milk

10) 2 loaves of bread
     2 pkgs. waffles
     1 cake

11) 2 lbs. apples
     1 pkg. ravioli
     2 doz. eggs
     1 cake

12) 1 pkg. 12 muffins
     8 cans soup
     2 pkgs. potato chips
     2 pkgs. lunch meat

STORE COUPONS

Food companies often offer money-off coupons to encourage sales. Study the following example.

Example: The price of Goody Chocolate Cake Mix is $1.29. Sarah has a coupon worth 25¢. How much will she pay for the cake mix?

Subtract.	$1.29	Price marked
	- .25	Coupon
	$1.04	Cost with coupon

25¢

Save 25¢ when you buy
Goody Chocolate Cake Mix

STORE COUPON

25¢

Exercise A: For each item below, find the cost if a coupon is used.

	Item	Price Marked	Coupon Value
1)	Cookies	$3.49	15¢
2)	Coffee	$4.89	40¢
3)	Popping corn	$2.75	13¢
4)	Frozen vegetables	$1.99	10¢
5)	Ice cream	$3.79	25¢
6)	Mayonnaise	$1.65	20¢
7)	Crackers	$1.95	12¢
8)	Spaghetti sauce	$2.09	40¢
9)	Orange juice	$2.19	25¢
10)	Cheese	$1.79	15¢

COUPONS FOR MORE THAN ONE

Several different types of store coupons are offered. Some store coupons are good only when the shopper buys more than one item.

Example: Mike had a coupon that offered a savings of 80¢ on any two Hearty Frozen Dinners. Each dinner was marked $2.89. How much did the two dinners cost with the coupon?

80¢ on 2 Dinners	SAVE 80¢ ON ANY TWO HEARTY DINNERS	
80¢ on 2 Dinners	STORE COUPON	80¢ on 2 Dinners

Step 1: Multiply.

$$\begin{array}{r} \$2.89 \\ \times\ \ 2 \\ \hline \$5.78 \end{array}$$

$2.89 — Price of 1 dinner

$5.78 — Price of 2 dinners

Step 2: Subtract.

$$\begin{array}{r} \$5.78 \\ -\ .80 \\ \hline \$4.98 \end{array}$$

$5.78 — Price of 2 dinners

- .80 — Value of coupon

$4.98 — Cost when coupon is used

Exercise A: For each set of items, find the cost when a coupon is used.

	Item	Price for 1 Item	Coupon Value
1)	Canned meat	$2.29	25¢ on 2 cans
2)	Tuna fish	$1.29	25¢ on 3 cans
3)	Evaporated milk	$ .69	35¢ on 4 cans
4)	Grape juice	$ .89	20¢ on 2 bottles
5)	Soup mix	$1.19	40¢ on 6 boxes
6)	Stuffing mix	$1.09	30¢ on 3 boxes
7)	Instant coffee	$4.19	80¢ on 2 jars
8)	Jelly	$2.79	35¢ on 2 jars
9)	Peanut butter	$4.15	80¢ on 2 jars
10)	Salad dressing	$1.59	12¢ on 2 bottles

COUPONS WITH CONDITIONS

Some coupons can only be used when certain conditions are met. Here is a sample of this type of coupon. Read the conditions.

<table>
<tr><td>40¢ OFF
TWO</td><td rowspan="2">CRUNCHO POTATO CHIPS

40¢ OFF when you purchase
TWO 8-oz. bags of CRUNCHO CHIPS

Store Coupon expires January 31, 1997
Limit one coupon per customer</td><td>40¢ OFF
TWO</td></tr>
<tr><td>40¢ OFF
TWO</td><td>40¢ OFF
TWO</td></tr>
</table>

Exercise A: Answer these questions about the coupon for Cruncho Chips.
1) What is the value of the coupon?
2) What product is the coupon good for?
3) How many items must you buy to use the coupon?
4) What size must the items be?
5) May the customer use two coupons to buy four items?
6) What is the last day that this coupon may be used?

Exercise B: Now answer the six questions above for this mayonnaise coupon.

12¢   **SAVE 12¢**   **12¢**

**when you buy two pints,
one quart, or one 48-oz. jar
of REAL MAYONNAISE**

REAL

ONE COUPON PER ITEM PURCHASED

Coupon expires July 31, 2001

12¢   STORE COUPON   **12¢**

EXPIRATION DATES

Many store coupons can be used for only a limited time. The *expiration date* will show when the coupon offer *expires,* or comes to an end.

Example: Heather cut from the newspaper a Cruncho coupon like the one shown on page 30. If the date is October 2, 1996, how much longer may she use the coupon? Since October has just begun, count October as one month. Count one month each for November, December, and January. Heather has 4 months in which to use the coupon: October 2, 1996, to January 31, 1997.

JANUARY							FEBRUARY							MARCH							APRIL						
S	M	T	W	T	F	S	S	M	T	W	T	F	S	S	M	T	W	T	F	S	S	M	T	W	T	F	S
					1	2		1	2	3	4	5	6		1	2	3	4	5	6					1	2	3
3	4	5	6	7	8	9	7	8	9	10	11	12	13	7	8	9	10	11	12	13	4	5	6	7	8	9	10
10	11	12	13	14	15	16	14	15	16	17	18	19	20	14	15	16	17	18	19	20	11	12	13	14	15	16	17
17	18	19	20	21	22	23	21	22	23	24	25	26	27	21	22	23	24	25	26	27	18	19	20	21	22	23	24
24	25	26	27	28	29	30	28							28	29	30	31				25	26	27	28	29	30	
31																											

MAY							JUNE							JULY							AUGUST						
S	M	T	W	T	F	S	S	M	T	W	T	F	S	S	M	T	W	T	F	S	S	M	T	W	T	F	S
						1				1	2	3	4						1	2	3	1	2	3	4	5	6	7
2	3	4	5	6	7	8	5	6	7	8	9	10	11	4	5	6	7	8	9	10	8	9	10	11	12	13	14
9	10	11	12	13	14	15	13	14	15	16	17	18	19	11	12	13	14	15	16	17	15	16	17	18	19	20	21
16	17	18	19	20	21	22	20	21	22	23	24	25	26	18	19	20	21	22	23	24	22	23	24	25	26	27	28
23	24	25	26	27	28	29	27	28	29	30				25	26	27	28	29	30	31	29	30	31				
30	31																										

SEPTEMBER							OCTOBER							NOVEMBER							DECEMBER						
S	M	T	W	T	F	S	S	M	T	W	T	F	S	S	M	T	W	T	F	S	S	M	T	W	T	F	S
			1	2	3	4						1	2		1	2	3	4	5	6				1	2	3	4
5	6	7	8	9	10	11	3	4	5	6	7	8	9	7	8	9	10	11	12	13	5	6	7	8	9	10	11
12	13	14	15	16	17	18	10	11	12	13	14	15	16	14	15	16	17	18	19	20	12	13	14	15	16	17	18
19	20	21	22	23	24	25	17	18	19	20	21	22	23	21	22	23	24	25	26	27	19	20	21	22	23	24	25
26	27	28	29	30			24	25	26	27	28	29	30	28	29	30					26	27	28	29	30	31	
							31																				

Exercise A: How much longer may each coupon be used?

Current Date	Expiration Date on Coupon
1) September 15, 1992	July 31, 1993
2) January 1, 1992	May 31, 1992
3) February 6, 1993	April 30, 1993
4) April 10, 1991	September 15, 1991
5) August 15, 1992	August 30, 1992
6) December 1, 1991	February 28, 1992
7) November 2, 1991	March 10, 1992
8) June 30, 1992	December 31,1992

FINDING THE COST OF ONE

To encourage shoppers to buy more items, food stores often mark a single price for two items. Study the following example.

$$\boxed{\textbf{Pudding} \ldots\ldots\ldots\ldots \text{2 boxes } \textbf{99¢}}$$

Example: Jim wanted one box of pudding. How much will it cost?

Divide.
$$
\begin{array}{r}
49\frac{1}{2}\,¢ \\
2\,)\overline{99¢} \\
\underline{8} \\
19 \\
\underline{18} \\
1
\end{array}
$$

The store charges a full penny for any fraction of a cent. One single box of pudding will cost Jim 50¢.

What would be the benefit of buying two boxes of pudding at the same time? Compare the following two ways of buying this product. Which price would give Jim a savings?

$ .50	One single box	$1.00	Two single boxes
x 2		- .99	Two boxes together
$1.00	Two single boxes	$ .01	Savings

When stores mark a single price for the purchase of two items, it is often helpful to compare prices. If Jim bought two single boxes of pudding at different times, he would pay 50¢ each, or a total of $1.00. If he bought two boxes of pudding at the same time, he would pay only 99¢, a savings of 1¢.

Any number of items may be offered for one price. Study the following example. How does the cost of buying one item compare to the cost of buying three iterms at the same time?

Example: Kelly wanted only one green pepper. The price was 3 for $1.48. How much will one pepper cost?

Divide.

$$\frac{.49\frac{1}{3}¢}{3\overline{)1.48}}$$

One pepper will cost 50¢.

How much would three peppers cost if they were bought at different times?

Multiply.

$ .50   One single pepper

x   3

$1.50   Three single peppers

How much do you save by buying the three peppers at the same time?

Subtract. $1.50 - $1.48 = $ .02 or 2¢ Savings

Exercise A: Copy this chart. Fill in the missing information.

Price	Cost of One Item	Total Cost of Single Items	Savings by Buying Items at the Same Time
1) 2 / 49¢			
2) 2 / 99¢			
3) 5 / 99¢			
4) 3 / $1.29			
5) 7 / 89¢			8¢
6) 12 / $1.00	9¢	10¢	
7) 5 / $1.00			5¢
8) 6 / 99¢		1.44	
9) 8 / $1.39	18¢		

THE KEY TO USING THE WORD "PER"

The word "per" in an expression means division. You can always replace the word "per" with the words "divided by." Study the following examples.

Examples: A. miles <u>per</u> gallon =
               miles <u>divided by</u> gallons =   gallons $\overline{)\text{miles}}$

B. cost <u>per</u> ounce =
    cost <u>divided by</u> ounces =   ounces $\overline{)\text{cost}}$

C. 5 <u>percent</u> =   .05
    5 <u>divided by</u> 100 =   100 $\overline{)\,5.00}$

(Remember that *percent* means "per hundred.")

Exercise A: Rewrite each of the following expressions. Use the words "divided by." Then set up the division problem. Look at the examples on the top of this page.

1) cost per liter
2) 17%
3) miles per hour
4) miles per minute
5) 6 percent
6) kilometers per year
7) feet per minute
8) cost per inch
9) kilometers per liter
10) attendance per game
11) cost per kilogram
12) miles per trip
13) meters per second
14) newspapers per day
15) cost per dozen
16) inches per second
17) 15%
18) cost per pound
19) liters per week
20) gallons per week

THE UNIT PRICE

The *unit price* is the cost of one unit of something. The unit price may be the cost per gram, cost per pound, cost per item, or any other unit. The word *per* means "for each" or "for one." The word *per* tells us to divide.

Example: A package of ground beef weighs 0.85 lb. The price marked is $1.69. What is the unit price, or the cost per pound?

$$\begin{array}{r} 1.988 \approx 1.99 \\ \text{pounds} \,\overline{)\,\text{cost}} \quad 0.85. \,\overline{)\,1.69.000} \\ 85 \\ \overline{840} \\ 765 \\ \overline{750} \\ 680 \\ \overline{700} \\ 680 \end{array}$$

Round your answer to the nearer cent.
1.988 ≈ 1.99

Note that you must move the decimal point so that you can divide by a whole number.

The unit price is $1.99 per pound.

Exercise A: Find the unit price for each item listed. Round your answer to the nearer cent.

✓	Price	Item	Unit	Unit Price
1)	$25.00	24 doz. eggs	dozen	_____
2)	$1.19	40 lollipops	lollipop	_____
3)	$3.09	18 oz. cookies	ounce	_____
4)	$3.79	1.59 kg. cat food	kilogram	_____
5)	$2.85	5 oz. cheese	ounce	_____
6)	$2.43	3.8 L milk	liter	_____
7)	$ .79	3 lbs. apples	pound	_____
8)	$2.29	12 oz. crackers	ounce	_____

COMPUTER APPLICATION

Use the following computer program to compute unit prices of various items. See the appendix in the back of this text for directions in using computer programs.

```
10    REM UNIT PRICE
20    REM CHAPTER 2
30    PRINT "U N I T   P R I C E"
40    PRINT "INPUT THE PRICE."
50    INPUT P
60    PRINT "INPUT THE NUMBER OF ITEMS."
70    INPUT N
80    PRINT "UNIT PRICE:  $"; INT( ( P / N + .005 ) * 100 ) / 100
90    END
RUN
```

COMPARING UNIT PRICES

Smart shoppers compare different products to help them decide which one to buy. For example, some items may be different in size:

Brand A contains $6\frac{1}{2}$ oz.   It sells for 98¢.

Brand B contains $12\frac{1}{2}$ oz.   It sells for $2.19.

Which size can has the lower unit price?

Study the example shown on the next page. Divide the cost by the number of ounces in each can to find the unit price of both Brand A and Brand B. You can then compare these unit prices to determine which size can has the lower unit price.

Compare the unit prices of Brand A and Brand B. Which size can has the lower unit price?

Brand	Size	Cost	Unit Price
A	$6\frac{1}{2}$ oz.	$ .98	$\begin{array}{r} \$\,.150 \text{ per oz.} \\ 6.5.\overline{)\,\$\,.9.800} \end{array}$
B	$12\frac{1}{2}$ oz.	$2.19	$\begin{array}{r} \$\,.175 \text{ per oz.} \\ 12.5.\overline{)\,\$2.1.900} \end{array}$

The smaller size, the $6\frac{1}{2}$ oz. can, has the lower unit price.

You may compare different brand names and sizes. A *brand name* identifies a product as being made by a single company or manufacturer. Compare the unit prices of Brands A, B, and C.

Brand A contains $12\frac{1}{2}$ oz.   It sells for $2.19.

Brand B contains $9\frac{1}{4}$ oz.   It sells for $1.49.

Brand C contains $9\frac{1}{4}$ oz.   It sells for $1.89.

Brand	Size	Cost	Unit Price
A	$12\frac{1}{2}$ oz.	$2.19	$\begin{array}{r} \$\,.175 \text{ per oz.} \\ 12.5.\overline{)\,\$2.1.900} \end{array}$
B	$9\frac{1}{4}$ oz.	$1.49	$\begin{array}{r} \$\,.161 \text{ per oz.} \\ 9.25.\overline{)\,\$1.49.000} \end{array}$
C	$9\frac{1}{4}$ oz.	$1.89	$\begin{array}{r} \$\,.204 \text{ per oz.} \\ 9.25.\overline{)\,\$1.89.000} \end{array}$

The $9\frac{1}{4}$ oz. can of Brand B has the lowest unit price.

Exercise A: Find the lowest unit price for each set of items.

1)	Rice cereals: Size: Price: Cost per ounce:	A 17 oz. $2.89	B 16 oz. $2.29	C 13 oz. $2.59	
2)	Cola drinks: Size: Price: Cost per liter:	A 2 L $1.53	B 2 L $1.03	C 2.83 L $2.01	D 2.124 L $2.71
3)	Potato chips: Size: Price: Unit price:	A 7 oz. $ .99	B 18 oz. $1.99	C 11 oz. $1.39	D 4 oz. $ .69
4)	Cheese pizzas: Size: Price: Unit price:	A 6.5 oz. $1.49	B 7 oz. $1.99	C 8 oz. $2.99	D 19 oz. $3.99

Remember that you must consider quality when deciding on the best buy. Paying less money for food that you do not like is never wise.

CONSUMER HUMOR

Millie is truly dedicated to thinking metric. She even eats graham crackers.

Review your ability to read and express prices.

1) Express this price as dollars: 89¢

2) Express this price as dollars: 7¢

3) Express this price as dollars: 1^{69}

Solve the following problems included on pages 39 and 40.

4) In the newspaper ad for a local food store, oranges are marked 4/99. What is the price of one orange?

5) You want to buy a stuffing mix.
   You have a $5 bill.
   There are three brands of stuffing mix available:

   a) Cook Top Stuffing Mix
      6 oz. for $1.49 or 12 oz. for $2.99

   b) Saltridge Farms Stuffing Mix
      6 oz. for $1.79

   c) Cousin Ben's Stuffing Mix
      6 oz. for $1.29

   You like the flavor of all three brands. However, you have a 10¢ off coupon for Cook Top Stuffing Mix.

   Find the best buy. Then compute your change.

6) You need some peanut butter.

You have a 40¢ off coupon for Creemy Peanut Butter. This coupon is good for one 40-oz. jar, or one 28-oz. jar, or two 18-oz. jars, or two 12-oz. jars.

The prices for Creemy Peanut Butter are:

12-oz. jar ....$1.85   28-oz. jar............................$4.15
18 oz. jar ....$2.49   40-oz. jar............................$5.29

What is the best buy? It may help to organize your work this way:

Size	Jars Needed	Cost per Jar	Total Cost	Cost with Coupon	Total Ounces	Cost per Ounce

Everyone must have clothes. There are many ways to shop for them. You may buy clothes in a clothing store or in a department store. You may buy materials and make your own clothes. You may order ready-to-wear clothes from a catalog. Shopping for clothes often involves mathematics. In this chapter you will learn to compute sale prices and discounts, order from a catalog, charge purchases to an account, and use a layaway plan.

READY-TO-WEAR

Here are some clothing items that were on sale at a department store. Read the price for each item. Then study the example on the next page.

Shirt	Vest	Socks	Jeans
$11.95	$25	79¢ pair	$21.95

Example: Jack Etts needed clothes for school. He bought 5 pairs of socks, 2 pairs of jeans, 2 shirts, and 1 vest. Look at the prices for these items on page 41. What was the total cost?

To find the total, make a list like the one shown below. Line up the decimal points. Add to find the cost of the clothes.

1)	socks	5	x	$ .79	=	$3.95
2)	jeans	2	x	$21.95	=	43.90
3)	shirts	2	x	$11.95	=	23.90
4)	vest	1	x	$25.00	=	+ 25.00
						$96.75 Cost of clothes

In most states, a *sales tax* is computed on the sale of goods and services. Jack had to pay a sales tax of 5%. How much was the tax? What was the total amount that Jack paid?

Example: To compute sales tax, multiply the cost by the rate. Round up to the next cent.

$96.75 x 5%
(Remember that 5% = .05)

$96.75   Cost of clothes
x   .05   Tax rate
$4.8375   ≈ $4.84   Sales tax

Add the sales tax to the cost to find the total amount Jack paid.

$96.75   Cost of clothes
+   4.84   Sales tax
$101.59   Total amount paid

Exercise A: Find the cost of each set of purchases. Find the sales tax. Then add the sales tax to the cost to find the total amount paid. The symbol @ means *at* and indicates unit price (the cost of one unit of something; for example, one sweater or one pair of socks).

	Consumer	Purchases	Sales Tax Rate
1)	Jean S. Pockets	Shirt, $9.95 Jeans, $29.99	5%
2)	Bo Lero	3 prs. socks @ $1.29 pr. Jacket, $34.59	6%
3)	Lacey Boots	Shoes, $17.99 3 prs. stockings @ $2.59	4%
4)	Chloe Thing	Dress, $15.99 2 sweaters @ $14.90 ea.	5%
5)	Pearl Button	Suit, $54.90 2 shirts @ $11.95	7%
6)	Dee Vest	Down-filled vest, $65.00 Flannel shirt, $14.99	5%
7)	Goldy Bukkel	Nightgown, $26.50 Slippers, $12.90 Robe, $44.80	3%
8)	Freud E. N. Slipp	Boots, $47.00 Overcoat, $129.99	None
9)	Roy L. Bloo	2 prs. pajamas @ $19.99 Robe, $35.00	8%
10)	A. Dora Bull	Cashmere coat, $259.99 Calfskin boots, $135.00	7%

SALE PRICES

Merchants often sell items at reduced prices. A careful shopper watches for these sales because they could provide good bargains.

Example: Dee Ziner jeans were regularly sold for $45.90. They are now on sale for $39.99. How much is saved by buying the jeans on sale?

To find the amount saved, subtract the sale price from the regular price. The *regular price* is the original or usual price of the item.

$45.90   Regular price
- 39.99   Sale price
$5.91   Amount saved

Exercise A: Find the amount saved on each item by using the sale price. Subtract to find the answer in each case.

	Item	Regular Price	Sale Price
1)	Dress	$50.00	$42.99
2)	Belt	$7.50	$5.99
3)	Coat	$75.00	$45.90
4)	Shoes	$15.80	$9.95
5)	Gloves	$10.00	$7.59
6)	Socks	$1.29	$ .79
7)	Sweater	$35.90	$26.95
8)	Shirt	$15.00	$9.65
9)	Pants	$21.00	$15.89
10)	Suit	$150.00	$79.98

PERCENT SAVED

Sometimes you may want to know what percent of the regular price is saved on a sale item.

To find the percent saved, divide the amount saved by the regular price. Then change the decimal to a percent.

Example: The Dee Ziner jeans were regularly sold for $45.90. $5.91 was saved by using the sale price. To find the percent saved, divide the amount saved, $5.91, by the regular price, $45.90.

$$\text{regular price} \overline{)\text{amount saved}} \qquad 45.90\overline{)5.91}$$

$$\qquad\qquad\qquad\qquad .128 \approx .13 \text{ or } 13\%$$
$$45.90.\overline{)5.91.000}$$

A consumer could save 13% by buying the jeans on sale. The sale price is 13% off the regular price.

Exercise A: Find the percent saved for each of the purchases listed in Exercise A on page 44.

You may want to use a hand calculator to do this exercise. Here's how:

Step 1: Key in the amount saved.

Step 2: Press $\boxed{\div}$.

Step 3: Key in the amount of the regular price.

Step 4: Press $\boxed{=}$. This answer is the decimal that you want.

Step 5: To change the decimal to the percent saved, press $\boxed{\text{X}}$. Key in 100. Press $\boxed{=}$.

Step 6: Round the answer to the nearer percent.

DISCOUNTS

A *discount* indicates an amount subtracted from the regular price. Stores may give discounts for cash or prompt payment or to reduce prices for a sale. Occasionally a store will offer a percent off every item in the store.

Sometimes this discount is given at the checkout counter and is not marked on the price tag. Before you check out of the store, you will need to compute the sale price to decide if it is a good bargain.

To compute a sale price after a discount:
1) Subtract the discount from 100%;
2) Multiply the difference times the regular price.

Example: A shirt is marked 20% off. What is the sale price if the regular price of the shirt is $49.99?

Step 1: 100%
        - 20%   Discount rate
         80%   Difference

Step 2: $49.99   Regular price
        x   .80   Difference found in Step 1 (80% = .80)
       $39.9920   ≈ $39.99 Sale price

How much is saved? $49.99   Regular price
                                 - 39.99   Sale price
                                $10.00   Amount saved

Buying the shirt at 20% off the regular price of $49.99 gives a sale price of $39.99 and a savings of $10.00.

Exercise A: Use the discount. Find the sale price of each item and the amount saved.

	Item	Regular Price	Discount
1)	Sweater	$19.99	10%
2)	Jeans	$34.99	15%
3)	Shirt	$14.99	10%
4)	Blouse	$39.95	20%
5)	Shoes	$24.99	25%
6)	Coat	$129.99	15%
7)	Dress	$64.00	10%
8)	Suit	$150.00	50%
9)	Vest	$17.99	12%
10)	Pants	$29.99	40%

COMPUTER APPLICATION

Use the following computer program to compute the sale price and the amount saved when a discount is used off the regular price of an item. See the appendix in the back of this text for directions in using computer programs.

```
10      REM DISCOUNTS
20      REM CHAPTER 3
30      PRINT " D I S C O U N T S "
40      PRINT "INPUT THE REGULAR PRICE."
50      INPUT P
60      PRINT "INPUT THE DISCOUNT (WITHOUT THE PERCENT SIGN)."
70      INPUT D
80      S = INT ( ( 100 - D ) * P + .5 ) / 100
90      PRINT "SALE PRICE:   $";S
100     PRINT "AMOUNT SAVED:   $";P - S
110     END
RUN
```

BUYING FROM A CATALOG

A *catalog* lists items in an organized way; for example, toys or household supplies. Descriptions are often included. Many companies send catalogs of their goods to people throughout the country. Customers look at the catalogs and decide what, if anything, they wish to buy. They may either mail their orders or phone them in to the store. Catalog buyers usually pay the cost of postage and handling in addition to the cost of the goods.

Example: Ray wanted two of the shirts he saw advertised in a catalog. Read the following ad. Then notice the way Ray filled out his order form.

Men's Shirt
Fine, lightweight cotton knit shirt for sports and casual wear.
Washable. 3-button opening. Short sleeves. White collar.
Three colors: Navy, Green, Red. Men's sizes S, M, L, XL.
A4610   Men's shirt, $35.00 postpaid

ORDER FORM						
Item No.	How Many?	Color	Size	Description	Amount	
A4610	1	Navy	M	Men's Shirt	35	00
A4610	1	Red	M	Men's Shirt	35	00
				Total of merchandise	70	00
				Add 6% state sales tax	4	20
				TOTAL AMOUNT	74	20

Exercise A: Compute the following answers. Include 6% sales tax.
1) What would the total amount be for three of these shirts?
2) What would the total amount be for one shirt?

Hooded Sweatshirt

Gray pullover.   80% cotton, 20% polyester. XSm. (32-34), Sm. (36-38), Med. (40-42), Lg. (44-46), XLg. (48). Weight 24 oz.
86395   Hooded Sweatshirt, $34.50

Buckskin Gloves

Elastic back.   Fully lined. Natural tan color. Sizes 7-11. Weight 5 oz.
1123   Buckskin Gloves, $24.00

Web Belts

1 ½ in. wide.   Steel ring buckles. Waist sizes S (30"-32"), Med. (34"-36"), Lg. (38"-40"), XLg. (42"-44"). Colors: White, Red, Navy. Weight 4 oz.
1166   Web Belt, $8.50

Classic Sweater

100% wool.   Crew neck. 3 initials monogrammed for $1.00. Colors: Red, Blue. Sizes: 34, 36, 38, 40. Weight 12 oz.
B3741 Classic Sweater, $32.00

Some mail order companies require the customer to pay shipping charges. Here is a table of these shipping charges from a catalog.

Example: Terry ordered a sweatshirt. It weighs 24 oz. How much is the shipping charge?

16 ounces = 1 pound

The sweatshirt weighs 1 pound, 8 ounces. The shipping charge is $3.56.

Shipping Charges	
Weight	
Up to 1 lb.	$3.04
1 lb. 1 oz. to 2 lbs.	$3.56
2 lbs. 1 oz. to 6 lbs.	$5.89
6 lbs. 1 oz. to 12 lbs.	$8.99
Over 12 lbs.	$13.87

Exercise B: Find the weight and shipping charge for each order.

1)   2 pair gloves
2 classic sweaters

2)   3 web belts
1 sweatshirt

3)   2 sweatshirts
1 pair gloves

4)   1 web belt
1 pair gloves
1 sweater

A person ordering clothes from a catalog must write the correct sizes on the order form. Some catalogs give directions for finding proper measurements and sizes. Read the following example.

Gloves. Measurement in inches of your right hand around the knuckles with the hand flat. Do not include the thumb.

Men's Jackets and Sweaters. Measurement in inches around chest and over shirt with tape well under arms and across shoulder blades.

Belts. Measurement in inches over shirt and around waist.

Exercise C: Determine the correct size for each item described in these problems. Use information from the ads on page 49.

1) Gary's chest measurement is 37". His hand measurement is $9\frac{1}{2}$". He is ordering a sweatshirt and gloves.

2) Meg's waist measurement is 30". Her sweater size is 36. She is ordering a belt and a sweatshirt.

3) Brad's waist measurement is 40". His chest measurement is 45". He wants a belt and a sweatshirt.

Exercise D: Find the cost of each order. Add 5% sales tax and shipping charges to find the total amount due.

1) 1 monogrammed sweater
   1 belt

2) 2 pairs gloves
   1 sweatshirt

3) 2 sweatshirts
   2 sweaters

4) 3 belts
   1 sweatshirt

5) 3 pairs gloves
   2 belts

6) 3 sweatshirts
   1 sweater

THE KEY TO SIMPLIFYING FRACTIONS

A fraction is made up of a *numerator* and a *denominator*. To simplify fractions, divide the numerator and the denominator by the *greatest common factor*.

$$\frac{2}{8} = \frac{2 \div 2}{8 \div 2} = \frac{1}{4} \qquad\qquad \frac{6}{9} = \frac{6 \div 3}{9 \div 3} = \frac{2}{3}$$

Exercise A: Write each fraction in simplest form.

1) $\frac{2}{4}$ 2) $\frac{8}{10}$ 3) $\frac{14}{16}$ 4) $\frac{9}{15}$

5) $\frac{6}{8}$ 6) $\frac{3}{9}$ 7) $\frac{6}{9}$ 8) $\frac{6}{16}$

9) $\frac{5}{10}$ 10) $\frac{12}{15}$ 11) $\frac{12}{32}$ 12) $\frac{8}{24}$

13) $\frac{13}{39}$ 14) $\frac{12}{16}$ 15) $\frac{14}{21}$ 16) $\frac{10}{45}$

If the numerator of a fraction is larger than the denominator, divide the numerator by the denominator. Write any remainder as a fraction.

$$\frac{11}{8} = \quad 8\overline{)11}^{\;1 \;=\; 1\frac{3}{8}} \atop \underline{\;8\;} \atop 3 \qquad\qquad \frac{20}{8} = \quad 8\overline{)20}^{\;2 \;=\; 2\frac{4}{8} \;=\; 2\frac{1}{2}} \text{ Simplify the fraction.} \atop \underline{16} \atop 4$$

Exercise B: Write each fraction in simplest form.

1) $\frac{5}{4}$ 2) $\frac{11}{7}$ 3) $\frac{12}{5}$ 4) $\frac{15}{8}$

5) $\frac{3}{2}$ 6) $\frac{13}{8}$ 7) $\frac{20}{9}$ 8) $\frac{10}{8}$

9) $\frac{7}{5}$ 10) $\frac{9}{5}$ 11) $\frac{19}{9}$ 12) $\frac{9}{4}$

13) $\frac{9}{2}$ 14) $\frac{17}{4}$ 15) $\frac{17}{3}$ 16) $\frac{27}{5}$

THE KEY TO COMMON DENOMINATORS

The number being multiplied is called a *factor*. To change the denominator of a fraction, multiply the numerator and the denominator by the same factor.

Example: Change the denominator of $\frac{1}{4}$ to 8. $\frac{1}{4} = \frac{?}{8}$

Think: $4 \times 2 = 8$

$$\frac{1}{4} = \frac{1 \times 2}{4 \times 2} = \frac{2}{8}$$

Exercise A: Change each numerator to the number shown.

1) $\frac{2}{3} = \frac{?}{9}$ 2) $\frac{1}{2} = \frac{?}{8}$ 3) $\frac{3}{8} = \frac{?}{16}$

4) $\frac{3}{4} = \frac{?}{8}$ 5) $\frac{3}{5} = \frac{?}{10}$ 6) $\frac{1}{2} = \frac{?}{4}$

7) $\frac{1}{8} = \frac{?}{16}$ 8) $\frac{7}{8} = \frac{?}{32}$ 9) $\frac{3}{4} = \frac{?}{16}$

To find the common denominator, find the smallest number which has both denominators as a factor.

Example: Find the common denominator of $\frac{3}{4}$ and $\frac{5}{6}$.

Think: $4 \times 3 = 12$ $6 \times 2 = 12$

$$\frac{3}{4} = \frac{3 \times 3}{4 \times 3} = \frac{9}{12} \qquad \frac{5}{6} = \frac{5 \times 2}{6 \times 2} = \frac{10}{12}$$

Exercise B: Write these pairs of fractions with common denominators.

1) $\frac{5}{8}$ and $\frac{1}{2}$ 2) $\frac{1}{2}$ and $\frac{3}{8}$ 3) $\frac{1}{3}$ and $\frac{1}{5}$

4) $\frac{3}{4}$ and $\frac{1}{8}$ 5) $\frac{3}{4}$ and $\frac{5}{8}$ 6) $\frac{3}{4}$ and $\frac{2}{3}$

7) $\frac{1}{4}$ and $\frac{1}{2}$ 8) $\frac{7}{8}$ and $\frac{1}{4}$ 9) $\frac{3}{10}$ and $\frac{4}{15}$

MAKING YOUR OWN CLOTHES

Many people sew their own clothes in order to match the right fabric with the right style. Besides saving money, sewing your own clothes provides a good fit. Buying fabric requires a knowledge of mathematics.

Example: Janice wanted to make herself a matching vest and pair of pants. She selected a pattern. On the back of the pattern envelope, she found a chart that showed how much fabric to use. Janice is a size 12. The fabric she wanted to use is 60 inches wide.

VEST A	**Size**	**6**	**8**	**10**	**12**	**14**	
60"		$^5/_8$	$^5/_8$	$^5/_8$	$^3/_4$	$^3/_4$	Yds.
PANTS B	**Size**	**6**	**8**	**10**	**12**	**14**	
60"		$1^3/_8$	$1^3/_8$	$1^3/_8$	$1^1/_2$	$1^5/_8$	Yds.

Patterns indicate fabric requirements in *yards*. From the chart, Janice found that she needed $\frac{3}{4}$ of a yard for the vest and $1\frac{1}{2}$ yards for the pants. How much fabric did she need altogether?

Add the two numbers.

$$1\tfrac{1}{2} = 1\tfrac{2}{4}$$
$$+ \quad \tfrac{3}{4} = \tfrac{3}{4}$$

The common denominator is 4.

$$1\tfrac{5}{4}$$

$$1\tfrac{5}{4} = 1 + \tfrac{5}{4} = 1 + 1\tfrac{1}{4} = 2\tfrac{1}{4}$$

Janice needed $2\frac{1}{4}$ yards of fabric to make the vest and pants.

Example: How much more fabric will be required to make a pair of size 14 pants than a pair of size 12 pants?

Step 1: Read the chart. Size 12.....................$1\frac{1}{2}$ yards
Size 14.....................$1\frac{5}{8}$ yards

Step 2: Subtract. $1\frac{5}{8} = 1\frac{5}{8}$ The common
$-1\frac{1}{2} = -1\frac{4}{8}$ denominator is 8.
$\frac{1}{8}$

The size 14 pants require $\frac{1}{8}$ of a yard more fabric than the size 12 pants.

Exercise A: Use the pattern chart on page 53 to answer these questions.

1) How much fabric is needed to make a size 6 vest and pants?

2) How much fabric is needed to make a size 14 vest and pants?

3) How much more fabric is required to make a size 14 vest than a size 6 vest?

4) How much more fabric is required to make a pair of size 12 pants than a pair of size 10 pants?

5) How much fabric is required to make two size 12 vests?

6) How much fabric is required to make two pairs of size 14 pants?

7) How much fabric is needed to make a size 10 vest and pants?

This chart appears on the back of Janice's *pattern* envelope: It includes fabrics, *notions,* and amounts of material needed to make the vest and pants in different sizes.

4759 Western Vest and Pants — 16 PIECES

Women's Sizes	6	8	10	12	14
VEST A	Number of Yards Needed				
35/36"	$1^1/_8$	$1^1/_8$	$1^1/_8$	$1^1/_4$	$1^1/_4$
44/45"	$5/_8$	$5/_8$	$7/_8$	$7/_8$	$1^1/_8$
60"	$5/_8$	$5/_8$	$5/_8$	$3/_4$	$3/_4$
PANTS B					
35/36"	$2^1/_4$	$2^1/_2$	$2^5/_8$	$2^5/_8$	$2^5/_8$
44/45"	$2^1/_4$	$2^3/_8$	$2^1/_2$	$2^1/_2$	$2^1/_2$
60"	$1^3/_8$	$1^3/_8$	$1^3/_8$	$1^1/_2$	$1^5/_8$

Men's Sizes	34	36	38	40	42
VEST C					
35/36"	$1^1/_8$	$1^1/_8$	$1^1/_8$	$1^1/_8$	$1^1/_4$
44/45"	$3/_4$	$3/_4$	$3/_4$	$7/_8$	$7/_8$
60"	$3/_4$	$3/_4$	$3/_4$	$3/_4$	$3/_4$
PANTS D					
35/36"	$2^5/_8$	$2^3/_4$	$2^7/_8$	$3^1/_8$	$3^1/_8$
44/45"	$2^3/_8$	$2^1/_2$	$2^5/_8$	$2^5/_8$	$2^5/_8$
60"	$1^3/_4$	$1^7/_8$	$1^7/_8$	$2^1/_4$	$2^3/_8$

FABRICS: Use leather, denim, or other sturdy fabrics.

NOTIONS: Thread, 4 snaps for A and C, 8 studs for B and D, 9" pants zipper for B and D, belt (optional)

Exercise B: Use the chart on page 55. Answer these questions.

1) How much 45" fabric is needed to make two pairs of women's size 8 pants? Add to find your answer.

2) How much 36" fabric is needed to make a man's size 42 pants and vest?

3) How much 45" fabric is needed to make both a woman's pair of size 6 pants and a man's pair of size 34 pants?

4) How much 60" fabric is needed to make both a woman's size 10 vest and a man's size 36 vest?

5) How much more 36" fabric is needed than 60" fabric for a woman's pair of size 10 pants? Subtract to find your answer.

6) How much more 60" fabric is needed to make a man's size 40 vest than a woman's size 10 vest?

7) How much more 36" fabric is needed to make a woman's size 14 vest than a size 10 vest?

8) How much more 36" fabric is needed than 45" fabric for a man's pair of size 36 pants?

9) Two people decide to make matching outfits. The man is size 38; the woman, size 12. They buy 60" wide fabric for the vest and 45" fabric for the pants. How much fabric is needed for the two outfits?

10) Two women are planning look-alike outfits. The mother is size 12; the daughter, size 8. They will use a 36" blue drill fabric for the vests and pants. How much total fabric must they buy for these outfits?

FINDING THE COST OF FABRIC

To find the cost of fabric, multiply the price per yard by the number of yards needed.

Example: What is the cost of $3\frac{1}{8}$ yards of fabric at $6.99 per yard?

Step 1: Write $3\frac{1}{8}$ as a decimal.

$$\frac{1}{8} = 8 \overline{)1.000} \quad .125$$

$$3\frac{1}{8} = 3.125$$

Step 2: Multiply 3.125 by $6.99.

$$\begin{array}{ll} 3.125 & \text{Amount of fabric} \\ \times\ \underline{\$6.99} & \text{Price per yard} \\ \$21.84375 & \approx \$21.84 \ \text{Cost} \end{array}$$

The cost of $3\frac{1}{8}$ yards of fabric is $21.84.

Exercise A: Write the decimal equivalent for each fraction.

1) $\frac{1}{8}$　　　　2) $\frac{1}{4}$　　　　3) $\frac{3}{8}$　　　　4) $\frac{1}{2}$

5) $\frac{5}{8}$　　　　6) $\frac{3}{4}$　　　　7) $\frac{7}{8}$　　　　8) $\frac{8}{8}$

Exercise B: Find the total cost of each fabric purchase.

	Length	Cost per Yard		Length	Cost per Yard
1)	2 yds.	$9.00	2)	$5\frac{1}{4}$ yds.	$7.99
3)	$4\frac{1}{2}$ yds.	$12.00	4)	$6\frac{1}{8}$ yds.	$8.00
5)	$5\frac{3}{8}$ yds	$5.49	6)	$9\frac{7}{8}$ yds.	$16.00
7)	$1\frac{7}{8}$ yds.	$15.00	8)	$8\frac{5}{8}$ yds.	$4.00
9)	$3\frac{3}{4}$ yds.	$8.99	10)	$7\frac{7}{8}$ yds.	$8.99
11)	$10\frac{1}{2}$ yds.	$4.99	12)	$24\frac{1}{4}$ yds.	$34.59

USING A CHARGE ACCOUNT

Many consumers find it convenient to charge their purchases and pay for them at a later date. People who use a *charge account* are expected to make a *minimum payment* each month. *Interest* is a fee charged on any unpaid balance.

Example: Adam Ion owes $126.60 on his charge account. The minimum payment due is $10.00. Part of his monthly record or *statement* is shown below. It indicates all payments and charges to date. Adam will mail a copy of this statement with his payment of $10.00.

Box 3030 Current, Utah	**AC Charge Card** STATEMENT	Amount Enclosed ....
To: Adam Ion 123 Static Street Positive, MD 20000		
Account Number: 1234-567-890-1	Period Ending 10/13	Payment Due Date 11/13
	Minimum Payment Due $10.00	Current Balance $126.60
Please return this portion with your payment.		

Adam's interest charge is 1.8% of the unpaid balance. How much will he owe next month if he makes no new purchases?

Step 1: Subtract his payment from the current balance.

$126.60   Current balance
- 10.00   Payment
$116.60   Unpaid balance, or amount owed

Step 2: Add the interest. Interest = Rate x Amount Owed (1.8% = .018)

$116.60   Amount owed $116.60   Amount owed
x   .018   Rate   +   2.10   Interest
$2.09880   Interest $118.70   New balance

Adam will owe $118.70 next month.

Exercise A: For each cardholder below, find the unpaid balance after the minimum payment is made. Then find the interest charge and the new balance in each case.

Cardholder	Current Balance	Minimum Payment	Interest Rate
1) E. Lectron	$245.78	$10.00	1.5%
2) Sir Kitt	$101.98	$15.00	1.6%
3) Cy Bernetics	$78.69	$10.00	1.9%
4) Ben Franklin	$2,889.76	$50.00	2.0%
5) Ona Kite	$99.87	$5.00	1.8%
6) I. C. Lightning	$100.00	$7.00	1.3%
7) Ann Ode	$105.05	$10.00	1.7%
8) Joel Ted	$88.88	$9.00	1.5%
9) Di Ode	$755.34	$6.00	$1\frac{3}{4}\%$
10) I. M. Shockt	$162.54	$10.00	$1\frac{1}{2}\%$

USING A LAYAWAY PLAN

Some customers prefer to buy their clothes by using a *layaway* plan. They pay part of the price as a deposit. The store keeps the item until the customer pays the remainder of the price. There are no interest charges. However, there is a limit to the time that the item may be laid away, usually a month.

CONSUMER HUMOR

I know that the beds are on sale in this store. But I don't think that sleeping in one is what is meant by layaway!

Example: Dee Lay put a swimsuit on layaway during a sale in January. It cost $25.00. She was required to make a 10% deposit. How much will she need to obtain her swimsuit in February?

$25	Cost		$25.00	Cost
x .10	Rate of deposit (10% = .10)		- 2.50	Deposit
$2.50	Deposit		$22.50	Remainder due

Dee will need $22.50 to get her swimsuit out of layaway.

Some stores allow the customer to pay one third of the cost as a deposit and one third each month until the item is paid for. When the total cost is paid, the garment can be taken home. Under this plan, how much would Dee pay each month on the swimsuit?

Example: To find one third of a price, divide the price by 3. Round to the nearest cent.

$$\frac{\$8.333}{3\,)\$25.000} \approx \$8.33$$

Notice that:

	$8.33
x	3
is only	$24.99

For the last payment, Dee would have to pay $8.34.
$8.33 + $8.33 + $8.34 = $25.00, the total amount owed.

Exercise A: These items are to be put on layaway. Find the amount of deposit and the remainder due in each case.

	Article	Cost	Deposit
1)	Dress	$85.00	10%
2)	Shoes	$48.00	$\frac{1}{3}$
3)	Hat	$24.00	15%
4)	Coat	$125.00	$10.00
5)	Jacket	$65.99	20%

CHAPTER REVIEW 3

Solve these problems on pages 61 and 62.

1) What is the total cost of three shirts @ $22.50 and two ties @ $14.90 with a 5% sales tax?

2) What is the amount saved on a coat that was regularly $179.00 and is now on sale for $149.99?

3) What is the amount saved on a dress that was regularly $69.99 and now has a 20% discount?

4) What is the shipping charge for a catalog order that weighs 7 lbs., 12 oz? Use the chart on page 49.

5) How much will $5\frac{3}{8}$ yards of fabric cost at $6.99 a yard?

6) What is the interest charge on $45.75 at 1.8% interest?

7) If a layaway plan required a 20% deposit, how much would the deposit be for a $58.90 dress?

8) What percent is saved when a dress costing $59.98 is bought on sale for $37.19?

9) A skirt requires $1\frac{5}{8}$ yards of fabric. A matching vest requires $\frac{3}{4}$ of a yard. How much fabric is needed for both garments?

10) A person owes $252.00 on his charge card. If he pays a minimum payment of $15.00, what will the unpaid balance be? If the interest rate is 1.5%, what will the interest charge and the new balance be?

What terms do these diagrams suggest?

1.

```
READY
WEAR  WEAR
```

2.

```
DIS 1
 DIS 2
  DIS 3
   DIS 4
    DIS 5
```

3.

```
PAYMENT
```

4.

```
A W A Y
```
(upside down)

CHAPTER 4

MANAGING A HOUSEHOLD

Wise consumers are well informed about the costs of their housing, of their utilities, and of the insurance on their homes. Mathematics skills are needed in order to manage a household effectively. For example:

- You may need to budget your money in order to pay rent on an apartment every month.

- You may be saving to buy a house and want to figure how much money you can borrow.

- You may wish to save money. If you learn to read utility meters, you can save on your gas and electric bills.

- You might also want to learn what factors affect the cost of mortgage and homeowners insurance.

Learning the information included in this chapter will help you to manage a household effectively.

RENTING A HOME

Many people rent their homes. They pay a monthly or weekly fee to the *landlord*, the owner of the property rented to another person. Renters also sign a *lease*. This contract or agreement states the amount of rent and the length of time that the property will be rented.

Renter's Rule: You should spend no more than one week's income for a month's rent.

Applying this *Renter's Rule* helps the renter to have enough money for other needs, such as food, clothing, transportation, and entertainment.

Example: Lisa Home earns $865 per month. What is the highest amount that she should pay for rent?
There are about 4.3 weeks in each month. To estimate Lisa's weekly income, divide her monthly income by 4.3.

$$\frac{\$201.16}{4.3.) \; \$865.0.00} \quad \text{One week's income}$$

Lisa can afford to spend about $200.00 per month for rent.

Exercise A: Find the maximum amount that may be spent for rent with each of these incomes. Remember that 1 year equals 12 months or 52 weeks.

1) $1,200 per month
2) $1,020 per month
3) $466 every 2 weeks
4) $610 every 2 weeks
5) $1,604 per month
6) $10,000 per year
7) $12,000 per year
8) $19,000 per year
9) $14,575 per year
10) $500 twice a month

Hourly Income: A 40-hour work week is considered typical for employees who earn hourly wages.

Exercise B: Multiply by 40 to find the maximum amount that should be spent for rent from each of these incomes.

1) $5.90 per hour
2) $4.39 per hour
3) $8.85 per hour
4) $4.80 per hour
5) $4.56 per hour
6) $6.50 per hour

Exercise C: Divide by 40 to find how much a person must earn per hour to be able to afford each of these monthly rents.

1) $400.00
2) $442.90
3) $564.50
4) $278.90
5) $369.80
6) $325.00

Annual Renting Costs: To find *annual,* or yearly, renting costs, multiply the monthly rent by 12, the number of months in a year.

Example: Lisa's ten aunts share a large townhouse. How much do they pay in rent per year if the monthly rent is $1,255.00?

$1255.00	Rent per month
x 12	Months per year
$15,060.00	Rent per year

Exercise D: Find the total rent paid in a year for each monthly rent.

1) $640.00
2) $307.00
3) $495.95
4) $256.50
5) $456.36
6) $578.50
7) $488.88
8) $367.89
9) $821.50
10) $248.90
11) $1,275.00
12) $380.00

Exercise E: Look in the local newspaper. Find three homes or apartments listed for rent. How much is the rent?

CHAPTER 4

BUYING A HOME

Many people wish to buy a home. Houses cost so much money that most people cannot pay the full price at the time of purchase. They borrow money from a bank or from a savings and loan association.

Lenders will require a certain percent of the price of the house to be paid in cash at the time of purchase. That amount is called a *down payment*. The remainder of the cost of the house will be borrowed or *financed*. This financed loan on property is called a *mortgage*. The amount of money borrowed is called the *principal*. The owners will repay the principal plus interest in monthly payments. The *interest* is a fee charged for borrowing money.

The following *Banker's Rule* is used to help determine how much money a person can borrow to buy a house.

Banker's Rule: You may borrow up to 2.5 times your annual income.

Example: How much can Moore Gedge borrow if his family's income is $20,000 per year?

$20,000	Annual income
x 2.5	Banker's Rule
$50,000	Amount that may be borrowed

Exercise A: Find the amount that may be borrowed for each annual income.

1) $26,000	2) $18,440	3) $20,570
4) $32,870	5) $24,390	6) $85,720
7) $63,560	8) $48,290	9) $50,500
10) $26,750	11) $22,500	12) $76,900

Exercise B: Look in the local newspaper. Find three homes listed for sale. What is the price of each home?

Hourly Income: Some people wanting to buy a house earn an hourly wage. Their annual income is estimated to find out how much money they may borrow. There are about 2,080 paid working hours in a year, so you can multiply the hourly rate by 2,080.

Example: Bill Payer earns $4.58 per hour. How much money may he borrow for a home?

$4.58	Hourly rate	$9,526.40	Annual income
x 2080	Hours per year	x 2.5	Banker's Rule
$9,526.40	Annual income	$23,816.000	May be borrowed

Exercise C: Find the amount that may be borrowed for each of these hourly wages.

1) $5.00   2) $8.00   3) $7.50
4) $6.49   5) $5.32   6) $16.00
7) $14.75   8) $5.15   9) $6.15
10) $8.50   11) $9.60   12) $7.35

Minimum Annual Income: You can estimate the amount a person should earn to qualify for a mortgage. Divide the amount of the mortgage by 2.5.

Example: Ann Yewell wants to borrow $125,000. What should her minimum annual income be?

$$\frac{\$50,000}{2.5\,)\$125,000.0.}$$ Minimum annual income / Mortgage

Ann should have a minimum annual income of $50,000 to borrow $125,000.

Exercise D: Find the minimum annual income for each mortgage.
1) $35,000   2) $80,000   3) $150,000
4) $40,000   5) $45,000   6) $50,000
7) $55,000   8) $60,000   9) $65,000

COMPUTING THE DOWN PAYMENT

To find the down payment, multiply the cost of the home by the rate of the down payment.

Example: Anita Place found the house of her dreams. The price tag was $159,900. What was her 20% down payment?

$159,900   Cost of the house
x   .20   Rate of down payment   (20% = .20)
$31,980.00   Down payment

How much remains to be financed? That is, what will the amount of the mortgage be? Subtract the down payment from the cost of the house.

$159,900   Cost of the house
- 31,980   Down payment
$127,920   Amount of mortgage

Exercise A: Find the amount of the down payment and the amount of the mortgage for each house.

	Cost of House	Rate of Down Payment
1)	$159,900	15%
2)	$159,900	10%
3)	$159,900	25%
4)	$159,900	30%
5)	$45,750	20%
6)	$138,990	17%
7)	$64,500	30%
8)	$72,950	18%
9)	$87,400	19%
10)	$249,900	23%

CONSUMER HUMOR

Would you say that the price of duck feathers is a down payment?

Oh, boy! That really quacks me up!

COMPUTER APPLICATION

Use this program to compute down payments and amounts of mortgages. Use only numbers for the cost of the house. Do not type dollar signs or commas. Do not use percent signs for rates of down payment. Type 13% as 13. See the appendix in the back of this text for directions in using computer programs.

```
10      REM COMPUTING THE DOWN PAYMENT
20      REM CHAPTER 4
30      PRINT "D O W N   P A Y M E N T   A N D   M O R T G A G E"
40      PRINT "NUMBER OF PROBLEMS TO SOLVE:  ";
50      INPUT N
60      FOR X = 1 TO N
70      PRINT "PROBLEM #"; X
80      INPUT "PRICE OF THE HOUSE:  $";
90      INPUT C
100     PRINT "RATE OF DOWN PAYMENT:  ";
110     INPUT P
120     LET D = P * .01 * C
130     LET A = C - D
140     PRINT "THE DOWN PAYMENT IS $"; D
150     PRINT "THE AMOUNT OF THE MORTGAGE IS $"; A
160     PRINT
170     NEXT X
180     END
RUN
```

Exercise A: Use the program to check your work from Exercise A on page 68.

Exercise B: Use the program to find the amount of each down payment and mortgage, given the cost of the house and rate of down payment.

1) $84,980 at 20%	2) $74,125 at 15%	3) $69,250 at 14%
4) $58,340 at 12%	5) $86,950 at 30%	6) $75,900 at 16%
7) $242,810 at 10%	8) $147,500 at 25%	9) $211,500 at 20%

PAYING THE MORTGAGE

Several kinds of mortgage loans exist. The most common loan is called a *fixed-rate mortgage*. The interest rate and the *monthly payments* on principal and interest remain the same until the loan is paid off. On a *variable-rate mortgage*, the interest rate and the monthly payments may change periodically.

Example: Hy Fynants wanted to buy a home. He had enough money for a large down payment. He took out a fixed-rate mortgage for $50,000, to be paid in 30 years. The bank charged him 13% interest. What was his monthly payment? Hy found out the answer quickly by using the following table. He looked down the column for 13%. He looked across the row for $50,000. Where these two lines met, he read, "553." His monthly payment would be $553.00.

Monthly Principal and Interest Payments for 30 Years

Mortgage Amount	9	9.5	10	10.5	11	11.5	12	12.5	13	13.5	14	14.5	15
$40,000	$322	$336	$351	$366	$381	$396	$411	$427	$442	$458	$474	$490	$506
→ $50,000	402	420	439	457	476	495	514	534	553	573	592	612	632
$60,000	483	505	527	549	571	594	617	640	664	687	711	735	759
$70,000	563	589	614	640	667	693	720	747	774	802	829	857	885
$80,000	644	673	702	732	762	792	823	854	885	916	948	980	1012
$90,000	724	757	790	823	857	891	926	961	996	1031	1066	1102	1138
$100,000	805	841	878	915	952	990	1029	1067	1106	1145	1185	1225	1264
$110,000	885	925	965	1006	1048	1089	1131	1174	1217	1260	1303	1347	1391

Exercise A: Find these monthly payments. Use the table given above.

	Mortgage	Interest Rate		Mortgage	Interest Rate
1)	$40,000	9%	2)	$50,000	9.5%
3)	$70,000	12%	4)	$60,000	13%
5)	$90,000	14.5%	6)	$60,000	11.5%
7)	$70,000	12.5%	8)	$80,000	15%
9)	$100,000	10%	10)	$110,000	14%

Example: How much will Hy pay the bank in 30 years?

Step 1: To find out how much Hy pays in one year, multiply the monthly payment by 12.

$553	Monthly payment (see table)
x 12	Months in a year
$6,636	Amount paid in 1 year

Step 2: Multiply the result by 30, the term of the mortgage.

$6,636	Amount paid in 1 year
x 30	Number of years
$199,080	Amount paid in 30 years

Example: How much of this money is *total interest* paid to the bank? Subtract the amount borrowed from the total amount paid to the bank over the term of the mortgage.

$199,080	Amount paid to the bank
- 50,000	Amount borrowed
$149,080	Total interest paid

Exercise B: Find the amount paid in 30 years and the total interest paid for each of these mortgages. Use the table on page 70.

	Amount of Mortgage	Rate of Interest
1)	$40,000	10%
2)	$70,000	12%
3)	$40,000	14%
4)	$60,000	13%
5)	$80,000	13.5%
6)	$50,000	15%
7)	$60,000	10.5%
8)	$90,000	11.5%
9)	$100,000	9.5%
10)	$60,000	15%

TERMS OF MORTGAGES DIFFER

Not all mortgages are for 30 years. Mortgages may be taken out for any term, or number of years.

Example: Anita Lone took out a 25-year mortgage for $35,000 at an interest rate of 11%. What was the monthly payment for this loan?

The table below shows the monthly payment (principal and interest) per $1,000 of mortgage.

Monthly Payments per $1,000							
Years	9%	10%	11%	12%	13%	14%	15%
15	$10.14	$10.75	$11.37	$12.00	$12.65	$13.32	$14.00
20	9.00	9.65	10.32	11.01	11.72	12.44	13.17
25	8.39	9.09	9.80	10.53	11.28	12.04	12.81
30	8.05	8.78	9.52	10.29	11.06	11.85	12.64
35	7.84	8.60	9.37	10.16	10.95	11.76	12.57
40	7.71	8.49	9.28	10.08	10.90	11.71	12.53

Step 1: Look down the column for 11%. Look across the row for 25 years. Read the amount where the two lines meet. This number, 9.80, means that $9.80 must be paid for every $1,000 of principal.

Step 2: Divide the principal by $1,000.

$$\overset{35}{\$1,000 \overline{)\$35,000}} \text{ Principal}$$

There are 35 $1000's in the principal.

Step 3: Multiply $9.80 by 35.

$9.80	Payment per $1,000
x 35	Number of $1,000's in principal
$343.00	Monthly payment

Anita's monthly payment (principal and interest) was $343.00.

Exercise A: Find the monthly payment for each of these mortgages. Use the table on page 72.

	Interest Rate	Term	Principal
1)	15%	15 years	$10,000
2)	9%	25 years	$30,000
3)	12%	30 years	$45,000
4)	11%	40 years	$50,000
5)	13%	20 years	$35,900
6)	15%	35 years	$45,900
7)	10%	15 years	$57,890
8)	14%	20 years	$100,000
9)	15%	40 years	$95,900
10)	9%	30 years	$85,900

Exercise B: Compute the total amount to be repaid on a mortgage for $90,000 under each of the following conditions.

	Interest Rate	Term	To Be Repaid
1)	15%	15 years	_____
2)	15%	20 years	_____
3)	15%	25 years	_____
4)	15%	30 years	_____
5)	15%	35 years	_____
6)	15%	40 years	_____
7)	13%	15 years	_____
8)	13%	30 years	_____
9)	10%	20 years	_____
10)	9%	40 years	_____

READING UTILITY METERS

Services for your home—such as gas, electricity, water, and telephone—are called *utilities*. The word *utility* comes from the word "use." Only one gas and electric company and one water company provide services to everyone living in a given community. The amount of gas, electricity, and water that a customer uses is measured with devices called *meters*. The *dials* on the meter show how many units of the product have been *consumed,* or used, since the meter was installed.

Reading a Meter: Sample dials from a gas meter are shown below. Each *dial* is divided into ten units. The numbers go in opposite directions because of the special *gears* that turn the pointers.

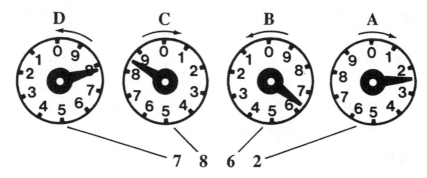

Begin with dial A. Read the number that the pointer has just passed. Take the lower number.

Then read dial B. If the pointer is between numbers, read the lower number. Even though the pointer appears to be exactly on a number, read the next lower number—unless the pointer to its right has passed zero. Dials C and D are read in the same way as dial B. The dials here read 7862.

CONSUMER HUMOR

"Did you hear that John got a job at the electric company?"

"Yes, I heard that he was a real live wire."

Exercise A: Record the readings on these sample utility meter dials. Follow the directions given on page 74.

1)

2)

3)

4)

5)

6)

7)

8)

9)

10)

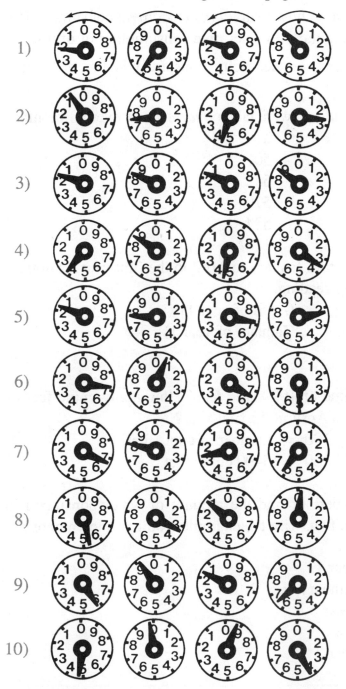

DETERMINING CONSUMPTION OF UTILITIES

How do utility companies know how many *units* customers consume? The companies send meter readers regularly to determine consumption of utilities.

Rule: The amount of water, gas, or electricity consumed is the difference between meter readings.

Example: These water meter readings were taken *quarterly,* or every 3 months.

	Year 1	Year 2
January	391	506
April	445	542
July	462	570
October	488	584

How many units were used from January to April in the first year? Subtract the earlier reading from the later reading.

445	Later reading	(April of year 1)
- 391	Earlier reading	(January of year 1)
54	Units used	

A water unit equals a volume of 100 *cubic feet.* How many cubic feet of water were used from January to April in the first year?

Number of units   x   100   =   number of cubic feet.

54   x   100   =   5400 cubic feet.

Exercise A: For each billing period, find the amount of water consumed in units and in cubic feet. Use the example readings shown above.

1) From April to July in year 1
2) From July to October in year 1
3) From October, year 1, to January, year 2
4) From January to April in year 2
5) From April to July in year 2
6) From July to October in year 2

Customers are billed for the number of units of water, gas, and electricity that they use.

Example: The Great Gas Company's rate is $ .75 per unit. A customer used 200 units. How much was the bill?

Multiply.

$$
\begin{array}{rl}
\$ .75 & \text{Charge per unit} \\
\underline{x \quad 200} & \text{Units used} \\
\$150.00 & \text{Total bill}
\end{array}
$$

Exercise B: Find how many units of gas were used each month. Subtract consecutive meter readings listed below. Then find the total bill for each month. Multiply by a rate of $ .75 per unit.

	December	8917
1)	January	9265
2)	February	9402
3)	March	0054
4)	April	0195
5)	May	0316
6)	June	0451
7)	July	0465
8)	August	0499
9)	September	0528
10)	October	0571
11)	November	0770
12)	December	0889

Exercise C: Subtract consecutive electric meter readings to find the number of units of electricity used each month. Then find the total bill for each month. Multiply by a rate of $ .09 per unit.

	December	65183
1)	January	65836
2)	February	66433
3)	March	66995
4)	April	67611
5)	May	68184
6)	June	68700
7)	July	69336
8)	August	70202
9)	September	71875
10)	October	73245
11)	November	73816
12)	December	74124

Consumers may also be interested in finding out the *average* use of utilities per month.

To find an average: 1. Find the total of the items to be averaged.
2. Divide the total by the number of items.

Example: Karen's family used the following units of electricity over four months. These units of electricity are measured by the *kilowatt hour*, or kwh. A *watt* is a unit of electrical power named after James Watt, a Scottish inventor. What was the average number of units used per month?

December   323 kwh
January   561 kwh
February   272 kwh
March   311 kwh

Step 1: Find the total.
323   kwh
561
272
+ 311
1467   kwh

Step 2: Divide by 4.

$$366.8 \approx 367 \text{ kwh}$$
$$4\overline{)1467.0}$$

Karen's family used an average of 367 kwh per month.

Exercise D: Find the average number of units consumed for the following sets. Round each answer to a whole number.

1) 653, 597, 562, 616
2) 542, 506, 488, 445, 391, 366
3) 36, 18, 26, 17, 54, 25, 19
4) 29, 29, 46, 348, 137, 652, 262, 135, 14
5) 1267, 573, 555, 558, 670, 532, 552, 480, 509, 747
6) 566, 653, 597, 562, 616, 572

TELEPHONE, GAS, AND ELECTRIC BILLS

Telephone customers receive a bill every month. It indicates basic *flat rates* plus additional charges for telephone *extensions* or for long distance calls.

Example: The Browns' telephone bill usually has these two charges.

Flat rate $17.19
1 Touchtone extension $3.15

Exercise A: Find the charge for this regular telephone service.

Exercise B: Find the monthly bill when these long distance charges and taxes are added to the Browns' usual charges.

	Long Distance	Taxes	Monthly Bill
1)	$1.21	1.44	_____
2)	$2.31	$1.48	_____
3)	$2.57	$1.31	_____
4)	$8.57	$1.49	_____
5)	0.00	$1.23	_____
6)	$14.98	$1.68	_____
7)	$5.78	$1.41	_____
8)	$4.94	$1.38	_____
9)	$5.66	$1.40	_____
10)	$11.99	$1.59	_____

Exercise C: On pages 79 and 80 is a summary of the gas, electric, and telephone bills for Ms. U. Tillie Tee during one year. Find the total expenses for these utilities for each month.

	Month	Gas	Electricity	Telephone
1)	January	$60.32	$31.44	$18.90
2)	February	$135.73	$30.95	$18.65
3)	March	$113.39	$33.23	$23.89

4) April	$71.72	$31.69	$30.18
5) May	$48.12	$31.05	$26.85
6) June	$24.67	$38.57	$19.05
7) July	$17.05	$55.74	$24.69
8) August	$14.68	$102.83	$27.36
9) September	$14.61	$84.93	$27.09
10) October	$18.31	$35.45	$29.00
11) November	$65.03	$21.61	$40.99
12) December	$93.27	$21.97	$28.36

Exercise D: Answer the following questions. Use the information given in Exercise C on pages 79 and 80 about Ms. U. Tillie Tee's expenses for gas, electricity, and telephone.

1) How much more did Tillie spend for gas in February than in March?

2) How much more did Tillie spend for electricity in August than in December?

3) How much more did Tillie spend for the telephone in November than in February?

4) In April, how much more was spent for gas than for electricity?

5) Compare the gas and electricity expenses for July. Which is more? By how much?

6) Did Tillie use the same amount of gas each month? Why or why not?

7) What accounts for the different charges for electricity in various months?

8) The utility companies will help Ms. U. Tillie Tee budget for her utility bills through the EMP, or Equal Monthly Payment plan. The customer pays the same amount each month. This amount is the average of the payments from the previous year. What was Tillie's average gas payment? Round your answer to the nearer cent.

9) What was Tillie's average electricity payment?

10) What was Tillie's average telephone payment?

Phone companies give discounts for long distance calls made outside business hours. Study this example. Then complete Exercise E.

Example: The Chime Telephone Company offers a 35% discount on evening calls (5 p.m. to 11 p.m.). For late night calls (11 p.m. to 8 a.m.) and weekend calls, it gives a 60% discount.

Exercise E: Answer these six questions based on the example shown above.

1) Dahlia Numbah made a call at 8 p.m. that would have cost $5.25 during business hours. How much did she save by calling during the evening?

2) Andy made a call on Saturday that would have cost $6.00 during business hours. How much did he save?

3) How much did Andy's call cost?

4) Pam called her sister at 10 p.m. Friday. If the call costs $8.36 during business hours, how much did this call cost?

5) Pam called her sister again at 10 p.m. on Saturday. If the call costs $8.36 during business hours, how much did this call cost Pam?

6) How much did Pam save on these two calls?

MORTGAGE INSURANCE

Homeowners can purchase insurance to protect their home. *Mortgage insurance* is a policy that can be purchased by owners of mortgaged property. It covers one or both owners of a house. If an insured owner dies, the insurance company will pay the balance owed on the house to the beneficiary.

The following table shows the percent of mortgage covered at different times for different mortgages.

Percent of Mortgage Covered					
Policy Year in Which Death Occurs	30 Year Mort.	25 Year Mort.	20 Year Mort.	15 Year Mort.	10 Year Mort.
1	100%	100%	100%	100%	100%
5	94%	92%	88%	80%	66%
10	84%	77%	67%	49%	12%
15	71%	59%	41%	9%	
20	55%	36%	8%		
25	34%	7%			
30	7%				

Example: Mr. Jack Benson had a $37,000 mortgage for a term of 25 years. He died in the fifteenth year. How much should the insurance company pay?

Step 1: Use the table on page 82.

Step 2: Look in the first column, "Policy Year in Which Death Occurs," for 15. The percentage to be paid will be found in this row.

Step 3: Find the column for "25 Year Mort." Go down this column to row 15. Read "59%."

Step 4: Multiply the mortgage by 59%, or .59.

$37,000	Amount of mortgage
x .59	Percent covered by insurance
$21,830.00	Amount to be paid by insurance company

Exercise A: Find the amount to be paid by the insurance company in each of these situations. Use the table on page 82.

	Policy Year in Which Death Occurs	Years of Mortgage	Amount of Mortgage
1)	10	15	$40,000
2)	5	25	$33,500
3)	25	30	$25,700
4)	15	15	$10,000
5)	30	30	$95,800
6)	20	25	$88,000
7)	15	20	$64,500
8)	1	25	$32,700
9)	5	15	$46,800
10)	10	25	$39,900

HOMEOWNERS INSURANCE

A *homeowners insurance* policy covers the home and its contents. The coverage is for damage or loss caused by such things as fire, smoke, theft, severe weather, or collision by any vehicle. Some policies also cover injuries incurred by people on the property.

The amount that a person pays for protection differs from home to home. Some factors that affect the *coverage rate* are:

- construction of brick or wood;

- location in a high or low crime area;

- distance from a fire hydrant or source of water;

- types of violent weather that occur in the area.

Sample Homeowners Rate Chart		
Area	Construction	Coverage Rate
A	Brick	.36%
	Wood Frame	.46%
B	Brick	.42%
	Wood Frame	.54%
C	Brick	.325%
	Wood Frame	.444%
D	Brick	.395%
	Wood Frame	.518%

Example: Les Thanmore owns a $65,000 brick home in Area A. How much would it cost him to insure the home each year with a homeowners insurance policy?

Step 1: Look in the chart on page 84.

Step 2: Find the coverage rate for a brick home in Area A. Read ".36%."

Step 3: Multiply the value of the dwelling by .36%, or .0036.

$$\begin{array}{ll} \$65,000 & \text{Value of dwelling} \\ \underline{\text{x} \quad .0036} & \text{Coverage rate} \\ \$234.00\cancel{0}\cancel{0} & \text{Annual insurance payment} \end{array}$$

His annual homeowners insurance payment would be $234.00.

Exercise A: Find the annual payment for homeowners insurance on the following homes. Use the information given in the chart on page 84.

	Area	Construction	Value of Dwelling
1)	A	Brick	$37,000
2)	C	Wood	$64,470
3)	B	Brick	$101,000
4)	D	Brick	$150,000
5)	C	Brick	$99,900
6)	A	Wood	$75,000
7)	B	Wood	$150,000
8)	D	Wood	$75,980
9)	C	Brick	$125,690
10)	D	Brick	$202,709

CHAPTER REVIEW

4

Solve these problems.

1) Brad pays $346.50 per month for his rent. How much does he pay in a year?

2) Use the banker's rule described on pages 66-67. Calculate the minimum annual income needed to borrow $75,000.

3) Use the table on page 70 to find the monthly payment on a 15% mortgage of $70,000 for 30 years.

4) How much will be repaid in 30 years on a 15% mortgage for $70,000?

5) Which is more—the amount repaid on a mortgage for $37,900 for 15 years at 15%, or the amount repaid on a mortgage for $37,900 for 40 years at 10%? Use the table on page 72.

6) What is this meter reading?

7) How many kilowatt hours were used between these meter readings?
   3049   April meter reading
   2750   March meter reading

8) Compute the average number of units consumed: 504, 519, 576, 321, 256, 101, 76, 75, 127, 289, 367, and 511.

9) What is the total amount due for these utility bills?
   $156.19   Electric
     25.16   Telephone
     32.78   Gas

10) Find the amount to be paid by the insurance company for a claim on an $89,000 mortgage. The company will pay 37%.

CHAPTER 5

BUYING AND MAINTAINING A CAR

The second largest purchase in a consumer's life is usually a car. You may need to compute total sticker price, finance a car, and purchase insurance. If you take a trip, you will need to read an odometer and compute mileage or fuel. You will need to buy gasoline and pay for repairs. People use mathematics when they buy, insure, operate, and maintain cars.

BUYING A NEW CAR

Each new car has a *base price* charged for standard equipment. Any extra items that the customer wants to add to the car—such as an AM/FM stereo radio or air conditioning or radial tires—increase this price. These extra items are called *options*.

On pages 88 and 89 are several examples of sticker prices on new cars. Notice the base price, the costs of various options, and the fee for transportation and handling in each case.

Example: Here is a sticker from a car that Gene wanted. The first amount is the base price. Then the options are listed. The last fee, *transportation and handling,* must be paid by the buyer.

Gene found that, with all the options, the car's total sticker price was $20,020.

$16,796	Base price
2,346	Options
+ 878	Trans./Hand.
$20,020	Total price

Sedan	$16,796
Vinyl roof	430
3.3 L 6-cylinder engine	313
Vinyl trim	149
Automatic transmission	570
4 radial tires	195
Factory air conditioner	624
Spare tire	65
Transportation/Handling	878

Exercise A: Find the total sticker price for each of these five new cars.

1)
Hatchback 3-door	$6,869
Metallic paint	50
Console	178
Automatic transmission	370
Radial tires	59
Power steering	176
Rear window defroster	115
Factory A/C	600
AM/FM stereo radio	188
Mirrors	39
Tinted glass	82
Transportation/Handling	338

2)
Station Wagon	$8,216
Luggage rack	115
Remote control mirror	60
Power steering	195
3.8 L 6-cylinder engine	170
Vinyl trim	29
2-way liftgate	105
Rear window defroster	124
Air conditioning	676
Radio: AM/FM stereo with cassette	172
Tinted glass	88
Power locks	152
Transportation/Handling	408

3)

Hatchback	$6,688
Automatic transmission	411
Clock	57
Power steering	190
Bucket seats	33
Power brakes	93
Rear defroster	120
Factory A/C	611
AM/FM stereo radio	106
Dual sports mirrors	66
Transportation/Handling	290

4)

4-door liftgate	$6,278
Power steering	176
Luggage rack	79
Rear window defroster	111
Air conditioning	563
AM/FM stereo radio	100
Dual remote-control sports mirrors	61
Vinyl molding	41
Tinted glass	76
Transportation/Handling	259

5)

Luxury Sedan	$23,465
Front floor mats	41
Rear floor mats	23
Keyless entry system	141
Door edge guard	27
License plate frames	20
Head lamp convenience group	175
AM/FM stereo w/cassette	107
Dual remote-control mirrors	114
Dual illuminated vanity mirrors	146
Sound system	181
Defroster group	151
Transportation/Handling	506

BUYING A USED CAR

New cars *depreciate* or lose value after they are bought. Many people buy used cars because of their lower prices. Sometimes used car dealers offer special sale prices to encourage people to buy these cars.

Example: The "Used But Not Abused" Car Lot is having a big sale. A two-year-old car that had been $5,200 is now sale priced at $4,750. How much money can be saved by buying this car on sale?

To find the savings, subtract the sale price from the original price.

$5,200   Price before sale
- 4,750   Sale price
$450   Savings

Exercise A: Find the amount that can be saved on each of these sales.

	Car	Years Old	Price Before Sale	Sale Price
1)	King	3	$4,889	$4,489
2)	Iguana	3	$5,389	$4,650
3)	Cat	4	$5,989	$5,589
4)	Mastery	1	$8,664	$6,894
5)	Windsprite	2	$5,689	$5,179
6)	Gazelle	4	$4,839	$3,959
7)	Checkmate	3	$9,199	$8,659
8)	Maria	1	$9,323	$6,895
9)	Fox	3	$9,783	$7,295
10)	Cheetah	5	$9,097	$7,495
11)	Traveler	2	$12,998	$10,295
12)	Destiny	1	$13,000	$10,495

Exercise B: Some buyers trade in their old car as part of the payment on a newer car. Find the cash price in each case. Subtract the trade-in value from the list price to find the cash price.

	List Price	Trade-in Value			List Price	Trade-in Value
1)	$6,895	$900		2)	$7,344	$795
3)	$5,595	$1,200		4)	$9,238	$877
5)	$9,908	$456		6)	$6,767	$869
7)	$10,345	$845		8)	$3,456	$1,457
9)	$10,449	$1,308		10)	$6,000	$879

The used-car dealer, Sue Perr, offered this special deal: "This week only! A guaranteed trade-in of $750 on any car driven onto our lot. OR...a $500 cash *rebate* on any car bought without a trade-in. Use your rebate for a down payment or put it in your pocket."

Exercise C: Find the sale price of each of these used cars from Sue Perr Car Sales. For a trade-in, subtract $750 from the original price. For a cash rebate, subtract $500 from the original price. The first answer has been provided for you.

	Price of Car	With Trade-in	With Rebate
1)	$6,395	$5,645	$5,895
2)	$4,195		
3)	$5,595		
4)	$5,395		
5)	$6,295		
6)	$4,095		
7)	$4,895		
8)	$4,995		

FINANCING A CAR

Few people pay cash for a car since cars are such expensive items. Financing terms vary with the car dealer, bank, or other lenders. Most finance plans require a down payment. The remainder is paid in monthly installments.

The total amount paid in down payment and monthly payments is called the *deferred price*. The amount of the down payment, the number of months to pay, and the amount of the monthly payment may all differ with each sale. Study the following example.

Example: Otto Mobile Used Cars offers the following deal on one of its cars: $199.00 down payment and $76.00 per month for 48 months. The cash price is $2,454. What is the total amount paid for the deferred price?

Step 1:	Multiply.	**Step 2:**	Add.
$76	Monthly payment	$3,648	Monthly payment total
x 48	Months	+ 199	Down payment
$3,648	Monthly payment total	$3,847	Deferred price

Exercise A: Find the deferred price of each of these cars sold at Otto Mobile Used Cars.

	Cash Price	Down Payment	Monthly Payment	Months to Pay
1)	$3,197	$99	$99	48
2)	$5,379	$299	$153	48
3)	$7,984	$499	$239	48
4)	$9,849	$999	$299	48
5)	$3,983	$299	$117	48
6)	$3,391	$199	$105	48
7)	$4,970	$399	$146	48

People who finance a car pay more than the cash price. They must pay an interest charge, which is included in their monthly payments.

Example: Look at the example shown on page 92. What is the total interest paid on this car loan?

Step 1: Subtract.

$2,454	Cash price
- 199	Down payment
$2,255	Amount financed

Step 2: Multiply.

$76	Monthly payment
x 48	Months
$3,648	Monthly payment total

Step 3: Subtract.

$3,648	Monthly payment total
- 2,255	Amount financed
$1,393	Interest paid

Exercise B: Find the total interest paid for each purchase.

	Cash Price	Down Payment	Monthly Payment	Months to Pay
1)	$3,989	$89.00	$129.41	42
2)	$3,989	$1,307.00	$89.00	42
3)	$3,789	$89.00	$129.72	42
4)	$4,798	$98.00	$130.06	48
5)	$4,798	$1,461.82	$98.00	48
6)	$5,601	$89.00	$188.65	42
7)	$5,398	None	$159.00	48
8)	$3,798	$99.00	$99.00	54

COMPUTER APPLICATION

Use this computer program to calculate the deferred price of a car and the total cost of financing a car. See the appendix in the back of this text for directions in using computer programs.

```
10      REM  FINANCING A CAR
20      REM  CHAPTER 5
30      PRINT " C O S T   O F   F I N A N C I N G   A   C A R "
40      PRINT "WHAT IS THE CASH PRICE";
50      INPUT C
60      PRINT "WHAT IS THE DOWN PAYMENT";
70      INPUT D
80      PRINT "WHAT IS THE MONTHLY PAYMENT";
90      INPUT M
100     PRINT "HOW MANY MONTHS TO PAY";
110     INPUT P
120     LET X = D + M * P
130     PRINT "  THE DEFERRED PRICE OF THIS CAR IS $"; X
140     PRINT "  THE COST OF FINANCING THIS CAR IS $"; X - C
150     END
RUN
```

CONSUMER HUMOR

Did you hear that John left his job at the loan department at the bank?

Yes, I understand that he lost interest in the job.

AUTOMOBILE INSURANCE

The owner of a car is *liable*, or legally responsible, for any damage done by the car to persons or property. *Liability* insurance protects the owner against claims resulting from an accident that is his or her fault. It covers personal injuries and property damage. The cost of the policy, or the *premium*, is affected by the age and sex of the driver, the location, and the distance traveled.

Liability Insurance

10 / 20 / 15

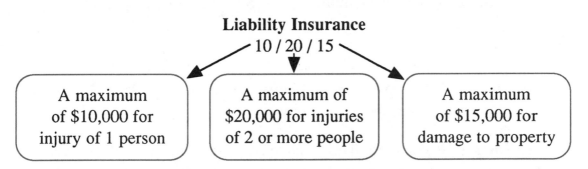

| A maximum of $10,000 for injury of 1 person | A maximum of $20,000 for injuries of 2 or more people | A maximum of $15,000 for damage to property |

	Liability Insurance Premiums							
	Personal Injury				Property Damage			
Area	10/20	20/40	40/80	75/150	5	10	25	50
High risk	$110	$154	$173	$204	$72	$84	$99	$148
Average	$67	$71	$89	$103	$56	$69	$77	$98
Low risk	$40	$52	$67	$89	$48	$52	$61	$73

Exercise A: Use this table to find the total premiums due in each case.

1) What is a person's premium for the 40/80/25 coverage if he lives in a high risk area? ($173 + $99 = ?)

2) Find the premium for a 10/20/25 policy in an average risk area.

3) What is the premium for a 75/150/50 policy in a low risk area?

4) Find the premium for a 20/40/5 policy in a high risk area.

Example: Because Bea Careful had such a good driving record, she earned a "Good Driver Discount." After finding her premium, the insurance agent multiplied her premium by the good driver factor, .86, to find her actual cost.

Bea bought 40/80/25 coverage in a high risk area.

$173	For the 40/80		$272	Regular premium
+ 99	For the 25		x .86	Good driver factor
$272	Regular premium		$233.92	Bea's premium

Exercise B: Find these premiums. Use the table on page 95. Multiply the factor times the regular premium.

1) Hy Rates is 18 years old, lives in an average risk area, and wants 10/20/10 coverage. Because young males have the highest rate of accidents, Hy will be charged a 1.77 factor on his policy. Find his premium.

2) I. C. Streets lives in a high risk area and wants 40/80/50 coverage. Because she also uses her car for business, she is charged a 1.29 factor on her policy. Find her premium.

3) Because Woody Stop has a poor driving record, he must pay a 1.48 factor on his policy for 20/40/25 coverage in a low risk area. What is his premium?

4) After six years of careful driving, Willy Crash got married. With the double discount of reaching age 25 and being married, Willy gets a .78 factor on his premium for 10/20/5 coverage in an average risk area. What is his premium?

5) Sue Everyone has a terrible driving record, drives 30 miles to work every day, and lives in a high risk area. She needs 75/150/50 coverage. Her factor is 2.08. What is Sue's premium?

READING AN ODOMETER

Operating a car involves working with distance. The *odometer* on a car's dashboard counts the number of miles that the car has traveled. There are usually five digits of one color and a sixth digit of another color. Imagine a decimal point between the last two digits.

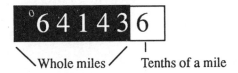

Whole miles   Tenths of a mile

This odometer reads, "64,143.6 miles."

The reading in words is: "Sixty-four thousand, one hundred forty-three and six tenths miles."

Notice that the word "and" stands for the decimal point. It is never used in any other part of the number.

Exercise A: Copy these odometer readings. Then write each reading in words.

1) 003046

2) 071235

3) 128905

4) 500701

5) 999999

6) 123456

7) 300567

8) 745820

9) 600062

10) 054173

Spelling Review of Some Number Names	
28	twenty-eight
30	thirty
44	forty-four
55	fifty-five
60	sixty
70	seventy
80	eighty
90	ninety
100	one hundred
1,000	one thousand

AVERAGE MILES DRIVEN PER YEAR

To find the average miles driven per year, divide the odometer reading by the age of the car.

Example: Kitty Karr's odometer reads 64,143.6 miles. Her car is six years old. On the average, how many miles did Kitty drive each year?

$$\frac{10690.6}{6 \overline{)64143.6}} \approx 10,691 \quad \text{Miles per year}$$

Exercise A: Find the average number of miles driven per year for each car. Round your answers to the nearer mile.

	Odometer Reading	Age of Car in Years
1)	3 0 3 6 5 7	3
2)	1 6 0 6 0 6	2
3)	4 9 7 5 6 7	5
4)	3 6 7 5 5 8	4
5)	1 2 4 8 9 5	5
6)	5 3 6 2 5 9	2
7)	9 5 8 9 7 6	10
8)	8 8 0 4 5 9	9
9)	7 0 2 0 7 0	6
10)	9 2 4 8 8 1	7
11)	2 6 3 9 4 2	2
12)	3 9 5 2 7 3	4

NUMBER OF MILES TRAVELED

To find the number of miles traveled, subtract the beginning odometer reading from the ending odometer reading.

Example: At the beginning of a trip, the odometer reading was 64,143.6. At the end of the trip, the odometer reading was 64,507.2. How many miles were traveled?

Subtract.   64,507.2   Reading at end of trip
       - 64,143.6   Reading at beginning of trip
          363.6   Miles traveled

If an odometer starts all over again, what number follows this reading?

9 9 9 9 9 9

Counting, we would go to 100,000.0. However, since the odometer has only six digits, the next number it shows is 0 0 0 0 0 0.   To find the distance traveled, use the 1 that you know should be the seventh digit.

Beginning of trip 9 9 3 0 4 7   100,006.9   End of trip
End of trip   0 0 0 0 6 9   - 99,304.7   Beginning of trip
                              702.2   Miles traveled

Exercise A: Find the miles traveled for each trip.   Use decimal points to indicate tenths of a mile.

	Beginning	End			Beginning	End
1)	123456	124890		2)	101011	101926
3)	003709	010008		4)	768423	769512
5)	368758	368792		6)	303067	317656
7)	993758	003059		8)	584104	589017
9)	008563	017465		10)	623076	632050

COMPUTING MILEAGE

The farther a driver can go on a unit of gasoline, the better. One measure of how well a car operates is the miles per gallon (mpg) or the kilometers per liter (km/L) the car can get. This figure is called the *mileage* or the mileage rating.

"Miles per gallon" means
$$\text{gallons} \overline{)\text{miles}}$$

Review the key to using the word "per" on page 34.

Example: Carla Carr traveled 274 miles on 15 gallons of gas. What was her mileage?

$$\begin{array}{r} 18.2 \\ \hline 15)274.0 \end{array} \approx 18 \text{ miles per gallon}$$

Carla's mileage was 18 miles per gallon.

Exercise A: Find the mileage for each trip. Round your answer to the nearer whole number.

	Distance		Gas Used	
1)	400	miles	20	gallons
2)	1,200	miles	70	gallons
3)	356	miles	15	gallons
4)	489	miles	12	gallons
5)	25	miles	1.2	gallons
6)	565	kilometers	62	liters
7)	256	kilometers	32	liters
8)	1,024	kilometers	128	liters
9)	245	kilometers	47	liters
10)	779	kilometers	89	liters

COMPUTING THE RANGE OF A CAR

How far can a car travel on a tank of gas? The Environmental Protection Agency (EPA) rates gas consumption for all cars and vans. The *EPA rating* is given for stop-and-start city driving as well as for highway driving on the open road.

To find the range of a car, multiply the miles per gallon rating or the kilometers per liter rating by the capacity of the tank.

Example: Hy Mileage's little import has an EPA rating of 35 mpg in the city and 40 mpg on the highway. His tank holds 12 gallons. What is the range of Hy's car?

City:	35	mpg	Highway:	40	mpg
	x 12	Gallons		x 12	Gallons
	420	Miles range		480	Miles range

Exercise A: Find the range for each car in the city and on the highway.

	EPA Rating		Tank
	City	Highway	Capacity
1)	40 mpg	50 mpg	10 gal.
2)	10 km/L	15 km/L	80 L
3)	20 mpg	30 mpg	19 gal.
4)	12 km/L	18 km/L	67 L
5)	21 mpg	29 mpg	17 gal.
6)	14 km/L	22 km/L	40 L
7)	27 mpg	38 mpg	19 gal.
8)	11 km/L	19 km/L	37 L
9)	29 mpg	37 mpg	18 gal.
10)	9 km/L	17 km/L	39 L

COMPUTING THE FUEL NEEDED

It is often helpful to estimate how many gallons or liters of gasoline will be needed for a trip. To find out how much fuel is needed for a trip, divide the distance by the mileage rating.

Example: Sue Perhighway is planning a 390-mile trip. Her car's EPA rating is 25 mpg on the highway. How many gallons of gas will she require for this trip?

$$\begin{array}{r} 15.6 \\ 25\overline{)390.0} \end{array} \approx \begin{array}{l} 16 \text{ Gallons needed for the trip} \\ \text{Miles} \end{array}$$

Exercise A: Find the amount of fuel needed for each trip. Round your answer to the nearer whole number.

	Distance		Mileage Rating	
1)	150	miles	20	mpg
2)	370	miles	27	mpg
3)	896	miles	35	mpg
4)	1,040	miles	40	mpg
5)	4,488	miles	44	mpg
6)	300	km	15	km/L
7)	247	km	12	km/L
8)	798	km	17	km/L
9)	2,211	km	11	km/L
10)	8,658	km	9	km/L

COMPUTING AVERAGE SPEED

Speed is measured in *miles per hour* (mph) or in *kilometers per hour* (km/h). To find the average rate of speed on a trip, divide the hours into the distance traveled. Study the example on the next page.

Example: Ann Jinn drove 360 miles in 8 hours and 36 minutes. What was her average rate of speed?

Step 1:

Convert minutes to a decimal part of an hour by dividing by 60.

$$\begin{array}{r} 0.6 \\ 60\overline{)36.0} \end{array}$$ Hour
Minutes

Step 2:

Write the hours as a decimal number.

8 hours and 36 minutes
8 hours + 0.6 hours = 8.6 hours

Step 3:

Divide the miles by the hours.

$$\begin{array}{r} 41.8 \approx 42 \text{ mph} \\ 8.6.\overline{)360.0.0} \end{array}$$

Ann's average rate of speed was 42 miles per hour.

Exercise A: Find the average rate of speed for each trip. Round your answer to the nearer whole number.

	Distance	Time
1)	180 miles	4 hours, 30 minutes
2)	340 miles	6 hours, 12 minutes
3)	1,100 miles	21 hours, 24 minutes
4)	65 miles	3 hours, 15 minutes
5)	385 miles	7 hours, 48 minutes
6)	299 kilometers	8 hours, 18 minutes
7)	68 kilometers	1 hour, 15 minutes
8)	302 kilometers	3 hours, 42 minutes
9)	343 kilometers	3 hours, 54 minutes
10)	384 kilometers	5 hours, 6 minutes

FINDING TRAVEL TIME

To find the time it should take for a trip, divide the distance by the speed.

Example: Carrie Meback plans a 418-mile trip to Virginia. Since she and her family will travel on the interstate highways for most of the trip, they hope to average 50 mph. How long should they expect the trip to last?

Step 1:

Divide the distance by the average speed.

$$\begin{array}{r} 8.36 \\ \hline 50\,\overline{)418.00} \end{array}\ \begin{array}{l} \text{Hours} \\ \text{Miles} \end{array}$$

Step 2:

Convert the decimal part of the quotient to minutes by multiplying it by 60.

$$\begin{array}{r} .36 \\ \times\ 60 \\ \hline 21.60 \end{array}\ \begin{array}{l} \text{Hours} \\ \text{Minutes per hour} \\ \approx 22 \text{ minutes} \end{array}$$

Step 3:

Write the hours and minutes.

8 hours, 22 minutes

Exercise A: Find the travel time for each of these trips. Round your answer to the nearer minute.

	Distance	Average Speed
1)	180 miles	45 mph
2)	91 miles	35 mph
3)	56 miles	42 mph
4)	360 miles	50 mph
5)	143 miles	37 mph
6)	420 kilometers	70 km/h
7)	1,042 kilometers	75 km/h
8)	240 kilometers	50 km/h
9)	976 kilometers	40 km/h
10)	36 kilometers	70 km/h

BUYING GASOLINE

Operating a car involves buying gasoline. Gasoline prices are quoted per gallon or per liter. Each price has three decimal places because gasoline is priced to the nearest tenth of a cent.

Example: EXOFF regular gasoline costs $1.459 per gallon. It is customary to read that price as "a dollar forty-five and $^9/_{10}$ cents." If we write that price in cents, it looks like this: 145.9¢. This number, 145.9¢, is read as "one hundred forty-five and nine-tenths cents."

To find the cost of gasoline, multiply the number of liters (or gallons) purchased times the cost per liter (or gallon). Round to the nearer cent.

Example: HEXACO lead-free gasoline costs 38.6¢ per liter. Find the cost of 72 liters.

38.6¢ = $ .386	

$ .386   Cost per liter
x   72   Number of liters purchased
$27.792 ≈ $27.79 for 72 liters

Exercise A: Find the cost for each of these gasoline purchases.
1) 17 gal. at $1.375 per gallon
2) 17 gal. at $1.489 per gallon
3) 17 gal. at $1.567 per gallon
4) 17 gal. at $1.299 per gallon
5) 17 gal. at $1.435 per gallon
6) 75 L   at 37.6¢ per liter
7) 75 L   at 42.2¢ per liter
8) 75 L   at $ .558 per liter
9) 75 L   at $ .459 per liter
10) 75 L   at $ .682 per liter

Gasoline from self-service pumps costs less per unit (liter or gallon) than gas from full-service pumps. Customers save money by pumping their own gas. The difference between the posted prices may seem small, but the savings per tankful are considerable.

Example: Millie Liter needs to buy 32 liters of gas. How much will she save by pumping her own? The price on the *self-serve pump* is .386 per liter. The price on the *full-service pump* is .453 per liter.

Step 1: Subtract. Find the difference in price per unit.	$ .453	Full-serve price
	- .386	Self-serve price
	$.067	Difference in prices

Step 2: To find the amount saved, multiply the difference by the number of units purchased.	$ .067	Difference in prices
	x 32	Liters purchased
	$2.144	≈ $2.14 Savings

Exercise B: Find the amount each customer saved by using the self-serve gasoline pump.

	Full-Serve	Self-Serve	Units	Savings
1)	$1.679	$1.599	20 gal.	_____
2)	$1.898	$1.779	19 gal.	_____
3)	$ .459	$ .420	42 L	_____
4)	59.6¢	52.8¢	57 L	_____
5)	135.8¢	129.4¢	15 gal.	_____
6)	55.5¢	44.4¢	79 L	_____
7)	$1.754	$1.689	14 gal.	_____
8)	64.3¢	57.4¢	68 L	_____
9)	$1.457	$1.398	17 gal.	_____
10)	45.7¢	39.9¢	59 L	_____

COMPUTING THE COST OF REPAIRS

Cars need occasional repair. Regular tuneups keep them running smoothly, but broken or worn parts must be replaced to prevent further damage. At an auto repair shop, you are charged for *parts and labor.* This term means that you must pay the mechanic a certain amount per hour for any work done. It also means that you must pay for all the new or *rebuilt* items that the mechanic installs.

Example: Anita Brakejob had her automatic transmission replaced for $500.00. The mechanic replaced 15 L of transmission fluid @ $3.50 per liter. (The symbol @ means *at* and indicates unit price.) It took three hours of labor to complete the job. The cost for labor is $35.00 per hour. There was a 5% sales tax for all parts. No sales tax is charged on labor. What was the total cost?

Step 1: Find the total cost of the parts.

15 L x $3.50 = $52.50.

$52.50	Cost of fluid
+ $500.00	Transmission repair
$552.50	Total parts

Step 2: Compute the sales tax. Hint: Instead of computing 5% tax and adding it on, multiply by 105% and do it in one step. Round up the answer to the next cent.

$552.50 x 105% (1.05)

$552.50	Total parts
x 1.05	Rate for parts plus tax
$580.125	≈ $580.13 Parts plus tax

Step 3: Compute the labor.

$35.00 per hour for 3 hours
$35.00 x 3 = $105.00   Labor

Step 4: Add the parts plus tax and the labor together to find the total cost.

$580.13	Parts plus tax
+105.00	Labor
$685.13	Total cost

Exercise A: Find the total cost of each repair job. Follow the steps given on page 107. Use $35 per hour as the labor rate. Include 5% tax on the parts.

1) Parts: Battery, $69.95   Labor: 0.3 hour

2) Parts: Muffler, $35.00   Labor: 1 hour
       Tail pipe, $18.00
       Clamps, $2.00

3) Parts: 4 Shock Absorbers @ $17.94   Labor: 2 hours

4) Parts: Rebuilt alternator, $85.00   Labor: $\frac{1}{2}$ hour
       Fan belt, $10.00

5) Parts: 4 Radial tires 6R78x14 @ $65 per tire   Labor: Included in
       Federal excise tax @ $2.50 per tire   price of tire
       Balanced and mounted @ $4.00 per tire

6) Parts: Filter, $7.50   Labor: 0.2 hours
       6 cans oil @ $1.95 per can

7) Parts: Radiator, $150.00   Labor: 1 hour
       2 gallons antifreeze @ $6.99

8) Parts: Disc brakes, $20.00   Labor: 2 hours
       2 turn rotors @ $5.00 each

9) Parts: Power steering pump, $95.00
       6 L fluid @ $1.75 per liter
  Labor: 2 hours

10) Parts: 2-Barrel carburetor, $75.00
       6 plugs @ $1.45 each
       Points, $4.50
  Labor: 3.2 hours

CONSUMER HUMOR

Did you hear John lost his job at the muffler shop?

Yes, I understand that he was always exhausted.

CHAPTER REVIEW 5

Solve these problems on pages 109 and 110.

1) Compute the total amount paid for a used car with the following financing arrangements. The buyer agreed to pay $89 down plus $128.57 per month for 36 months.

2) Stan Dardshift has a good driver discount on his insurance policy. Compute his actual premium if he pays 86% of the $279 regular premium rate.

3) Write this odometer reading in words: 7 3 8 0 4 5

4) At the beginning of a trip, the odometer read 04157.8. At the end of the trip, the odometer read 04360.7. Compute the distance traveled.

5) Calculate the cost of 67.4 liters of gasoline at a price of 32.4 cents per liter.

6) Find the mileage for a car that travels 473.3 miles on 13.6 gallons of gas.

7) Compute the range of a car with EPA rating of 19 km/L and a tank that holds 38 liters.

8) Calculate the average rate of speed on a 510-mile trip that took 17 hours.

9) Find the number of hours it will take to drive 360 miles if a person averages 50 miles per hour.

10) Calculate the cost of 7.3 hours of mechanical labor at a rate of $35 per hour.

11) The odometer in Ingrid's 3-year-old car read 38465.2. What was her average yearly mileage?

12) Brad is planning a 285-mile trip. His car's EPA rating is 18 mpg. How many gallons of gas will Brad need for this trip?

CHAPTER 6

WORKING WITH FOOD

Knowing the nutritional value of the foods you eat can help you to plan better meals. You can learn to count calories and understand recommended daily allowances. Exercise can also burn off excess calories and tone your body. You may want to lose weight, need to change the yield of a recipe, or time food preparation. This chapter discusses some of the mathematics involved in preparing and eating food.

COUNTING CALORIES

Many people are concerned about calories. A *calorie* is a measure of heat energy. It is the amount of energy needed to raise the temperature of 1 kilogram of water one degree *Celsius*. Calories measure food consumption because food contains energy for our bodies. The more energy that a food provides, the higher the number of calories that it contains.

Example: The following chart shows everything that Ann R. Gee ate in one day plus the calories in each food item.

Food for One Day		
Meal	**Item**	**Calories**
Breakfast:	Milk (1 cup)	150
	Egg (1 medium)	95
	Toast (1 slice)	65
	Orange juice (1 cup)	120
Lunch:	Hamburger	305
	French fries	155
	Cola (12 oz.)	145
	Ice Cream (1 cup)	270
Dinner:	Chicken pot pie	
	($\frac{1}{3}$ of 9" pie)	545
	Milk (1 cup)	150
Snacks:	Cheese pizza ($\frac{1}{8}$ pie)	186
	Popcorn (1 cup)	25
	Potato chips (10)	115
	3 Colas (12 oz.)	435

Exercise A: Find the number of calories that Ann consumed in each case.

1) For breakfast
2) For lunch
3) For dinner
4) For snacks
5) During the entire day
6) For breakfast, lunch, and dinner

Exercise B: Find the answers. Use the chart on page 112 to solve the first four problems.

1) If Ann had a second egg and a second slice of toast for breakfast, how many more calories would she have consumed?

2) How many total calories are there in the French fries and the ice cream?

3) How many calories are in a whole chicken pot pie?
   Hint: There are 545 calories in $\frac{1}{3}$ of the pie. There are three $\frac{1}{3}$'s in a whole pie, so multiply 545 by 3 to find the total number of calories.

4) How many calories are in a whole cheese pizza?

5) How many calories are contained in a gingerbread cake if $\frac{1}{9}$ of the cake contains 175 calories?

6) In $\frac{1}{7}$ of a banana cream pie are 285 calories. What is the caloric content of the whole pie?

7) How many calories are in a whole pound cake if $\frac{1}{17}$ of the cake contains 160 calories?

8) Dark fruit cake contains 55 calories in $\frac{1}{30}$ of a loaf. How many calories are in the whole loaf?

9) One-sixth of a coffee cake has 230 calories. Compute the total calories in the cake.

10) How many calories are in a devil's food cake if $\frac{1}{16}$ of it contains 235 calories?

THE KEY TO RATIO

A *ratio* is a comparison of two quantities. Study the following examples.

Example: Suppose that there are 18 girls and 14 boys in your class.
The ratio of boys to girls is 14 to 18.
The ratio of girls to boys is 18 to 14.

A short way to write ratios is with fractions.
The ratio of boys to girls is $\frac{14}{18}$.
The ratio of girls to boys is $\frac{18}{14}$.

You can simplify the fraction by dividing both terms by their greatest common factor.

Examples: 14 to 18 $\rightarrow$ $\frac{14}{18}$ = $\frac{14 \div 2}{18 \div 2}$ = $\frac{7}{9}$

18 to 14 $\rightarrow$ $\frac{18}{14}$ = $\frac{18 \div 2}{14 \div 2}$ = $\frac{9}{7}$

Exercise A: Write each ratio as a fraction in simplest terms.

1) 2 to 4
2) 160 calories to 2 cups
3) 4 to 7
4) 34 miles to 2 gallons
5) 6 to 8
6) 40 minutes to 50 miles
7) 5 to 10
8) 120 miles to 3 hours
9) 8 to 36
10) 145 calories to 15 ounces
11) a million to 1
12) eight to twelve
13) two to three
14) ten to fifteen
15) 100 to 150
16) six to nine

THE KEY TO PROPORTION

When two ratios are equal, we say that they form a *proportion*. One way to tell if two ratios are equal is to compare the *cross products*. This answer is obtained by multiplying the denominator of one fraction by the numerator of another.

Example: Are $\frac{2}{3}$ and $\frac{4}{6}$ equal?

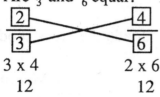

3 x 4   2 x 6 $\frac{2}{3} = \frac{4}{6}$

12   12

The cross products are both 12.
The cross products are equal, so the ratios form a proportion.

Example: Do $\frac{7}{8}$ and $\frac{28}{32}$ form a proportion?

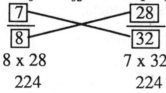

8 x 28   7 x 32 $\frac{7}{8} = \frac{28}{32}$

224   224

The cross products are both 224.
The cross products are equal, so the ratios form a proportion.

Exercise A: Copy the following ratios. See if the ratios are equal. Write an equal sign if the ratios form a proportion.

1) $\frac{3}{6}$ $\frac{5}{10}$ 2) $\frac{2}{3}$ $\frac{9}{12}$ 3) $\frac{1}{3}$ $\frac{5}{6}$

4) $\frac{1}{4}$ $\frac{2}{8}$ 5) $\frac{10}{16}$ $\frac{5}{8}$ 6) $\frac{4}{5}$ $\frac{20}{25}$

7) $\frac{5}{8}$ $\frac{3}{4}$ 8) $\frac{7}{8}$ $\frac{15}{16}$ 9) $\frac{10}{19}$ $\frac{30}{39}$

You may use cross products to find an unknown term in a proportion.

Example: $\dfrac{2}{5} = \dfrac{?}{15}$

Step 1: Find one cross product.

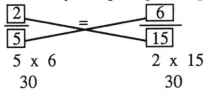

$\rightarrow$ 2 x 15 = 30

Step 2: To find the missing term, divide the cross product by the other term.

6 Missing term

5 $\overline{)30}$ Cross product

Step 3: Write the complete proportion.

$$\dfrac{2}{5} \quad = \quad \dfrac{6}{15}$$

Step 4: Check by comparing cross products.

5 x 6   2 x 15

30   30

Exercise B: Find the missing term in each proportion.

1) $\dfrac{1}{3} = \dfrac{?}{12}$ 2) $\dfrac{3}{4} = \dfrac{6}{?}$ 3) $\dfrac{?}{12} = \dfrac{27}{36}$

4) $\dfrac{8}{150} = \dfrac{?}{75}$ 5) $\dfrac{5}{16} = \dfrac{25}{?}$ 6) $\dfrac{3}{?} = \dfrac{9}{45}$

7) $\dfrac{2}{7} = \dfrac{24}{?}$ 8) $\dfrac{96}{180} = \dfrac{16}{?}$ 9) $\dfrac{72}{?} = \dfrac{9}{7}$

10) $\dfrac{108}{18} = \dfrac{?}{3}$ 11) $\dfrac{2}{4} = \dfrac{4}{?}$ 12) $\dfrac{3}{9} = \dfrac{9}{?}$

13) $\dfrac{5}{25} = \dfrac{25}{?}$ 14) $\dfrac{4}{?} = \dfrac{16}{64}$ 15) $\dfrac{1}{?} = \dfrac{2}{4}$

FINDING CALORIES WITH PROPORTION

Read the calorie chart shown on the right. When you drink a glass of cola, you do not always drink 12 ounces. Not all pizzas are cut into eight pieces. How can you use the calorie chart to tell the number of calories in any amount of food? Use proportions!

Calorie Chart		
Food Item	Amount	Calories
Cola	12. oz.	145
14" Pizza	$\frac{1}{8}$ pie	186
Spaghetti	1 cup	250
Ginger Ale	12 oz.	115
Clam Chowder	8 oz.	80
Tomato Soup	8 oz.	90
Gelatin Dessert	8 oz.	140

Example: How many calories are in 16 ounces of cola?

Step 1: Write a proportion.

$$\frac{12 \text{ ounces}}{145 \text{ calories}} = \frac{16 \text{ ounces}}{? \text{ calories}}$$

Step 2: Find the cross product.

$$145 \times 16 = 2320$$

Step 3: Divide and round to the nearer whole number.

$$12\overline{)2320} \quad 193\frac{1}{3} \approx 193 \text{ calories}$$

Example: At the Leaning Tower of Pizza Shop, pizzas are cut into six pieces instead of eight. How many calories are in one prtion, or $\frac{1}{6}$ of a pie?

Step 1: Write a proportion.

$$\frac{\frac{1}{8} \text{pie}}{186 \text{ calories}} = \frac{\frac{1}{6} \text{pie}}{? \text{ calories}}$$

Step 2: Find the cross product.
$$186 \times \frac{1}{6} = 31$$

Step 3: Divide. When dividing by a fraction, invert the divisor and multiply.
$$31 \div \frac{1}{8}$$
$$\rightarrow 31 \times \frac{8}{1} = 248 \text{ calories}$$

CONSUMER HUMOR

Do you want your pizza cut into eight pieces today?

No, cut it into six pieces. I'm not sure I could eat eight.

Exercise A: Calculate the number of calories in each portion by using a proportion. Round your answer to the nearer calorie.

1)   8 oz. of cola   12 oz. = 145 calories

2)   3 cups of spaghetti   1 cup = 150 calories

3)   10 oz. of ginger ale   12 oz. = 115 calories

4)   12 oz. of clam chowder   8 oz. = 80 calories

5)   16 oz. of tomato soup   8 oz. = 90 calories

6)   4 oz. of gelatin dessert   8 oz. = 140 calories

7)   1,000 grams of cookies   10 g = 50 calories

8)   100 grams of rice   205 g = 225 calories

9)   One-sixth of a pie   one-seventh of a pie = 350 calories

10) One-fourth of a pizza   one-eighth of a pie = 186 calories

11) 100 g of layer cake   54 g = 200 calories

12) 100 g of brownies   20 g = 95 calories

13) One cup of buttermilk contains 90 calories. How many calories are in one-third of a cup?

14) One-seventh of a custard pie contains 185 calories. Find the number of calories in the following parts of this pie.
     a) one-eighth   b) one-fourth   c) one-sixth

15) One-seventh of a pineapple chiffon pie has 265 calories. Find the number of calories in the following parts of this pie.
     a) one-fifth   b) one-tenth   c) one-twelfth

16) One-sixteenth of a chocolate cake has 275 calories. Find the number of calories in the following parts of this cake.
     a) one-eighth   b) one-half   c) one-tenth

17) One-ninth of a 9" square cake contains 400 calories. Find the number of calories in the following parts of this cake.
     a) one-eighth   b) one-fourth   c) one-sixth

RECOMMENDED DAILY ALLOWANCES

Nutritionists have determined *nutrient* levels that people need each day to maintain energy and growth. These amounts are shown in the following table.

Recommended Daily Allowances of Chief Food Elements
Source: Food and Nutrition Board, National Research Council

Age	Weight (lbs.)	Calories	Protein (grams)	Calcium (mg,)	Iron (mg.)	Vit. A (I.U.)	Thia-min (mg.)	Ribo-flavin (mg.)	Niacin (mg.)	Ascorbic Acid (mg.)
11-14	97	2,800	44	1,200	18	5,000	1.4	1.5	18	45
15-18	134	3,000	54	1,200	18	5,000	1.5	1.8	20	45
19-22	147	3,000	54	800	10	5,000	1.5	1.8	20	45
23-50	154	2,700	56	800	10	5,000	1.4	1.6	18	45
51+	154	2,400	56	800	10	5,000	1.2	1.5	16	45
11-14	97	2,400	44	1,200	18	4,000	1.2	1.3	16	45
15-18	119	2,100	48	1,200	18	4,000	1.1	1.4	14	45
19-22	128	2,100	46	800	18	4,000	1.1	1.4	14	45
23-50	123	2,000	46	800	18	4,000	1.0	1.2	13	45
51+	126	1,800	46	800	10	4,000	1.0	1.1	12	45

The U.S. Department of Agriculture lists these nutrients in beverages:

Nutritional Value of Beverages

Beverage	Volume (fluid oz.)	Calories	Protein (grams)	Calcium (milligrams)	Iron (milligrams)	Vitamin A (I.U.)	Thiamin (milligrams)	Riboflavin (milligrams)	Niacin (milligrams)	Ascorbic Acid (milligrams)
Whole milk	8	160	9	288	.1	350	.07	.41	.2	2
Apple juice	8	120	T	15	1.5	—	.02	.05	.2	2
Cranberry juice	8	165	T	13	.8	T	.03	.03	.1	40
Grapefruit juice	8	100	1	20	1.0	20	.07	.04	.4	84
Grape juice	8	165	1	28	.8	—	.10	.05	.5	T
Orange juice	8	120	2	25	.2	550	.22	.02	1.0	120
Prune juice	8	200	1	36	10.5	—	.03	.03	1.0	5
Carbonated water	8	77	0	—	—	0	0	0	0	0
Cola	8	97	0	—	—	0	0	0	0	0
Orange soda	8	113	0	—	—	0	0	0	0	0
Ginger ale	8	77	0	—	—	0	0	0	0	0
Root beer	8	100	0	—	—	0	0	0	0	0

T = Trace   — = Not Determined   I.U. = International Units

Exercise A: Write the answers. Use information from the tables on page 119.

1) Which beverage is highest in Vitamin A?

2) Which beverage is highest in ascorbic acid (Vitamin C)?

3) Which beverages are lowest in calories?

4) Which beverage is highest in calcium?

5) Which juice is lowest in thiamin?

6) List the juices and milk in order of their thiamin content. Begin with the highest.

7) List the juices and milk in order of their iron content. Begin with the highest.

8) List the juices and milk in order of their niacin content. Begin with the lowest.

9) What two beverages supply more than the Recommended Daily Allowance (RDA) of ascorbic acid?

10) Compared with the Recommended Daily Allowance (RDA) for protein, are juices high or low in protein?

11) What is meant by this statement: "Soft drinks contain empty calories"?

One serving of food may provide part of a Recommended Daily Allowance. You can find out what percent of the RDA for a certain nutrient is supplied by one serving by using a ratio.

Example: What percent of the RDA of iron for an 18-year-old is provided by 8 ounces of prune juice? Follow these two steps.

Step 1: Write the ratio. $$\frac{\text{iron in prune juice}}{\text{RDA of iron}} = \frac{10.5 \text{ mg}}{18 \text{ mg}}$$

Step 2: Change the fraction to a percent by dividing.

$$\frac{10.5}{18} = 18\overline{)10.500} \quad .583 = 58.3\% \approx 58\%$$

Eight ounces of prune juice supplies an 18-year-old with 58% of the RDA for iron.

Exercise B: Find the percent of the RDA of the nutrient that is supplied by 8 ounces of each beverage. Use the tables on page 119.

1) Calcium in grape juice for a 16-year-old
2) Ascorbic acid in orange juice
3) Iron in apple juice for a 17-year-old
4) Calcium in milk for a 15-year-old
5) Niacin in grape juice for a 13-year-old male
6) Riboflavin in apple juice for a 17-year-old male
7) Protein in grapefruit juice for a 14-year-old male

COMPUTER APPLICATION

Use this program to check your answers from Exercise B given above. See the appendix in the back of this text for directions in using computer programs.

```
10      REM  RECOMMENDED DAILY ALLOWANCES
20      REM  CHAPTER 6
30      PRINT " R D A "
40      PRINT "AMOUNT OF NUTRIENT IN 8 OZ. OF JUICE";
50      INPUT J
60      PRINT "RDA OF NUTRIENT";
70      INPUT R
80      PRINT "  PERCENT OF RDA IN JUICE:  "
90      PRINT INT ( J / R * 100 + .5 ) ; "%"
100     END
RUN
```

USING CALORIES

Calories are necessary for carrying on *basic processes* such as heartbeat, breathing, and digestion. The average person uses 1,400 to 1,650 calories each day just to live. Other activities may require between 700 and 1,400 more calories.

The graph below shows how many calories are burned per hour by different activities. The amount shown may vary from person to person, depending on age, weight, and sex.

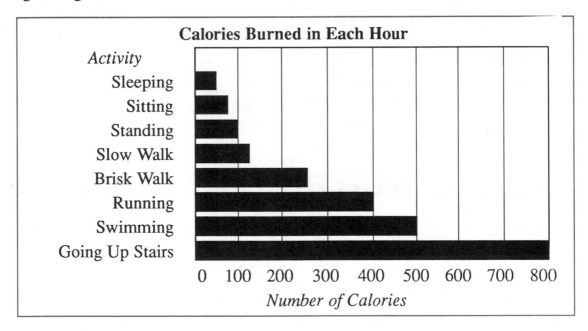

Exercise A: Use the graph to answer these questions.
1) How many calories are used in an hour's brisk walk?
2) How many calories are burned by swimming for 2 hours?
3) How many calories are burned in 8 hours of sleep?
4) How many more calories are used in one hour by a person who stands than by a person who sits?
5) In two hours, how many more calories are burned while swimming than while running?

You may use proportions to find out how many calories are burned during a different length of time than one hour.

Example: Ms. X. R. Size ran for 45 minutes. How many calories did she use? Use information from the graph on page 122.

Step 1: Write a proportion. The ratio will be minutes to calories.

$$\begin{array}{ccc} & \textit{Graph} & \textit{Ms. X. R. Size} \\ \text{minutes} \rightarrow & \dfrac{1 \text{ hour}}{400 \text{ calories}} = & \dfrac{45 \text{ minutes}}{? \text{ calories}} \end{array}$$

Step 2: Change the time to minutes. $\dfrac{60}{400} = \dfrac{45}{?}$

Step 3: Find the cross product. $400 \times 45 = 18{,}000$

Step 4: Divide by 60.
$$\begin{array}{r} 300 \text{ calories} \\ 60 \overline{)18{,}000} \end{array}$$

Ms. X. R. Size used 300 calories.

Exercise B: Calculate the number of calories used in each activity. Use the graph on page 122. Round your answer to the nearer calorie.

Activity	Time Spent
1) Walking slowly	20 minutes
2) Sleeping	$1\frac{1}{2}$ hours
3) Running	1 hour, 25 minutes
4) Walking up stairs	15 minutes
5) Sitting in class	45 minutes
6) Swimming	9 hours, 15 minutes
7) Standing	2 hours, 15 minutes
8) Walking briskly	55 minutes
9) Sleeping	4 hours, 35 minutes
10) Sitting in front of TV	3 hours, 40 minutes

LOSING POUNDS

Each extra pound in a person's body contains about 3,500 calories. One way to lose a pound is to exercise enough to burn 3,500 calories.

Example: How long does Cal O'Ree have to run to burn up one extra pound? Use information from the graph on page 122.

Divide 3,500 by the number of calories burned while running one hour.

$$8 \frac{300}{400} = 8 \frac{3}{4} \text{ hours}$$
$$400 \overline{)3500}$$
$$\underline{3200}$$
$$300$$

Exercise A: Find the length of time each exercise must be carried out to lose weight. Use the graph on page 122.

	Exercise	Pounds to Lose
1)	Walking briskly	1
2)	Standing	1
3)	Swimming	2
4)	Walking up steps	1
5)	Walking slowly	2
6)	Running	2
7)	Swimming	1
8)	Walking briskly	2

Note: Of course, these exercises should not be overdone. They should be spread over a number of days. Stamina and conditioning are also important factors in exercise and in maintaining a healthy body.

A second way for a person to lose a pound is to consume 3,500 calories less than the body uses. A person's body will burn a pound of body fat for the energy he or she needs.

Desirable Weight	
Height	Weight
5'0"	105 pounds
5'2"	115 pounds
5'4"	125 pounds
5'6"	135 pounds
5'10"	145 pounds
6'0"	155 pounds

Example: Y. M. I. Plump wants to lose 2 pounds in 21 days. How many fewer calories must he consume each day?

Step 1: Multiply 3,500 times the number of pounds to be lost.
3,500 x 2 = 7,000 total number of calories

Step 2: Divide the total number of calories by the number of days.
333 calories per day
21)7,000 total number of calories

Y. M. I. Plump must consume 333 fewer calories per day for 21 days to lose 2 pounds.

Exercise B: Compute how many fewer calories per day must be consumed to lose the following amounts of weight. Remember to change all time periods to days.

1) 1 pound in 7 days
2) 4 pounds in 10 days
3) 2 pounds in 1 week
4) 10 pounds in 3 months
5) 3 pounds in 2 weeks
6) 4 pounds in 3 weeks
7) 5 pounds in 8 weeks
8) 12 pounds in 6 months

CONSUMER HUMOR

Did you look at the height and weight chart on this page?

I weigh 155 pounds. According to that chart, I'm not too fat—I'm too short!

CHANGING RECIPE YIELDS

Recipes are designed to provide a given number of servings. For example, this recipe for Chicken Casserole has a *yield* of 6 servings. You may need to make a larger or smaller casserole.

Chicken Casserole

6 chicken breasts, cooked and sliced
2 packages of frozen broccoli, cooked
$10\frac{1}{2}$ oz. condensed cream of chicken soup
$\frac{1}{2}$ cup mayonnaise
1 Tbsp. lemon juice
4 oz. cheddar cheese, shredded

Spread broccoli in a glass baking dish. Arrange chicken over broccoli. Mix soup, mayonnaise, and lemon juice. Pour over chicken. Sprinkle cheese over top. Microwave 20 minutes on low.
Yield: 6 servings

Example: Compute the quantity of each ingredient in Chicken Casserole needed to serve 3 people.

Step 1: Find the ratio of desired portions (3) to recipe portions (6).
$$\frac{\text{desired}}{\text{recipe}} = \frac{3}{6} = \frac{1}{2}$$

Step 2: Multiply every quantity by the ratio $\frac{1}{2}$.

Remember: Use these steps to multiply fractions.
1. Multiply the numerator times the numerator.
2. Multiply the denominator times the denominator.
3. Simplify your answer if possible.

Examples: $\dfrac{\text{Numerator} \rightarrow}{\text{Denominator} \rightarrow}$ $\quad \dfrac{2}{5} \times \dfrac{3}{7} = \dfrac{6}{35}$ $\qquad \dfrac{2}{10} \times \dfrac{4}{8} = \dfrac{8}{80} = \dfrac{1}{10}$

Recipe for 6 Servings

1) 6 chicken breasts

2) 2 pkgs. broccoli

3) $10\frac{1}{2}$ oz. soup

(Write mixed numbers as fractions, $10\frac{1}{2} = \frac{21}{2}$)

4) $\frac{1}{2}$ cup mayonnaise

5) 1 Tbsp. lemon juice

6) 4 oz. cheddar cheese

Recipe for 3 Servings

$\frac{6}{1}$ x $\frac{1}{2}$ = 3

$\frac{2}{1}$ x $\frac{1}{2}$ = 1 pkg.

$10\frac{1}{2}$ x $\frac{1}{2}$ =

→ $\frac{21}{2}$ x $\frac{1}{2}$ = $\frac{21}{4}$ or $5\frac{1}{4}$ oz.

$\frac{1}{2}$ x $\frac{1}{2}$ = $\frac{1}{4}$ cup

1 x $\frac{1}{2}$ = $\frac{1}{2}$ Tbsp.

$\frac{4}{1}$ x $\frac{1}{2}$ = 2 oz.

Example: Find how much of each ingredient is needed to serve 8 people.

Step 1: Write the ratio: $\dfrac{\text{desired}}{\text{recipe}} = \dfrac{8}{6} = \dfrac{4}{3}$

Step 2: Multiply each amount by $\frac{4}{3}$.

Recipe for 6 Servings

1) 6 chicken breasts

2) 2 pkgs. broccoli

3) $10\frac{1}{2}$ oz. soup

4) $\frac{1}{2}$ cup mayonnaise

5) 1 Tbsp. lemon juice

6) 4 oz. cheddar cheese

Recipe for 8 Servings

$\frac{6}{1}$ x $\frac{4}{3}$ = $\frac{24}{3}$ = 8

$\frac{2}{1}$ x $\frac{4}{3}$ = $\frac{8}{3}$ = $2\frac{2}{3}$ pkgs.

$\frac{21}{2}$ x $\frac{4}{3}$ = $\frac{84}{6}$ = 14 oz.

$\frac{1}{2}$ x $\frac{4}{3}$ = $\frac{4}{6}$ = $\frac{2}{3}$ cup

1 x $\frac{4}{3}$ = $\frac{4}{3}$ = $1\frac{1}{3}$ Tbsp.

$\frac{4}{1}$ x $\frac{4}{3}$ = $\frac{16}{3}$ = $5\frac{1}{3}$ oz.

Exercise A: Find the amounts of ingredients needed to make Chicken Casserole for each of these numbers of servings.

1) 12   2) 3   3) 36   4) 9   5) 4

6) 18   7) 15   8) 21   9) 24   10) 30

TIMING FOOD PREPARATION

Perhaps the most difficult part of making a meal is scheduling the preparation so that all of the food is ready at the same time.

Example: Cassie Roll is planning to serve the following items at 7:30 p.m. When must each item be put on to cook if all is to be ready at 7:30?

Item	Cooking Time
Roast lamb (7 lbs.)	30 min./pound + 15 minutes standing time
Brown rice	40 minutes
Broccoli	12 minutes

Roast Lamb: Multiply the weight times the cooking time per pound. Add the standing time.

$$7 \times 30 = 210 \text{ min.} \qquad 210 + 15 = 225 \text{ minutes}$$

Change to hours and minutes by dividing by 60.

$$
\begin{array}{r}
3 \\
60\,\overline{)\,225} \\
180 \\
\hline
45
\end{array}
$$
3 Hours   Total time: 3 hours, 45 minutes.

45 Minutes

Subtract 3 hours, 45 minutes from 7:30.

$$
\begin{array}{rl}
7 \text{ hrs. } 30 \text{ min.} & = 6 \text{ hrs. } 90 \text{ min.} \\
- 3 \text{ hrs. } 45 \text{ min.} & - 3 \text{ hrs. } 45 \text{ min.} \\
\hline
 & 3 \text{ hrs. } 45 \text{ min.}
\end{array}
$$

The lamb must go in the oven at 3:45 p.m.

Brown Rice: Subtract 40 minutes from 7:30.

$$
\begin{array}{rl}
7 \text{ hrs. } 30 \text{ min} & = 6 \text{ hrs. } 90 \text{ min.} \\
- 40 \text{ min.} & - 40 \text{ min.} \\
\hline
 & 6 \text{ hrs. } 50 \text{ min.}
\end{array}
$$

The rice must begin cooking at 6:50 p.m.

Broccoli: Subtract 12 minutes from 7:30.

7 hrs.	30 min.
-	12 min.
7 hrs.	18 min.

The broccoli must begin cooking at 7:18 p.m.

Exercise A: Calculate the times these foods must begin cooking to be ready at a given time.

1) Dinner at 8:00 p.m.
Roast beef (6 lbs.)	35 min./lb. + 20 min. standing time
Mixed vegetables	18 minutes
Boiled potatoes	40 minutes
Rolls	17 minutes

2) Dinner at 7:00 p.m.
Baked chicken (5 lbs.)	25 minutes per pound
Noodles Romanoff	55 minutes
Acorn squash	$1\frac{1}{2}$ hours
Biscuits	15 minutes

3) Dinner at 4:30 p.m.
Roast turkey (20 lbs.)	20 min./lb. + 25 min. standing time
Sauerkraut casserole	1 hour, 20 minutes
Baked potatoes	$1\frac{1}{2}$ hours
Lima beans	35 minutes

4) Dinner at 6:30 p.m.
Oxtail stew	$3\frac{1}{2}$ hours
Celery, carrots, and tomato paste	Add to stew during last 35 minutes
Dumplings	Add to stew during last 10 minutes

5) Dinner at 5:15 p.m.
Chicken Kiev	Deep fry 10 minutes
Noodles	20 minutes
Spinach	17 minutes
Garlic bread	35 minutes

Solve these problems.

1) There are 350 calories in $1\frac{1}{2}$ cups of spaghetti. How many calories are in two cups?

2) Simplify the ratio $\frac{10}{15}$.

3) Use cross products to see if these ratios are equal.

$$\frac{5}{6} \qquad \frac{30}{360}$$

4) Find the missing term in this proportion.

$$\frac{60}{360} = \frac{?}{12}$$

5) There are 1.5 mg of iron in 8 ounces of apple juice. How many ounces would contain 100% of the RDA for iron if 18 mg are recommended?

6) Running consumes 400 calories per hour. How many calories are used in 40 minutes of running?

7) A salad recipe that serves 10 people requires $1\frac{1}{2}$ cups of celery. How much celery is needed for 5 servings?

8) How many fewer calories per day must be consumed in order to lose 6 pounds in 5 weeks?

9) A recipe, which serves six, calls for 125 mL of tomato sauce. Compute the amount of tomato sauce necessary to serve eight people.

10) A roast requires 3 hours and 40 minutes to prepare. When must it be put into the oven in order to be ready to be served at 6:30 p.m.?

CHAPTER 7

IMPROVING YOUR HOME

Almost every home improvement involves mathematics. You may want to improve your home in one of the following ways:

- You may want to buy furniture and appliances.

- You may need to figure perimeter and area in order to fence a yard, to wallpaper or paint a room, or to cover a floor with carpeting.

- You may want to make an addition to an existing home, insulate walls, or improve your lawn.

In this chapter you will practice math skills needed for making improvements in and around your home.

BUYING FURNITURE AND APPLIANCES

Furniture and appliances are expensive. Smart shoppers may find the items that they want on sale.

Example: Sophia Davenport purchased a couch at a "40% off" sale. If the sale price was $239.99, what was the original cost?

Rule: To find the original cost, subtract the discount rate from 100%. Then divide the sale price by this difference.

Step 1: Subtract the discount from 100%.

100%
- 40%   Percent discounted
  60%   Percent paid

Sophia paid 60% of the original cost.

Step 2: Round the sale price to the nearer dollar to make the calculations easier.

$239.99 ≈ $240.00   Rounded sale price

Step 3: To find the original cost, divide the rounded sale price by the percent paid.
60% = .60

$$\begin{array}{r} \$400. \\ .60\,\overline{)\,\$240.00.} \end{array}$$
  $400.   Original cost
.60.) $240.00.   Rounded sale price

The original cost was $400. Note that this original price may have actually been listed as $399.99!

Exercise A: Find the original cost of each item. Round your answer to the nearer dollar.

	Item	Discount	Sale Price
1)	Full mattress set	50%	$169.99
2)	Twin mattress set	50%	$129.99
3)	4-piece living room set	35%	$499.00
4)	Rocking chair	26%	$169.97
5)	Cocktail table	25%	$59.97
6)	Ottoman	50%	$29.97
7)	Recliner rocker	27%	$269.97
8)	Swivel rocker	28%	$199.97
9)	Dining set	20%	$399.97
10)	Refrigerator	12%	$499.97
11)	Refrigerator in colors	16%	$999.97
12)	Deluxe refrigerator	16%	$1,009.97
13)	Side by side refrigerator	5%	$807.97
14)	Microwave/convection oven	20%	$599.97
15)	Microwave oven	10%	$269.97
16)	Television	32%	$399.97
17)	Canopy bed	50%	$199.88
18)	Family room sofa bed	40%	$299.88
19)	Washing machine	13%	$479.95
20)	Dryer	23%	$299.95

You can compute the sale discount when you know the sale price and the regular price of the item.

Example: Otto Mann bought a footstool for $49.99. The regular price was $79.99. What discount did he receive?

Step 1: Round the prices to the nearer dollar.

$49.99 ≈ $50
$79.99 ≈ $80

Step 2: Subtract the sale price from the regular price to find the amount saved.

$80   Regular price
- 50   Sale price
$30   Amount saved

Step 3: Write the ratio. $\dfrac{\text{amount saved}}{\text{regular price}}$

Simplify this ratio.

$$\frac{\$30}{\$80} = \frac{3}{8}$$

Step 4: Write the ratio as a percent.

$$8\overline{)3.000} \quad .375$$

$.375 ≈ .38 = 38\%$

CONSUMER HUMOR

What a sale! I bought a dresser and a refrigerator and a console TV! I saved over $300!

Now the bills are coming due. I don't know if I can afford to save that much money.

Exercise B: Find the discount in each case.

	Item	Regular Price	Sale Price
1)	Maple bed	$249.99	$149.50
2)	Chest to match bed	$159.99	$99.88
3)	4-piece bedroom suite	$779.99	$549.99
4)	Sectional sofa	$899.99	$599.50
5)	Colonial sofa	$599.99	$379.88
6)	Traditional sleep sofa	$599.99	$399.88
7)	Colonial sleep sofa	$699.99	$399.88
8)	Pine finish rocker	$109.99	$79.88
9)	5-piece dinette group	$309.99	$239.50
10)	Early American dining room	$899.99	$699.88
11)	5-piece dining room	$1,149.99	$849.50
12)	Ceiling fan	$329.99	$249.99
13)	Crystal chandelier	$529.99	$328.59
14)	Color television	$429.95	$359.95
15)	19-cubic ft. refrigerator	$599.95	$469.95
16)	16-cubic ft. freezer	$499.95	$399.95
17)	Black and white portable TV	$109.95	$89.95
18)	Console TV	$699.95	$599.95
19)	Washing machine	$319.95	$279.95
20)	Clothes dryer	$219.95	$199.95

90-DAY PURCHASE PLAN

Rather than pay interest on a charge account to purchase an expensive item, some customers use a plan called a *Ninety Days Same As Cash* plan. This term means that within 90 days after the date of purchase, the purchase price must be paid in full. No interest is charged for the use of this plan.

Example: Mr. E. Z. Chair purchased a living room suite on January 14 and used the "Ninety Days Same As Cash" plan. By what date must he pay the total purchase price?

Step 1: Find the number of days left in January. January has 31 days.

31	Days in January
- 14	Date of purchase
17	Days left in January

Step 2: Subtract the days left in January from 90, the total number of days in the purchase plan.

90	Days in plan
- 17	Days left in January
73	

Step 3: Subtract the days in February from 73. There are usually 28 days in February.

73	Days left in plan
- 28	Days in February
45	

Step 4: Subtract the days in March from 45. March has 31 days.

45	Days left in plan
- 31	Days in March
14	Days left in plan

There are 14 days left after March. The next month is April. April 14 is the final payment date.

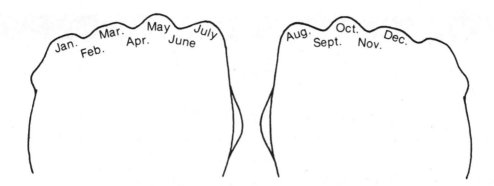

Use a Knuckle Calendar to help you remember how many days are in each month. Make a fist with your left hand. Name the months as you touch each knuckle and valley in succession. When you reach July at your last knuckle, make a fist with your right hand, and name August through December.

All the months named on the knuckles have 31 days. All the rest have 30 days, except February, which has 28 (29 days in a leap year).

Exercise A: Find the payment date for each of these "Ninety Days Same As Cash" plans. The purchase dates are listed below. Any leap years are indicated.

1) January 20
2) November 10
3) March 10
4) July 30
5) December 30
6) June 6
7) June 22
8) December 24 (Next year is a leap year.)
9) May 10
10) July 10
11) June 28
12) February 6
13) September 7
14) December 7
15) August 22
16) July 4
17) July 16
18) February 22
19) February 2 (Leap year)
20) May 5

THE KEY TO PERIMETER AND AREA

Perimeter is the distance around a figure. Notice the word "rim" in **perime**ter. Remember that perimeter is the measure of the **rim** of a figure.

Area is the number of squares of a given size that cover a surface. It is the surface included inside a perimeter. Notice that the last three letters in sq**are**e are in **are**a.

Certain figures have formulas to be used for finding their perimeter and area. Study the following examples for a rectangle and a square. Note that some symbols are used in this chapter: 5" means 5 inches; 5' means 5 feet.

Rectangle

	Perimeter	Area
width = w	$P = 2(l + w)$	$A = l \times w$
length = l		

Example: What is the perimeter of this rectangle?
What is the area of this rectangle?

Perimeter

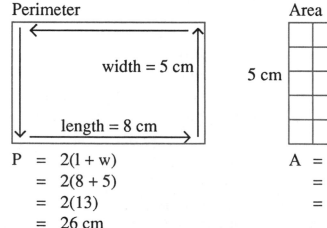

width = 5 cm
length = 8 cm

$$
\begin{aligned}
P &= 2(l + w) \\
&= 2(8 + 5) \\
&= 2(13) \\
&= 26 \text{ cm}
\end{aligned}
$$

Area

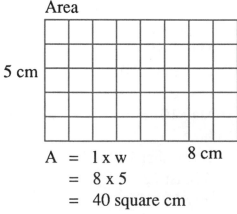

5 cm

8 cm

$$
\begin{aligned}
A &= l \times w \\
&= 8 \times 5 \\
&= 40 \text{ square cm}
\end{aligned}
$$

Square

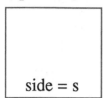

side = s

Perimeter
P = 4 x s
or
P = 4s

Area
A = s x s
or
$A = s^2$

Example: What is the perimeter of this square?
What is the area of this square?

Perimeter

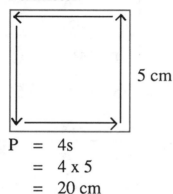

5 cm

$$P = 4s$$
$$= 4 \times 5$$
$$= 20 \text{ cm}$$

Area

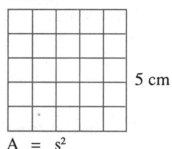

5 cm

$$A = s^2$$
$$= 5 \times 5$$
$$= 25 \text{ square cm}$$

Exercise A: Find the perimeter and area of each of the following figures. Label each answer with the correct units.

Rectangles
1) l = 4 cm   w = 6 cm
3) l = 2"   w = 10"
5) l = 1"   w = 5"

Squares
2) s = 3"
4) s = 5 cm
6) s = 10 m

Round to the nearer tenth.
7) l = 7.5 m   w = 2.7 m
9) l = 13.8 cm   w = 10.9 cm
11) l = 25.6 cm   w = 14.8 cm
13) l = 38.7'   w = 39.6'

Round to the nearer hundredth.
8) s = 6.28 cm
10) s = 7.94"
12) s = 32.50 m
14) s = 187.4'

Irregular Shapes: You can find the area of some irregular shapes by dividing them into rectangles.

Example: What is the area of this irregular shape?

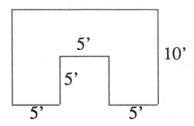

Step 1: Divide the irregular shape into rectangles.

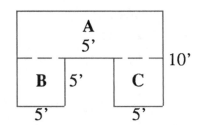

Step 2: Find any missing dimensions.

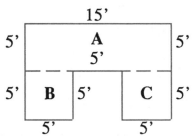

Step 3: Calculate the areas of the rectangles.
Rectangle A: 5' x 15' = 75 sq. ft.
Rectangle B: 5' x 5' = 25 sq. ft.
Rectangle C: 5' x 5' = 25 sq. ft.

Step 4: Add these areas to find the total area of the irregular shape.

   75 sq. ft.   Rectangle A
   25 sq. ft.   Rectangle B
<u>+ 25 sq. ft.</u>   Rectangle C
 125 sq. ft.   Total area

The area of this irregular shape is 125 square feet.

Exercise B: Find the area of each irregular shape.

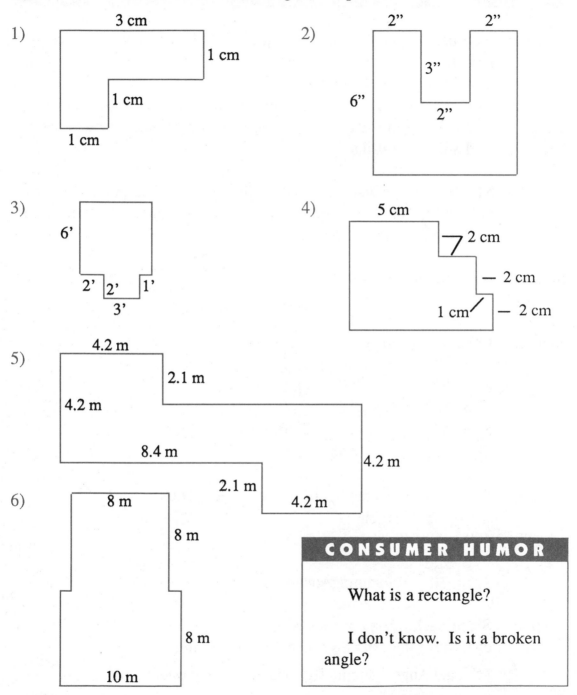

1)

3 cm

1 cm

1 cm

1 cm

2)

2"   2"

3"

6"

2"

3)

6'

2' 2' 1'

3'

4)

5 cm

2 cm

— 2 cm

1 cm — 2 cm

5)

4.2 m

2.1 m

4.2 m

8.4 m

2.1 m

4.2 m

4.2 m

6)

8 m

8 m

8 m

10 m

CONSUMER HUMOR

What is a rectangle?

I don't know. Is it a broken angle?

PAINTING A ROOM

How much paint to buy? That's the question! If you buy too much, you waste money. If you buy too little, you have to return to the store for more. Mathematics will help you to buy the correct amount.

Each can of paint is marked with the area of wall that it is supposed to cover. This *coverage* is listed in square feet per *quart* or per *gallon*. Painters need to know the total area to be painted.

Example: Michael Angelo wants to paint his living room. The paint he selected will cover 100 square feet per quart or 400 square feet per gallon. How many gallons should he buy?

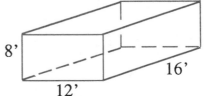

Step 1: Measure the living room. Round to the nearer foot.

Step 2: Calculate the total area of the walls.

8'	x 12'	=	96	sq. ft.
8'	x 12'	=	96	sq. ft.
8'	x 16'	=	128	sq. ft.
8'	x 16'	=	128	sq. ft.
Total area		=	448	sq. ft.

Step 3. Divide the total area by the coverage per gallon.

```
         1   Gallon
400 ) 448   Total area in square feet
      400
       48   Remaining square feet
```

Step 4: Since each quart covers 100 square feet, one quart should be purchased for the extra 48 square feet remaining.

Michael Angelo should buy one gallon and one quart.

Exercise A: Find these answers.

1) Suppose that Michael Angelo wanted to paint the ceiling of the living room in the example given on page 142. How much paint does he need?

2) Van Go wants to paint three rooms the same color. The total area to be painted is 1,375 square feet. How many gallons of paint will he need if each gallon covers 500 square feet?

Exercise B: Mason Ree wants to paint his basement walls with waterproof paint. Each gallon covers 75 square feet. The dimensions of this basement are 20' by 30'. The walls are 7' high.

1) Draw a diagram of the basement (like the diagram on page 142).

2) Find the area of each wall.

3) Find the total area to be painted.

4) Find the number of gallons needed.

Exercise C: Find the amount of paint Anne Artist needs to paint the walls of each of these rooms.

	Length	Width	Height	Coverage	
1)	8'	10'	8'	100	sq. ft./quart
2)	11'	20'	8'	125	sq. ft./quart
3)	15'	7'	7'	75	sq. ft./quart
4)	25'	17'	8'	100	sq. ft./quart
5)	18'	19'	10'	110	sq. ft./quart

COMPUTER APPLICATION

Use this computer program to determine the number of cans of paint that you will have to buy to paint a room. You will need to know:
- the length of the room to be painted;
- the width of the room to be painted;
- the height of the room to be painted;
- the coverage per can of paint.

The term *coverage* means the amount of square feet that one quart or gallon of paint will cover.

See the appendix in the back of this text for additional directions in using computer programs.

```
10     REM  PAINTING A ROOM
20     REM  CHAPTER 7
30     PRINT " P A I N T I N G   A   R O O M "
40     PRINT "LENGTH OF ROOM";
50     INPUT L
60     PRINT "WIDTH OF ROOM";
70     INPUT W
80     PRINT "HEIGHT OF ROOM";
90     INPUT H
100    PRINT "WHAT IS THE COVERAGE PER CAN OF PAINT";
110    INPUT C
120    LET T = ( ( 2 * L + 2 * W ) * H ) / C
130    IF T = INT(T) THEN GOTO 150
140    LET T = 1 + INT(T)
150    PRINT T; "CANS ARE NEEDED."
160    END
RUN
```

BUYING PAINT

Paint is sold by the quart and by the gallon. Sometimes you need to purchase paint in both of these sizes to get the best value for your money.

Example: Sarah Painter-in-the-House must decide whether to buy paint in 9 individual quart cans or to buy it in both gallon and quart cans. Here are the facts:

4 quarts = 1 gallon

1 quart costs $3.99

1 gallon costs $11.99

What should Sarah do?

Step 1: Find the cost of 4 quarts.

$$\begin{array}{ll} \$3.99 & \text{Cost of 1 quart} \\ \underline{\text{x} \quad 4} & \text{Number of quarts} \\ \$15.96 & \text{Cost of 4 quarts} \end{array}$$

Step 2: Find the difference in price between 1 gallon and 4 quarts.

$$\begin{array}{ll} \$15.96 & \text{Cost of 4 quarts} \\ \underline{- \ 11.99} & \text{Cost of 1 gallon} \\ \$3.97 & \text{Difference} \end{array}$$

One gallon of paint is cheaper to buy than 4 quarts. The amount you save, $3.97, is just about the price of 1 quart of paint. When you buy the gallon, you practically get 1 quart free.

Step 3: Find out how many gallons to buy. Divide the total number of quarts needed by 4. This answer will tell Sarah the number of gallons and quarts she needs.

$$\begin{array}{r} 2 \\ 4\,\overline{)9} \\ \underline{8} \\ 1 \end{array}$$ Gallons

1   Quart

Two gallons and 1 quart are equal to 9 quarts.

Step 4: Find the cost.

$11.99	Cost per gallon
x 2	
$23.98	Cost of 2 gallons

$3.99	Cost per quart
x 1	
$3.99	Cost of 1 quart

$23.98	Cost of 2 gallons
+ 3.99	Cost of 1 quart
$27.97	Total cost

Exercise A: Copy and complete this chart. The first line describes the completed sample problem above. Its answers are provided for you.

	Quarts Required	Amount to Buy		Cost		
		Gallons	Quarts	Gallons	Quarts	Total
1)	9	2	1	$23.98	$3.99	$27.97
2)	10					
3)	6					
4)	7					
5)	13					
6)	46					

BUYING WALLPAPER

Each *single roll* of wallpaper covers 72 square feet. Some patterns are sold only by the *double roll*. Before you purchase wallpaper, you need to calculate the area to be covered.

Example: Paul Paperhanger developed an easy way to estimate the area to be papered.

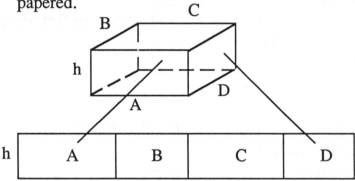

Visualize the walls moved into a straight line to form a large rectangle. The length of this rectangle is the perimeter of the original floor. The width of this rectangle is the height of the original room. The total *wall area* of the room equals the perimeter of the floor times the height of the room.

Rule: Wall area = perimeter of floor x height of room

Example: Ann E. Z. Job plans to paper her bedroom, which measures 10' by 12' by 8'. How much wallpaper should she buy?

Step 1: Find the perimeter of a floor 10' x 12'.

$$P = 2(10' + 12')$$
$$= 2(22')$$
$$= 44'$$

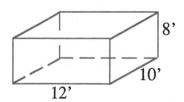

Step 2: Find the area of the room. Multiply the perimeter by the height.

$$\begin{array}{rl} 44' & \text{Perimeter} \\ \underline{x \qquad 8'} & \text{Height} \\ 352 \text{ sq. ft.} & \text{Area of room} \end{array}$$

Step 3: Divide the area by 72 square feet to find the number of single rolls needed.
Because of the remainder, Ann will need to buy 5 single rolls.

$$\begin{array}{rl} 4 & \text{Single rolls of wallpaper} \\ 72\overline{)\,352} & \text{Area of room} \\ \underline{288} & \\ 64 & \text{Square feet remaining} \end{array}$$

Step 4: Divide the number of single rolls by 2 to find the number of double rolls.
Because of the remainder, Ann will need to buy 3 double rolls.

$$\begin{array}{rl} 2 & \text{Double rolls} \\ 2\overline{)\,5} & \\ \underline{4} & \\ 1 & \text{Roll remaining} \end{array}$$

Exercise A: Calculate the number of double rolls of wallpaper needed to paper each of these rooms. The third measurement for each room is the height.

1) 7' x 10' x 8'
2) 8.25' x 11.75' x 8'
3) 11' x 12' x 8'
4) 16.3' x 14.8' x 8.5'
5) 15' x 12' x 10'
6) 9.7' x 11.6' x 8.5'
7) 9' x 10' x 8'
8) 13.5' x 21.8' x 8'
9) 9.5' x 10.5' x 8'
10) 25.5' x 17.7' x 8.25'

COVERING THE FLOOR

Whenever a person decides to buy floor covering, the area of the floor needs to be determined before the purchase is made.

Example: Vi Nill decided to buy square tiles to cover her kitchen floor. Each square measures 12" by 12" and costs $1.39. How much will it cost to cover her 10' x 7' floor?

> **Step 1:** Find the area that each tile covers.
> 12 inches = 1 foot
> 1' x 1' = 1 square foot

```
┌──────────┐
│ 1 square │  12"
│   foot   │
└──────────┘
     12"
```

> **Step 2:** Find the number of square feet of floor that needs to be covered.
> Area = l x w
> = 10' x 7'
> = 70 square feet

```
┌──────────┐ 10'
│          │
│          │ 7'
└──────────┘
```

> Since each tile covers 1 square foot, Vi will need 70 tiles.

> **Step 3:** Multiply the number of tiles by the cost per tile.
> $1.39   Cost per tile
> x   70   Number of tiles
> $97.30   Total cost

Exercise A: Find the cost of covering these floors with 12" by 12" tiles.

	Cost per Tile	Floor Dimensions		Cost per Tile	Floor Dimensions
1)	$.89	10' x 7'	2)	$.99	10' x 16'
3)	$1.29	8' x 11'	4)	$2.79	13' x 17'
5)	$2.59	10' x 15'	6)	$4.39	18' x 17'
7)	$1.89	11' x 16'	8)	$3.59	9' x 17'
9)	$1.79	12' x 18'	10)	$1.59	19' x 16'

The dimensions of a floor rarely measure a whole number of feet. To simplify calculations and to be sure you get enough covering, round to the next foot.

Example: Help Flora compute the cost of covering the floor of her dining room. The floor measures 15 feet 6 inches by 12 feet 7 inches. Each tile covers 1 square foot. A box of 45 tiles costs $29.25.

Step 1: Round the dimensions to the next foot.

15' 6" → 16'

12' 7" → 13'

Step 2: Find the area of the floor.

Area = l x w

= 16' x 13'

= 208 square feet

Since each tile covers 1 square foot, Flora needs 208 tiles.

Step 3: Find the number of boxes needed. Divide the number of tiles by 45, the number of tiles in one box. Round your answer up to the next whole number.

$$\frac{4.6}{45 \overline{)208.0}} \quad \rightarrow \quad 5 \text{ boxes}$$

Number of tiles

Step 4: Find the cost. Multiply the cost per box by the number of boxes.

$29.25   Cost per box

x   5   Number of boxes

$146.25   Total cost

Flora needs 5 boxes of tiles to cover the floor of her dining room. The cost of putting floor tiles in her dining room will be $146.25.

Exercise B: Find the cost of covering the floor of each room below with tiles measuring 12" by 12". Round floor dimensions to the next foot. Round the number of boxes of floor tiles to the next whole number.

	Cost per Box (45 tiles)	Floor Dimensions
1)	$39.95	10' 5" x 9' 8"
2)	$14.99	15' 6" x 17' 10"
3)	$26.59	25' 3" x 15' 8"
4)	$10.85	11' 2" x 7' 9"
5)	$16.39	12' 3" x 8' 3"
6)	$20.99	14' 6" x 15' 2"
7)	$16.17	10' 11" x 7' 9"
8)	$15.99	12' 4" x 16' 7"
9)	$17.99	13' 10" x 14' 6"
10)	$26.85	26' 10" x 17' 5"

COMPUTING LENGTH OF MOLDING

Molding is a decorative strip used to finish a room. After the floor is covered, molding is usually installed at the base of the walls. You can determine the length of molding you need by finding the perimeter of the room.

Example: Vi Nill wanted to finish her kitchen by installing molding around the room. How much quarter-round molding must she buy for the 10' by 7' room?

Find the perimeter of the room.

$$P = 2(l + w)$$
$$= 2(10' + 7')$$
$$= 2(17')$$
$$= 34'$$

Vi needs 34 feet of molding.

Exercise A: Find the amount of molding needed for each of the floors described in Exercise A, page 149.

Example: Flora wishes to finish her dining room with quarter-round molding. The room is 15' 6" by 12' 7". How much molding must she buy? Follow these steps to calculate the perimeter of the room.

Step 1: Write the formula to find the perimeter of the room.

$$P = 2(l + w)$$
$$= 2(15'\ 6" + 12'\ 7")$$

Step 2: Add the feet and inches.
a) Add feet together.
b) Add inches together.
c) If total inches are 12 or more, rename to feet and inches.

$$
\begin{array}{ll}
15 \text{ feet} & 6 \text{ inches} \\
+\ 12 \text{ feet} & 7 \text{ inches} \\
\hline
27 \text{ feet} & 13 \text{ inches} \quad (13 \text{ inches} = 1 \text{ foot, 1 inch})
\end{array}
$$

or   28 feet 1 inch or 28 feet + 1 inch
P = 2(28 feet + 1 inch)

Step 3: Multiply the feet and inches by the whole number.
a) Multiply the feet by the whole number.
b) Multiply the inches by the whole number.
c) Rename the inches to feet if necessary.

$$
\begin{aligned}
P &= 2(28 \text{ feet} + 1 \text{ inch}) \text{ or } 2(28' + 1") \\
&= (2 \times 28') + (2 \times 1") \\
&= 56' + 2" \\
&= 56'\ 2"
\end{aligned}
$$

Flora needs 56 feet and 2 inches of molding.

Exercise B: Find the length of molding needed for each of the floors listed in Exercise B on the top of page 151.

WALL-TO-WALL CARPETING

Wall-to-wall carpeting is sold by the square yard. You can estimate the amount needed.

Example: Wally wanted wall-to-wall carpeting in his den, which measures 8' by 11'. Carpeting is on sale for $7.99 per sq. yd. Estimate his cost. Round answers where possible.

Step 1: Find the area of the floor in square feet.

$$A = l \times w$$
$$= 8' \times 11'$$
$$= 88 \text{ square feet}$$

Step 2: Find the area in square yards. One square yard = 9 square feet. Divide by 9 to find the number of square yards.

$$9 \text{ sq. yds.} \approx 10 \text{ sq. yds.}$$

```
      9 sq. yds. ≈ 10 sq. yds.
    9 )88
      81
       7 sq. ft.
```

1'	1'	1'
1	2	3	1'
4	5	6	1'
7	8	9	1'

1 sq. yard

Step 3: Round the cost per square yard to the next whole number. Multiply the number of square yards by the cost per square yard. Wally's estimated cost was $80.00.

$$\$7.99 \approx \$8.00$$

$$10 \times \$8.00 = \$80.00$$

Exercise A: Estimate the cost of carpeting for each room.

	Room	Cost per Sq. Yd.		Room	Cost per Sq. Yd.
1)	8' x 10'	$5.99	2)	12' x 15'	$7.99
3)	25' x 18'	$10.95	4)	10' x 17'	$8.90
5)	14' x 16'	$9.98	6)	9' 6" x 11'	$7.99
7)	10' 3" x 15' 8"	$10.99	8)	13' 5" x 16' 9"	$12.99
9)	15' 8" x 17' 9"	$14.99	10)	12' 6" x 13' 10"	$15.99

ADDITIONS TO EXISTING HOMES

Some families who outgrow their houses add to their existing home. *Contractors* who erect buildings or additions estimate a job based on its area and on the cost of the *materials* required.

Example: Brad and Penny Nails plan to build a family room. The new 10' by 15' room will cost an average of $42 per square foot. The fireplace will cost $1,500 more. What will be the total cost?

Step 1: Find the area of the addition.

$A = l \times w$
$= 10' \times 15'$
$= 150$ square feet

Step 2: Multiply the area by the cost per square foot.

150	Square feet
x $42	Cost per square foot
$6,300	Cost of addition

Step 3: Add the cost of any extras to find the total cost.

$6300	Cost of addition
+ 1500	Cost of fireplace
$7,800	Total cost of addition

Exercise A: Compute the total cost of each of these additions.

	Addition	Dimensions	Cost per Sq. Ft.	Cost of Extras
1)	Family room	18' x 10'	$36.00	$2,400
2)	Sun porch	14' x 25'	$10.00	$150
3)	Master bedroom	20' x 30'	$30.00	$3,200
4)	Bathroom	7' x 10'	$28.50	$156
5)	Garage	20' x 30'	$15.50	$309
6)	Breakfast nook	8' x 8'	$20.75	$497
7)	Sun deck	25' x 30'	$4.85	None
8)	Bedroom and bath	12' x 13'	$16.50	$379
9)	Family room	10' x 12'	$18.57	$1,847
10)	Den and TV room	16' x 25'	$27.50	$1,575

INSULATION

Insulation is a term describing materials used to prevent transfer of electricity, heat, or sound. Installing insulation in an attic will cut heating bills. Consumers compare prices to decide which insulation is least expensive.

Exercise A: Find the cost per square foot of insulation described in each of the following ads. Round answers to the nearer cent.

1) Brand A

SALE	
88 sq. ft. roll Insulation	**$17.49**

2) Brand B

SPECIAL!	135 sq. ft.
$26.79	Rolls of Insulation

3) Brand C

SELL OUT ON **INSULATION!**	
$13.99 per roll	49 sq. ft. in each roll

4) Brand D

INSULATION CLEARANCE
$15.79
48 sq. ft. per roll

Example: Ms. N. Sue Late plans to put Brand A insulation in her attic. How much will it cost? The dimensions are as shown.

Step 1: Divide the irregular figure into rectangles.

Step 2: Find the missing dimensions.

Step 3: Find the areas.

Area 1 = l x w
      = 20' x 21'
      = 420 square feet

Area 2 = l x w
      = 30' x 21'
      = 630 square feet

Step 4: Add these areas to find the total area.

$$\begin{array}{ll} 420 & \text{sq. ft.} \\ +\,630 & \text{sq. ft.} \\ \hline 1{,}050 & \text{sq. ft.} \end{array}$$

Step 5: Divide total area by the number of square feet per roll of insulation.

$$\begin{array}{r} 11.9 \\ 88\,\overline{)\,1050} \end{array} \rightarrow \begin{array}{l} 12 \text{ rolls} \\ \text{Round up for} \\ \text{any remainder.} \end{array}$$

Step 6: Multiply the cost per roll times the number of rolls of insulation needed.

$$\begin{array}{ll} \$17.49 & \text{Cost per roll} \\ \underline{x\quad 12} & \text{Number of rolls} \\ \$209.88 & \text{Total cost to insulate attic} \end{array}$$

Exercise B: Find the cost of insulating each of these attics.

1) Brand A

24'
24'

2) Brand B

37'
25'

3) Brand C

51'
25'
9'
17'

4) Brand D

41'
21'
15'
11'
13'
13'

5) Brand A

47'
24'
36'
36'
11'
12'

6) Brand C

23'
17'
17'
17'
17'

SEEDING AND FEEDING LAWNS

Grass seed and fertilizer are sold in quantities to cover a certain size area. Before you buy grass seed or fertilizer, you need to know how much ground is to be covered.

The table below shows the coverage rates and prices for sample grass seeds and fertilizer. The coverage figures are for *established lawns* that have thin grass and are in need of more seed and fertilizer. The coverage rates are listed in *square meters* (m²).

Coverage Rates		
Variety	Coverage per Box	Cost per Box
A. Shady Seed	275 m²	$11.79
B. Show Seed	200 m²	$7.59
C. Hardy Seed	450 m²	$9.99
D. Kentucky Bluegrass Seed	400 m²	$8.49
E. Generic Seed	400 m²	$5.69
F. Fertilizer	100 m²	$4.49

Exercise A: Find the cost per square meter of each of the five grass seeds. Round your answer to the nearer cent.

1) Shady seed ($11.79 ÷ 275 = ?)
2) Show seed
3) Hardy seed
4) Kentucky Bluegrass seed
5) Generic seed

Example: Moe Orr wanted to reseed his lawn. He selected variety A, Shady Seed. The total area of his property was 600 m². His house and driveway cover 150 m². What did the seed cost?

Step 1: Find the area to be seeded. Subtract the area of the house and driveway from the total area.

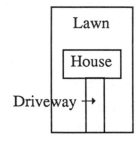

$$\begin{array}{r} 600 \ \text{m}^2 \\ - \ 150 \ \text{m}^2 \\ \hline 450 \ \text{m}^2 \end{array}$$
To be seeded

Step 2: Find the number of boxes of seed needed. Divide the area to be seeded by the coverage per box. Round up your answer.

$$\overset{\displaystyle 1.6}{275 \overline{)450.0}} \quad \rightarrow \quad 2 \ \text{Boxes}$$

Step 3: Multiply the cost per box times the number of boxes needed.

$$\begin{array}{r} \$11.79 \\ \text{x} \quad 2 \\ \hline \$23.58 \end{array}$$
Cost per box
Number of boxes
Total cost

The cost of seed for Moe's lawn was $23.58.

Exercise B: Find the cost of the seed for each of these lots.

	Area of Lot	Area of House	Variety of Seed
1)	1,000 m²	100 m²	A
2)	975 m²	75 m²	B
3)	827 m²	129 m²	C
4)	2,010 m²	68 m²	D
5)	1,575 m²	103 m²	E

Exercise C: Find the annual cost of fertilizing each lawn above twice a year. Use Fertilizer F mentioned in the chart on page 157.

FENCING A YARD

People fence their property for privacy or for protection. The amount of fencing you need is determined by the perimeter of the property that you are enclosing.

Example: Dee and O. Fentz decided to fence their property. They live on a rectangular lot 30 meters long by 20 meters wide.

$$P = 2(l + w)$$
$$= 2(30 \text{ m} + 20 \text{ m})$$
$$= 2(50 \text{ m})$$
$$= 100 \text{ m}$$

20 m

30 m

Dee and O. will need 100 meters of fencing to surround their lot.

Exercise A: Find the length of fencing needed for each of these lots.

1) 17 m x 19 m
2) 15 m x 25 m
3) 27 m x 39 m
4) 10.5 m x 18.9 m
5) 22.3 m x 22.8 m
6) 43 m x 86.7 m
7) 23.9 m x 45.7 m
8) 22.8 m x 43.9 m
9) 23.7 m x 32.9 m
10) 41.8 m x 32.3 m

CONSUMER HUMOR

Why did your cousin take barbed wire to the Olympic Games?

He wanted to participate in the fencing event.

Solve these problems.

1) Find the original cost of a rocker selling for $79.95 at 20% off.

2) Find the discount if a $69.99 item is on sale for $39.99.

3) Find the due date on a "Ninety Days Same As Cash" agreement. The purchase date was October 10.

4) Calculate the number of cans of paint needed to cover the walls of a room 11' x 12' x 8'. Each can covers 300 square feet.

5) A special variety of wallpaper covers only 60 square feet per roll. How many single rolls are needed to paper a room measuring 19' by 12' by 8' 6"?

6) Estimate the number of square yards of carpeting needed to cover a floor 10' 3" by 15' 9".

7) Paint sells for $4.99 a quart and $15.99 a gallon. How many gallons and quarts should be purchased if 9 quarts are needed? What will this paint cost?

8) Compute the cost of insulation for this attic. The insulation comes in 49 sq. ft. rolls, which cost $15.97 each.

9) Compute the length of fencing needed to enclose this yard.

10) Calculate the length of fencing needed to enclose this yard.

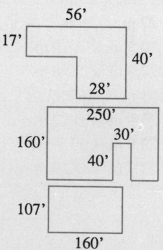

CHAPTER 8

TRAVELING

Many people travel often, both in our country and abroad. Sometimes traveling poses questions. Notice the following examples.

- How far is it to a given destination?

- How much will the ticket cost?

- How many hours will be spent in traveling?

- What will be the arrival time?

- Is a rental car needed?

- How much is a U.S. dollar worth in another country?

Travelers frequently use mathematics to answer their questions. In this chapter, you will learn to read maps and train schedules. You will learn to compute the costs of fares, hotel stays, car rentals, and parking expenses. You will learn how to exchange currencies and to compare time zones when traveling by air. These skills will help you to prepare for your trip.

READING A MAP

Using a map can simplify travel by car. The distances between towns and road junctions are shown by small numbers. A road map usually has a *legend* on it to explain the symbols used on that particular map. The legend may tell about highway markers, different kinds of roads, sizes of towns and cities, mileages, and points of interest. A sample legend is shown below.

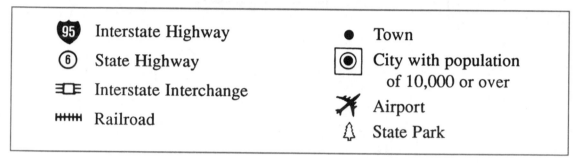

Study the following road map. Notice the names of the towns, the highways, and the symbols used on this map. Then answer the questions in Exercise A on page 163.

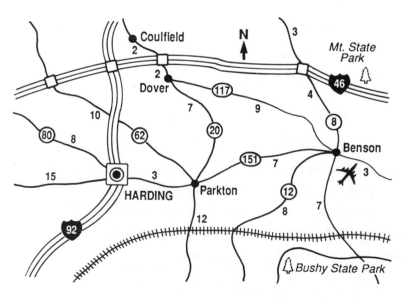

Exercise A: Answer these questions. Use the road map shown on page 162.

1) How many interstate highways are shown on this map?

2) What is the route number of the interstate highway that heads north and south?

3) What is the route number of the interstate highway that heads east and west?

4) What is the route number of the state highway that goes from Benson towards Mt. State Park?

5) Is an airport located near Benson?

6) How many state parks are located near Benson?

7) What route would you take to travel from Benson to Harding?

8) How many miles is it from Benson to Harding?

9) How many miles is it from Interstate 46 to Bushy State Park?

10) Does the train stop in Benson?

11) What city has a population over 10,000?

12) What cities have populations under 10,000?

13) In what direction do you travel to go from Parkton to Dover?

14) Is Dover closer to Parkton or Benson?

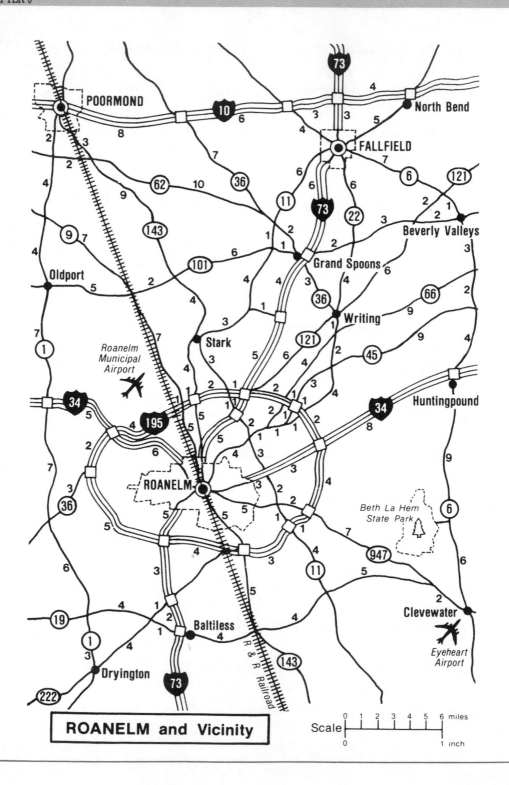

ROANELM and Vicinity

Scale

0 1 2 3 4 5 6 miles

0   1 inch

Example: Rhoda Carr drove from Dryington to Huntingpound. How many miles did she travel?

Step 1: Read the map on page 164 and choose a route. Locate Dryington. Use Route 222 to Route 73 to Route 34 to Huntingpound.

Step 2: Read each mileage number along the route.

Route 222	4
	1
Route 73	3
	5
Route 34	3

Step 3: Find the total.

	3
	+ 8

It is 27 miles from Dryington to Huntingpound. Total 27

Exercise B: Read the map on page 164. Find the distance in miles in each case.
1) Between Grand Spoons and Beverly Valleys
2) Between Poormond and Stark
3) Between Poormond and Dryington
4) Between Beverly Valleys and Poormond
5) Between state highways 1 and 11 on Route 101
6) From Grand Spoons to Poormond on 36 and 10
7) From Grand Spoons to Poormond on Routes 36, 62, and 143
8) From Fallfield to North Bend on Routes 73 and 10
9) From Fallfield to North Bend on Route 11
10) From Oldport to Roanelm on Routes 1 and 34
11) From Oldport to Roanelm on Routes 101 and 9

Exercise C: Read the map on page 164. Answer the following questions.
1) What is the road distance between the airports?
2) How far is it from Fallfield to the state park?
3) What is the shortest route from Baltiless to Oldport?
4) What is the shortest road distance from Clevewater to Dryington?

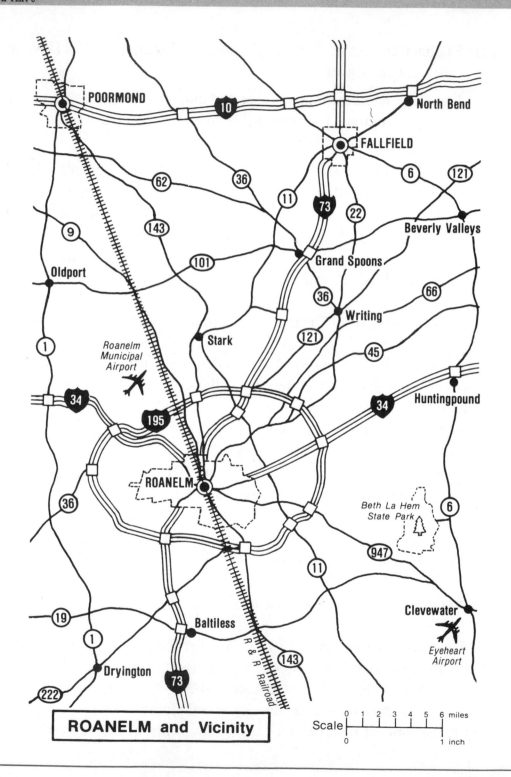

ROANELM and Vicinity

Scale

| 0 | 1 | 2 | 3 | 4 | 5 | 6 miles |

0 .... 1 inch

ESTIMATING DISTANCES

You can estimate the shortest or *straightline distance* between towns by using the *scale*. It indicates the relationship between the distances on a map and the corresponding actual distances. Look at the map and the scale on page 166.

Example: Rhoda Rider wants to know about how far it is between Baltiless and Fallfield.

> **Step 1:** With a ruler, measure the distance between Baltiless and Fallfield. It is about $5\frac{1}{4}$".
>
> **Step 2:** Read the scale at the bottom of the map. It indicates that 1 inch = 6 miles.
>
> **Step 3:** Multiply the measured distance in inches by the number of miles to the inch.

$$\begin{array}{r} 5.25 \\ \times \quad 6 \\ \hline 31.50 \quad \text{Miles} \end{array}$$

It is about $31\frac{1}{2}$ miles between Baltiless and Fallfield.

According to the map shown on page 164, what is the driving distance between Baltiless and Fallfield? Compare the estimate above (from the map and scale on page 166) with that driving distance. Which is larger? Why?

Exercise A: Use the scale on the map on page 166 to estimate the distance between these towns. Copy the following chart and complete it.

Towns	Distance in Inches	Distance in Miles
1) Writing to Stark		
2) Clevewater to Poormond		
3) Oldport to Clevewater		
4) Beverly Valleys to Baltiless		
5) Grand Spoons to Dryington		
6) Roanelm to Dryington		
7) Huntingpound to North Bend		

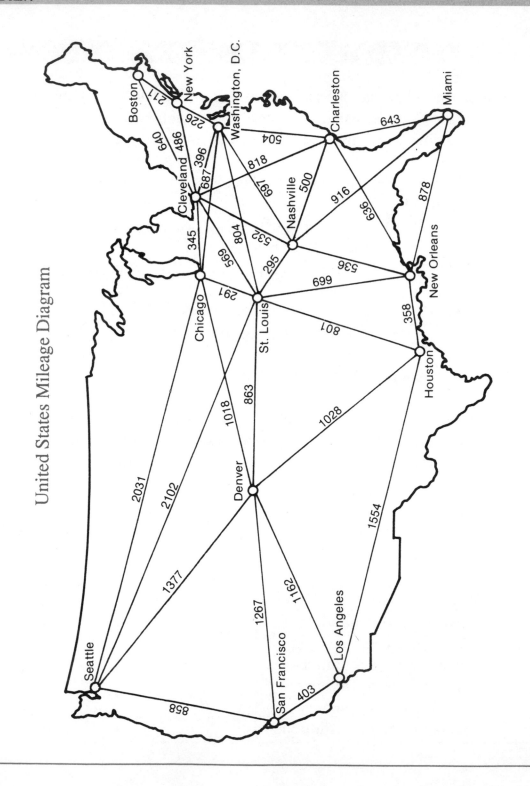

United States Mileage Diagram

Example: The *mileage diagram* shown on page 168 gives the driving distance in miles between major cities. Di Agram wants to know the shortest route between Nashville and Chicago.

Step 1: Find a likely route and add the distances.

Nashville to St. Louis   295 miles
St. Louis to Chicago   + 291 miles
                           586 miles

Step 2: Find another likely route and add the distances.

Nashville to Cleveland   532 miles
Cleveland to Chicago   + 345 miles
                           877 miles

Step 3: Choose the route with the shorter distance: 586 miles.

Exercise B: Copy this table and complete it with the shortest distance between each pair of cities. Use the mileage diagram shown on page 168. Leave plenty of room for the numbers.

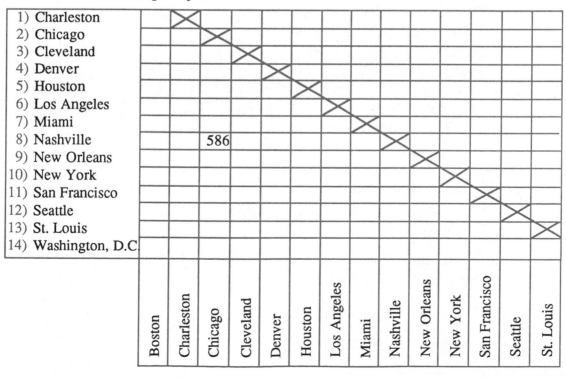

	Boston	Charleston	Chicago	Cleveland	Denver	Houston	Los Angeles	Miami	Nashville	New Orleans	New York	San Francisco	Seattle	St. Louis
1) Charleston														
2) Chicago														
3) Cleveland														
4) Denver														
5) Houston														
6) Los Angeles														
7) Miami														
8) Nashville			586											
9) New Orleans														
10) New York														
11) San Francisco														
12) Seattle														
13) St. Louis														
14) Washington, D.C.														

READING A TRAIN SCHEDULE

Train schedules are charts or tables that indicate arrival and departure times at all the stops on a given route. To find the time to travel any given distance, subtract the departure time from the arrival time.

THE NUMBER LINE		
READ UP ⬆	STOPS	READ DOWN ⬇
3 52 p	Able	5 44 p
3 45 p	Bell	5 49 p
3 15 p	Davis	6 01 p
2 43 p	Evans	6 39 p
1 43 p	Ford	7 47 p
12 50 p	DP Hope AR	8 58 p
12 40 p	AR Hope DP	9 08 p
11 48 a	Largo	10 00 p
11 10 a	DP Taft AR	10 40 p
10 55 a	AR Taft DP	11 00 p
10 40 a	Opal	11 15 p
9 52 a	Peru	12 08 a
9 15 a	Union	12 50 a
DP = Departure Time		a = a.m.
AR = Arrival Time		p = p.m.

Example: Find the time for the trip from Opal to Ford.

Step 1: To get from Opal to Ford on the schedule, you read up. Therefore, use the times given in the first column, "READ UP."

  1 43 p Ford
10 40 a Opal

Step 2: Subtract 10:40 (the departure time) from 1:43 (the arrival time). Rename 1:43. Add the 12 morning hours to 1:43 so that it becomes 13:43.

Arrival time at Ford	1:43	+12 hours →	13:43
Departure time at Opal	- 10:40		- 10:40
			3:03

The trip from Opal to Ford takes 3 hours and 3 minutes.

Example: Find the time for the trip from Bell to Evans.

Step 1: Read down to get from Bell to Evans.

Bell 　　　　　　　　5 49 p

Evans 　　　　　　　6 39 p

Step 2: Subtract the departure time from the arrival time. Rename 1 hour to 60 minutes so that 6:39 becomes 5:99.

Arrives at Evans 　　6:39 　　Rename → 　　5:99

Departs Bell 　　　　- 5:49 　　(1 hour = 　　- 5:49

　　　　　　　　　　　　　　　　60 minutes) 　　50

The trip from Bell to Evans takes 50 minutes.

Exercise A: Use the schedule on page 170. Find the time for each trip.

Point of Departure	Destination		Point of Departure	Destination
1) Able	Union		2) Union	Able
3) Taft	Peru		4) Largo	Evans
5) Peru	Hope		6) Ford	Hope
7) Davis	Opal		8) Bell	Ford
9) Peru	Bell		10) Evans	Davis

Exercise B: Use the schedule on page 170. Answer the following questions.

1) How long does the train stay in the station at Hope on the trip from Union to Able?

2) How long does the train stay in the station at Hope on the trip from Able to Union?

3) How long does the train stay in the station at Taft on the trip from Union to Able?

4) How long does the train stay in the station at Taft on the trip from Able to Union?

COMPUTING TRAIN FARES

Knowing the special rates for train fares can help travelers to save money. A sample rate chart is shown below. *Coach* fares are lower. Extra fares are charged for *parlor cars* since they are equipped with individual seats.

Train Fares Rate Chart		
Service Between Able and:	Coach	Parlor Car
Bell	$1.50	$3.00
Davis	$2.00	$4.25
Evans	$3.75	$8.00
Ford	$8.50	$13.25
Hope	$12.00	$17.75
Largo	$15.50	$21.75
Taft	$16.50	$23.75
Opal	$17.75	$26.50
Peru	$20.90	$33.50
Union	$24.25	$37.25

Here are money-saving plans that apply to this rate chart:
1. Children under 12 may ride at half price when accompanied by one or more adults. Otherwise, full price is charged.
2. One infant under 2, not occupying a separate seat and accompanied by a person aged 12 or older, may ride free. Otherwise, half fare is charged.
3. All coach fares are reduced 25% when a trip is not taken at peak times. These lower fares are called *excursion rates*.
4. A round-trip fare is double the one-way fare.

Example: Anne Trak, her husband, and their three children (ages 6, 8, and 10) will ride the train from Able to Largo. If they choose the coach fare and the excursion rates, what will their fares be?

Step 1: Read the rate table for adult coach fare between Able and Largo.

$15.50 Coarch fare for adult

Step 2: Multiply the coach fare by 2. (2 adults)

$15.50 Coach fare
x   2
$31.00 Fare for parents

Step 3: Find the child's fare by dividing by 2.

$7.75 Fare for child under 12
2)$15.50

Step 4: Multiply child's rate by number of children. (3)

$7.75 Fare for child under 12
x   3
$23.25 Fare for children

Step 5: Add the adult fares and children's fares to find total fares.

$31.00 Fare for parents
+ 23.25 Fare for children
$54.25 Fare for family

Step 6: Find the excursion rate. Multiply the total fare by 75%. (100% - 25% = 75%.)

$54.25 Fare for family
x   .75
$40.6875 ≈ $40.69 Excursion Fare

The family will pay $40.69 for their excursion train fares.

Exercise A: Find the fares from Able for each of these groups.

	Adults	Children	Infants	Destination	Trip	Service
1)	1	0	0	Opal	One way	Parlor
2)	2	0	0	Hope	One way	Excursion
3)	2	3	0	Ford	Round	Coach
4)	1	2	1	Taft	Round	Parlor
5)	2	3	0	Bell	One way	Coach
6)	3	0	1	Union	Round	Excursion
7)	4	5	1	Largo	One way	Coach
8)	2	0	2	Evans	One way	Parlor
9)	3	1	0	Peru	Round	Excursion
10)	4	2	0	Davis	Round	Coach

STAYING IN HOTELS

Most hotel rooms are designed for *single* or *double* occupancy. Those terms mean rooms for one or two persons. *Suites,* or sets of rooms, are usually designed for groups of more than two persons. Rates, or prices, for the rooms may change depending on the *tourist season.* The highest prices are in effect during the peak season when many people visit a given area. The term *peak season* is used to describe the time of year when business is at its best; for instance, at the beach in summer or in the mountains during ski season. Below is a list of the rates available at the Dew Drop Inn in Sunnyvale, Florida.

Daily Rates—Dew Drop Inn			
April 20 - Sept. 8		Sept. 9 - Dec. 19	
Single	$23.50	Single	$19.50
Double	$29.50	Double	$24.50
Suite	$67.50	Suite	$57.50
Dec. 20 - Jan. 31		Feb. 1 - April 19	
Single	$29.50	Single	$39.50
Double	$33.50	Double	$43.50
Suite	$85.00	Suite	$95.00

Daily rates apply to persons who arrive after 1 p.m. on the first day and leave by checkout time (11 a.m.) on the last day. Anyone who arrives too early or leaves too late must pay for an extra day.

Example: Virginia and Georgia plan to stay at the Dew Drop Inn from March 24 to March 31. They plan to arrive on March 24 and leave by checkout time on March 31. They will not be charged for March 31. What will be the cost per person?

Use a four-step method to solve this problem.

Step 1: Calculate the number of days. Subtract the earlier date from the later date.

March 31
- March 24
        7   Days

Step 2: Find the daily rate in the schedule. A double room from February 1 to April 19 is $43.50 daily.

Step 3: Multiply the daily rate times the number of days to find the total cost.

$43.50   Daily rate
x   7   Days
$304.50   Total cost

Step 4: To find the cost per person, divide the total cost by the number of people.

$152.25   Cost per person
2) $304.50   Total cost

The cost per person will be $152.25.

Exercise A: Copy and complete the information for this table.

| Dates | | Number of | Number of | Daily | Total | Cost per |
Arrive	Depart	Days	Persons	Rate	Cost	Person
1) Jan. 4	Jan. 11		1			
2) Oct. 10	Oct. 11		2			
3) Apr. 11	Apr. 19		2			
4) May 10	May 20		5			
5) Dec. 5	Dec. 14		4			
6) Feb. 14	Feb. 20		2			
7) May 5	May 9		1			
8) Aug. 10	Aug. 21		2			
9) June 7	June 21		3			
10) Dec. 25	Dec. 31		3			

Exercise B: Hotel guests are often charged a special tax. Find a 15% tax for each cost per person in Exercise A. To find a 15% tax, multiply .15 times the cost per person. What would the tax be in each case?

Often a person's stay in a hotel happens to include days in two different months.

Example: Della Ware is staying at the Dew Drop Inn from July 29 to August 15. What is the cost?

Step 1:	Calculate the number of days she stays in July. Subtract the arrival date from the number of days in the month. Add one day. (Why?)	31 - 29 2 + 1 3	Days in July Arrival date Add a day Days stayed
Step 2:	Find the number of days in August that Della stays. She leaves on the 15th, so she will not be charged for that day. Subtract 1 from the date she leaves. (Why?)	15 - 1 14	Departure Days stayed
Step 3:	Add the days stayed in each month.	3 + 14 17	July August Total days
Step 4:	Find the total cost. Multiply the daily rate by the number of days. Della's total cost is $399.50.	$23.50 x 17 $399.50	Daily rate Days Total cost

Exercise C: Copy and complete the information for this table.

	Dates		Number of	Number of	Daily	Total	Cost per
	Arrive	Depart	Days	Persons	Rate	Cost	Person
1)	Apr. 25	May 5		2			
2)	Dec. 28	Jan. 3		5			
3)	Oct. 25	Nov. 4		2			
4)	Nov. 20	Dec. 10		1			
5)	Mar. 29	Apr. 10		7			

Sometimes a guest's stay spans two rental seasons. Study this example.

Example: Ms. Zuri and Ms. S. Zippy visited the Dew Drop Inn from September 5 to 15. What was their cost per person?

		Season 1 Sept. 5-8	**Season 2** Sept. 9-15
Step 1:	Find the number of days stayed.	8 3 - 5 +1 Add a day 3 4 Days	15 - 9 6 Days
Step 2:	Find the daily rate.	$29.50	$24.50
Step 3:	Multiply the rate by the number of days.	$29.50 x 4 $118.00	$24.50 x 6 $147.00
Step 4:	Find the total cost. Add.	$118.00 Cost for Sept. 5-8 + 147.00 Cost for Sept. 9-15 $265.00 Total cost	
Step 5:	Find the cost per person. Divide the total cost by the number of persons.	$132.50 Cost per person 2) $265.00 Total cost	

The cost per person was $132.50.

Exercise D: Copy and complete the information for this chart.

	Dates		Number of	Number of	Daily	Total	Cost per
	Arrive	Depart	Days	Persons	Rate	Cost	Person
1)	Apr. 15	Apr. 25		3			
2)	Sept. 1	Sept. 14		2			
3)	Jan. 27	Feb. 4		1			
4)	Aug. 28	Sept. 12		2			
5)	Dec. 15	Jan. 15		5			

PACKAGE TRAVEL PLANS

Travel agencies and travel groups will plan a trip for a large number of people. Because of the big volume of such sales, discounts are given. These low-priced trips are called *package plans*. They often provide for hotel rooms, transportation, some meals, tours or side trips, and other special services.

Example: Mary and Rode I. Land each purchased a $939 package plan to travel to London for seven days. What was their daily cost?

Divide the number of days into the total cost.

$$\begin{array}{r} \$134.14 \quad \text{Cost per day} \\ 7\,)\overline{\$939.00} \quad \text{Total cost} \end{array}$$

Exercise A: Find the cost per day for each of these package plan tours.

	Trip	Cost	Number of Days
1)	Cruise to Nassau	$795	7 days
2)	Health Spa and Inn	$70	3 days
3)	Hawaii	$699	7 days
4)	Hawaii	$689	8 days
5)	Bermuda	$1,044	7 days
6)	Italy	$1,420	10 days
7)	Spain	$1,499	8 days
8)	China	$2,037	12 days
9)	Peru	$1,519	7 days
10)	Ireland	$1,255	8 days

EXCHANGING CURRENCY

Sometimes Americans who travel must exchange their dollars for another nation's money, or currency.

The following table shows various countries' currencies and their values compared to the United States dollar. These values can change daily. Travelers must find out the correct *exchange rates* at the time of their trip.

Comparison of Currencies			
Country	Currency Name	Number of Units That Equal One U.S. Dollar	Value of Unit in U.S. Dollars
1) Australia	dollar	.92 dollars	$1.09
2) Austria	schilling	10.51 schillings	$0.095
3) Belgium	franc	40 francs	$0.025
4) Brazil	cruzeiro	106 cruzeiros	$0.009
5) Britain	pound	.60 pounds	$1.66
6) Canada	dollar	1.22 dollars	$0.82
7) China	yuan	1.51 yuan	$0.66
8) Denmark	krone	7.70 krones	$0.13
9) Finland	markka	4.49 markkas	$0.22
10) France	franc	5.02 francs	$0.199
11) Germany	mark	1.50 marks	$0.67
12) Greece	drachma	152 drachmas	$0.0066
13) India	rupee	18.14 rupees	$0.055
14) Israel	shekel	1.98 shekels	$0.50
15) Italy	lira	1481 lire	$0.0006
16) Japan	yen	127.75 yen	$0.0078
17) Mexico	peso	29.21 pesos	$0.0003
18) Sweden	krona	5.73 krona	$0.18
19) Switzerland	franc	2.21 francs	$0.45

Example: Penny Wise wants to exchange 25 United States dollars for Japanese yen. How many yen will she receive?

Rule: To convert United States dollars to foreign currency, multiply the currency rate from the third column (see chart on page 179) by the number of U.S. dollars.

127.75	Currency rate of yen per dollar
x 25	U.S. dollars
3,193.75	Yen

Penny will receive 3,193.75 yen for $25.

Exercise A: For each of the countries listed on page 179, find out how much currency you would receive for 70 United States dollars. Use the currency rate listed in the third column. Round answers to the nearer whole number.

Exercise B: Convert the United States currency below to currency of other countries.

	U.S. Dollars	Country	Number of Units
1)	$100	Britain	_____
2)	$50	Canada	_____
3)	$25	Mexico	_____
4)	$40	Germany	_____
5)	$85	Italy	_____
6)	$37	France	_____
7)	$423	China	_____
8)	$10,500	Israel	_____
9)	$798	Japan	_____
10)	$25,000	Greece	_____

Example: Bill Fold sees a chess set for sale in Switzerland for 65 francs. How much would it cost in United States dollars?

Rule: To convert foreign currency to United States dollars, multiply the currency rate in the fourth column (see chart on page 179) by the amount of foreign money.

65	Swiss Francs
x .45	Currency rate (value in U.S. dollars)
$29.25	U.S. Dollars

The chess set costs $29.95 in U.S. dollars.

Exercise C: Convert the currency below to United States dollars. Round each answer to the nearer cent.

	Country	Amount
1)	Australia	26 dollars
2)	Austria	304 schillings
3)	Belgium	6,754 francs
4)	Brazil	30,985 cruzeiros
5)	Britain	75 pounds
6)	Canada	50 dollars
7)	China	403 yuan
8)	Denmark	987 krones
9)	Finland	100 markkas
10)	Greece	309 drachmas
11)	India	1,300 rupees
12)	Israel	967 shekels
13)	Italy	135,879 lire
14)	Mexico	685 pesos
15)	France	50 francs
16)	Germany	300 marks
17)	Sweden	6,790 krona

COMPUTER APPLICATION

Use the following computer program to change U.S. dollars to foreign currency or to change foreign currency to U.S. dollars. See the appendix in the back of this text for directions in using computer programs.

```
10      REM  EXCHANGING CURRENCY
20      REM  CHAPTER 8
30      PRINT "E X C H A N G I N G   C U R R E N C Y"
40      PRINT "     MENU"
50      PRINT " 1.  U.S. DOLLARS TO FOREIGN CURRENCY"
60      PRINT " 2.  FOREIGN CURRENCY TO U.S. DOLLARS"
70      PRINT "      DO YOU WANT 1 OR 2";
80      INPUT M
90      IF  M = 2 THEN GOTO 160
100     PRINT "HOW MUCH IN U.S. DOLLARS";
110     INPUT D
120     PRINT "WHAT IS THE EXCHANGE RATE FOR U.S. DOLLARS TO
        FOREIGN CURRENCY";
130     INPUT R
140     PRINT "YOU GET "; D * R ; " IN FOREIGN CURRENCY."
150     GOTO TO 210
160     PRINT "HOW MUCH IN FOREIGN CURRENCY";
170     INPUT F
180     PRINT "WHAT IS THE EXCHANGE RATE FOR FOREIGN CUR-
        RENCY TO U.S. DOLLARS";
190     INPUT R
200     PRINT "YOU GET $"; F * R
210     END
RUN
```

RENTING A CAR

A traveler may find it necessary or convenient to rent a car while away from home. Two sample rate charts are shown below. As you can see on one chart, rates are often higher for larger cars than for smaller cars.

Hurts Rents	Bevis Rent-A-Car
Daily Rates Subcompact $43 Compact $50 Midsize $54 Full Size $57	Daily Rates $18.98 + 20¢/mile $22.95 + 20¢/mile $24.95 + 20¢/mile
Weekly Rates Subcompact $159 Compact $189 Midsize $209 Full Size $229	Monthly Rates (No charge for first 3,000 miles) $420 + 20¢/mile > 3,000 $525 + 20¢/mile > 3,000 $545 + 20¢/mile > 3,000

Example: Carlotta Miles rented a midsized car from Bevis Rent-A-Car for three days. She drove 657 miles. What was the rental fee?

Step 1: Find the daily rate.

$22.95

Step 2: Multiply the daily rate by the number of days.

$22.95	Daily rate
x 3	Number of days
$68.85	Daily cost

Step 3: Find the mileage cost. Multiply the mileage by $.20.

657	Mileage
x $.20	Rate per mile
$131.40	Mileage cost

Step 4: Add the daily cost and the mileage cost to find the total rental fee.

$68.85	Daily cost
+ 131.40	Mileage cost
$200.25	Total rental fee

Here is another sample rate chart for car rentals.

Carl Eece Rentals

Daily Rate — $19.95 + 10¢/mile + $3.50 insurance
For all models

Weekly Plan 1 — Daily rate (plus $3.50 insurance fee) x 7
with unlimited mileage.

Weekly Plan 2 — $125/week + $3/day insurance +
18¢/mile over 1,000 miles/week

Example: Kitty Carr rented a small automobile from Carl Eece Rentals. She selected Weekly Plan 2 and traveled 1,156 miles in seven days. What was her rental fee?

Step 1: Find the weekly rate.

$125 + $3 Per day for insurance

Step 2: Find the insurance cost for one week. Multiply the insurance rate by 7.

$3 Cost of insurance per day
x 7 Number of days
$21 Insurance per week

Step 3: Find the number of miles over 1,000 that Kitty drove.

1156 Miles traveled
- 1000 Miles allowed free
156 Excess miles

Step 4: Find the mileage cost. Multiply the excess miles by the rate per mile.

156 Excess miles
x .18 Mileage rate
1248
156
$28.08 Mileage cost

Step 5: Find the total cost by adding the separate costs.

$125.00 Weekly rate
21.00 Insurance per week
+ 28.08 Mileage cost

Kitty's total rental fee was $174.08.

$174.08 Total rental fee

Exercise A: Find the cost of renting each of these cars. Use the rate charts given on pages 183 and 184.

	Rental Agency	Size of Car	Time Rented	Miles Traveled
1)	Bevis	Midsize	5 days	329
2)	Hurts	Full Size	2 weeks	897
3)	Carl Eece	Midsize	3 weeks, Plan 1	2,567
4)	Hurts	Subcompact	3 days	158
5)	Carl Eece	Compact	6 weeks, Plan 2	2,514
6)	Bevis	Full Size	3 months	9,254
7)	Hurts	Subcompact	8 days	1,400
8)	Bevis	Compact	4 months	14,259
9)	Carl Eece	Midsize	4 weeks, Plan 1	5,000
10)	Carl Eece	Midsize	4 weeks, Plan 2	5,000

Exercise B: Find the cost of renting each of these cars from Hurts Rents and Bevis Rent-A-Car. Then choose one plan from Carl Eece and find its cost for each car.

	Size of Car	Time Rented	Miles Traveled
1)	Compact	1 week	1,500
2)	Midsize	6 days	759
3)	Full Size	2 weeks	1,100
4)	Compact	3 days	548
5)	Full Size	8 weeks	6,623

PARKING EXPENSES

One of the expenses of driving a car in a city is parking.

Example: Otto Parker left his car at Manny Carr's Garage. Otto returned 2 hours and 15 minutes later. What was his parking fee?

Manny Carr's Garage		
PARKING		
$1.00	For first hour	
75¢	Each extra hour	
$5.00	Maximum	

Add: $1.00   First hour
       .75   Second hour
   + .75   15 minutes   (Note that any portion of an
  $2.50   hour counts as a whole hour.)

Otto's parking fee was $2.50.

Exercise A: Find the total parking fee at Manny's for each of these times.

1) 2 hours
2) 3 hours
3) 4 hours
4) 5 hours
5) 6 hours
6) 10 hours
7) 5 hours, 30 minutes
8) 3 hours, 20 minutes
9) 4 hours, 5 minutes
10) 2 hours, 54 minutes

CONSUMER HUMOR

I was so sorry to hear that you were in the hospital. How did your accident happen?

Everything was fine until I passed the sign for the town of Merging Traffic.

December 4
09:15
○
December 4
13:12

— — — —

Grand City
Garage

Some parking lots use an electronic ticket dispenser. It prints the date and time of your car's arrival at the parking lot. When you leave, an attendant uses another electric device that prints the leaving time and date. The attendant subtracts the times and computes your parking fee.

Notice the use of the 24-hour clock. Any number below 12:00 stands for morning hours. Numbers greater than 12:00 stand for afternoon and evening times.

12-Hour Clock	24-Hour Clock
1:00 a.m.	01:00
2:00 a.m.	02:00
3:00 a.m.	03:00
⋮	⋮
10:00 a.m.	10:00
11:00 a.m.	11:00
12:00 noon	12:00
1:00 p.m.	13:00
2:00 p.m.	14:00
⋮	⋮
11:00 p.m.	23:00
12:00 p.m.	24:00

Example: Max E. Otto uses an electric ticket machine at his parking lot. His rates are posted on a big sign.

PARKING

$1.25 First hour
$1.00 Each additional hour
$6.00 Maximum per day

A sample ticket from Max E. Otto's lot is shown at the right. The numbers 5/12 stand for the date, May 12. The other numbers stand for the times. What is the cost for parking for a car with this ticket?

5/12 — 08:45
5/12 — 12:20

Step 1: Find the parking time. Subtract the earlier time from the later time. Round answers to the next full hour.

$$\begin{array}{ll} & 11{:}80 \\ 12{:}20 & \text{Rename 12:20 to 11:80} \rightarrow \quad \cancel{12{:}20} \\ \underline{-\ 8{:}45} & \qquad\qquad\qquad\qquad\qquad \underline{-\ 8{:}45} \\ & \qquad\qquad\qquad\qquad\qquad\ \ 3{:}35 \quad \rightarrow \quad 4 \text{ hours} \end{array}$$

Step 2: Find the total cost. Add the hourly rates.

$$\begin{array}{ll} \$1.25 & \text{First hour} \\ \underline{+\ 3.00} & \text{3 additional hours} \\ \$4.25 & \text{Total cost} \end{array}$$

The parking fee for this ticket is $4.25.

Exercise B: Find the cost to park at Max's lot for each of these tickets.

1)
11/10 — 12:15
11/10 — 15:20

2)
10/20 — 20:30
10/20 — 23:30

3)
5/10 — 07:00
5/10 — 09:15

4)
7/10 — 10:12
7/10 — 12:15

5)
2/2 — 09:01
2/2 — 12:58

6)
6/6 — 14:15
6/6 — 16:02

7)
6/28 — 11:28
6/28 — 15:12

8)
7/30 — 09:10
7/30 — 17:02

9)
9/7 — 06:30
9/7 — 15:29

10)
12/24 — 04:25
12/24 — 19:20

TIME ZONES

The world is divided into 24 different *time zones*. The same standard time is used within each zone. The United States falls into seven different time zones of the world. Beginning at the Atlantic Ocean and moving west, one crosses these four time zones: Eastern, Central, Mountain, and Pacific.

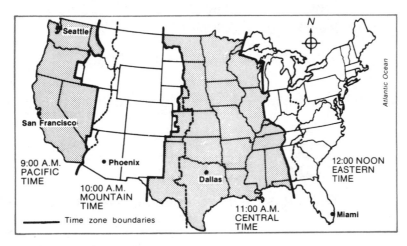

The state of Alaska is so large that it falls into the next three time zones: Yukon, Alaska-Hawaii, and Bering. Hawaii is also located in the Alaska-Hawaii time zone.

When every zone is using standard time, each zone's time is one hour later than the next zone to the west.

For example: When it is 12:00 noon in the Eastern Time Zone, it is 11:00 a.m. in the Central Time Zone.

Likewise, each zone is one hour earlier than the next zone to the east.

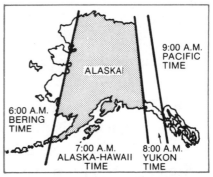

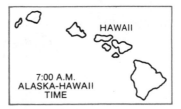

Example: What is the time in San Francisco when it is 7 p.m. in Miami?

Step 1: Look at the map on page 189. Start at Miami in the Eastern Time Zone. Count the number of time zones one passes through to reach San Francisco.

Central   — 1 hour
Mountain — 2 hours
Pacific   — 3 hours

The difference in time is three hours.

Step 2: You are moving west. So you will subtract 3 hours.

  7:00   p.m.
- 3:00   Hours
  4:00   p.m.

When it is 7 p.m. in Miami, it is 4 p.m. in San Francisco.

Example: What is the time in Dallas when it is 11 a.m. in Seattle?

Step 1: Dallas is two time zones away from Seattle. The difference in time is two hours.

Step 2: You are moving east. So you will add 2 hours.

  11:00   a.m.
+ 2:00   Hours
  13:00

13:00 is the same as 1:00 p.m. When it is 11 a.m. in Seattle, it is 1 p.m. in Dallas.

Example: When it is 1:43 p.m. in Phoenix, what time is it in Hawaii?

> **Step 1:** The time zones are Pacific, Yukon, and Alaska-Hawaii. Three time zones mean a difference of three hours.
>
> **Step 2:** You are moving west, so you will subtract the 3 hours.
>
> 1:43 p.m. + 12 Hours → 13:43   Rename 1:43 as 13:43
> - 3:00 Hours   - 3:00
>   10:43

When it is 1:43 p.m. in Phoenix, it is 10:43 a.m. in Hawaii.

Exercise A: Find the missing time for each of the zones indicated.

1) 2:00 p.m. Central
   ? Time Eastern

2) 6:25 a.m. Mountain
   ? Time Eastern

3) 3:04 p.m. Eastern
   ? Time Pacific

4) 8:59 a.m. Central
   ? Time Bering

5) 9:37 p.m. Alaska-Hawaii
   ? Time Mountain

6) 2:48 a.m. Central
   ? Time Yukon

7) 10:15 a.m. Bering
   ? Time Mountain

8) 1:36 a.m. Mountain
   ? Time Pacific

9) 4:01 p.m. Eastern
   ? Time Yukon

10) 11:52 p.m. Eastern
    ? Time Alaska-Hawaii

CONSUMER HUMOR

Did you ever wonder about times around the world?

No. But one time I did stay up all night and wondered where the sun went. Finally, it dawned on me.

TRAVELING BY AIR

For each airline flight, a schedule is available that states the time of departure and the time of arrival at its destination. Notice the following example.

Flight	Departure from Baltimore	Arrival in New York City	
1	7:00 a	8:00 a	Kennedy
2	10:10 a	11:15 a	Kennedy
3	11:45 a	1:05 p	Kennedy
4	5:24 p	7:09 p	La Guardia

Rule: To find the length of flying time for a trip, subtract the departure time from the arrival time.

Example: How long does Flight 2 take?

$$\begin{array}{ll} 11:15 & \text{Arrival} \\ -10:10 & \text{Departure} \\ \hline 1:05 & \end{array}$$

Flight 2 takes 1 hour and 5 minutes.

Example: How long does Flight 3 take?

Arrival   1:05   →   13:05   →   12:65 ~~13:05~~

Departure - 11:45   - 11:45   - 11:45

                                                 1:20

Flight 3 takes 1 hour and 20 minutes.

Exercise A: Calculate the length of time for each flight.

	Departure	Arrival			Departure	Arrival
1)	3:35 p	6:46 p		2)	10:35 p	1:20 a
3)	5:05 p	7:10 p		4)	7:44 p	11:15 p
5)	3:45 p	8:00 p		6)	9:35 p	2:12 a
7)	9:50 a	2:20 p		8)	12:30 a	8:15 a
9)	7:50 a	5:00 p		10)	11:40 a	4:13 p

| Time Differences Between Some Cities and U.S. Time Zones | | | | | | | | |
City	PST	MST	CST	EST	City	PST	MST	CST	EST
Baltimore	3	2	1	—	Nome	3	4	5	6
Bermuda	4	3	2	1	Ottawa	3	2	1	—
Chicago	2	1	—	1	Paris	9	8	7	6
Detroit	3	2	1	—	Phoenix	1	—	1	2
Dallas	2	1	—	1	St. Louis	2	1	—	1
Honolulu	2	3	4	5	San Diego	—	1	2	3
Juneau	—	1	2	3	San Francisco	—	1	2	3
Los Angeles	—	1	2	3	San Juan	4	3	2	1
Miami	3	2	1	—	Seattle	—	1	2	3
Minneapolis	2	1	—	1	Vancouver	—	1	2	3
New York City	3	2	1	—	Washington, D.C.	3	2	1	—

When calculating travel time, you need to consider the time differences between zones. Use the chart shown above.

Example: What is the time of a flight that leaves Baltimore at 8 a.m. (EST) and arrives in Honolulu at 3:15 p.m. (A-HST)?

Step 1: Express both times in terms of the same time zone. Find the equivalent time in EST for 3:15 p.m. Honolulu time. Use the table to find the differences in time zones.

Step 2: According to the table, there is a 5-hour difference in time between Honolulu and EST. Since you are converting to eastern time, add hours.

$$\begin{array}{r} 3:15 \text{ p.m.} \\ + 5:00 \text{ Hours} \\ \hline 8:15 \text{ p.m.} \end{array}$$

Step 3: Subtract the departure time from the converted arrival time.

$$\begin{array}{r} 8:15 \text{ p.m.} \quad + 12 \text{ hours} \rightarrow \\ - 8:00 \text{ a.m.} \end{array} \quad \begin{array}{r} 20:15 \\ - 8:00 \\ \hline 12:15 \end{array}$$

The trip takes 12 hours and 15 minutes.

Exercise B: Calculate the travel time for each flight. Use the chart on page 193.

	Departure		Arrival	
1)	Baltimore	11:10 a	San Francisco	6:05 p
2)	St. Louis	2:15 p	Washington, D.C.	5:07 p
3)	Chicago	4:05 p	Seattle	6:58 p
4)	Los Angeles	7:20 a	New York City	4:47 p
5)	Detroit	10:35 a	Bermuda	2:19 p
6)	Vancouver	7:45 a	Baltimore	5:00 p
7)	Miami	4:40 p	Ottawa	9:03 p
8)	Nome	2:05 a	New York City	10:15 p
9)	Honolulu	7:15 p	San Francisco	1:05 a
10)	Baltimore	6:20 p	Los Angeles	9:00 p
11)	Los Angeles	9:30 a	Baltimore	5:15 p
12)	Washington, D.C.	10:50 a	Minneapolis	1:35 p
13)	Minneapolis	5:05 p	Washington, D.C.	9:30 p
14)	Phoenix	3:25 p	Dallas	6:13 p
15)	Dallas	8:45 p	Phoenix	9:50 p
16)	San Diego	3:15 p	Juneau	7:10 p
17)	Juneau	11:10 a	San Diego	3:15 p
18)	Washington, D.C.	11:10 a	Chicago	12:06 p
19)	Chicago	11:35 a	Washington, D.C.	2:10 p
20)	Chicago	5:10 p	San Juan	2:10 a
21)	San Juan	5:40 p	Chicago	11:35 p
22)	New York City	5:10 p	Paris	8:30 a
23)	Paris	12:45 p	New York City	4:30 p
24)	Washington, D.C.	11:45 a	Paris	7:50 p
25)	Paris	4:35 p	Washington, D.C.	3:05 p

CHAPTER REVIEW   8

Solve these problems on pages 195 and 196.

1) Three towns are on a route. What is the distance between Town A and Town C?

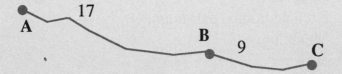

2) A map has a scale of 1 cm = 5 km. What distance is represented by a line 6 cm long? What distance is represented by a line 2.5 cm long?

3) A train leaves Station A at 3:44 p.m. and arrives at Station B at 6:03 p.m. How long is the trip?

4) A passenger on a train paid the excursion rate of 25% off the regular fare of $48.75. How much did he pay?

5) How many nights were spent in a hotel by a guest who arrived on May 28 and left early on June 11?

6) What is the cost per day of a 7-day trip that has a total cost of $756.00?

7) The conversion rate for Swiss francs is 2.21 francs = 1 U.S. dollar. How many Swiss francs can be exchanged for $79.00 in U. S. currency?

8) What is the cost of renting a car for 4 days at $17.59 per day and driving 237 miles at 19¢ per mile?

9) Use the chart for parking rates shown below. What is the cost of parking 3 hours and 15 minutes?

PARKING RATES	
$1.75	First hour
.75	Each additional half hour
$6.25	Maximum

10) When it is 3:45 p.m. in Phoenix, what time is it in New York City? Use the time zone map found on page 189. New York is located in the Eastern Time Zone.

CHAPTER 9

BUDGETING YOUR MONEY

A *budget* is a plan for managing income and expenses. It is usually figured for a set period of time, such as month, year, etc. Budgets contribute to financial stability. The federal government plans a budget every year. Large corporations and small businesses also make budgets.

People make budgets to plan their spending so that they can afford necessary expenses. Is there enough money for the rent or mortgage payment? How much can be spent for food? What about buying a new appliance or a car? Many people who are concerned about these questions make budgets.

In this chapter, you will learn to find the average income available for budgeting. You will practice the steps necessary for preparing, adjusting, and balancing a budget. You will also learn to read and create circle graphs that are used to represent budgets. This chapter will help you to develop the mathematical skills to plan for financial stability.

FINDING AVERAGE INCOME

When you compute the average monthly income available for budgeting, use only the *net,* or *take-home, pay.* This figure shows the actual amount of money available for budgeting.

Example: Bud Jett is paid $276.56 *biweekly.* This term means that he is paid every other week. What is his average monthly net income?

Step 1: Find his yearly income. Multiply his biweekly income by the number of pay periods per year.

$$\frac{26}{2)52} \text{ Pay periods} \qquad \begin{array}{r} \$276.56 \\ \times \quad 26 \\ \hline \$7,190.56 \end{array} \begin{array}{l} \text{Biweekly income} \\ \text{No. of pay periods} \\ \text{Yearly income} \end{array}$$

26 Pay periods
2)52 Weeks in a year

Step 2: Find monthly income. Divide yearly income by 12 months.

$$\frac{\$599.21}{12)\$7190.56} \begin{array}{l} \text{Monthly income} \\ \text{Yearly income} \end{array}$$

Bud's average monthly net income is $599.21.

Rule: To find average monthly income, multiply the regular take-home pay by the number of pay periods per year. Then divide this yearly income by 12 months.

Exercise A: Find the average monthly income for each pay. *Semimonthly* means twice a month.

	Pay Period	Net Pay		Pay Period	Net Pay
1)	Biweekly	$357.84	2)	Semimonthly	$282.47
3)	Biweekly	$135.96	4)	Weekly	$159.32
5)	Weekly	$89.21	6)	Biweekly	$287.16
7)	Weekly	$128.75	8)	Biweekly	$312.10
9)	Semimonthly	$376.89	10)	Weekly	$196.88

Example: O'Vera Time works different hours each week and wants to estimate her average monthly income. These figures show her net pays for the last seven weeks.

| $156.19 | $154.57 | $167.98 | $148.76 |
| $137.82 | $172.08 | $187.19 | |

Step 1: Find the average weekly income. Add the seven net pays. The sum of the net pays is $1,124.59.

Step 2: Divide this sum by the number of pays. The average weekly income is $160.66.

$160.66 Average weekly income
7) $1124.59 Total of net pays

Step 3: Compute the yearly income. Multiply the weekly income by 52.

$160.66   Average weekly income
x   52
$8354.32   Yearly income

Step 4: Divide the yearly income by 12 to find the average monthly income.

$696.19 { Average monthly income
12) $8354.32   Yearly income

O'Vera's average monthly income is $696.19.

Exercise B: Find the average monthly income for each set of weekly net pays.

1) $356.10 $159.25 $267.84 $192.90 $212.88
2) $105.16 $174.87 $97.59 $110.03 $126.48 $95.70
3) $88.88 $102.15 $90.76 $101.18 $129.87 $135.18 $116.05
4) $256.00 $243.50 $252.05 $261.18 $225.93 $250.47
5) $131.07 $139.10 $133.48 $128.79 $127.56
6) $75.89 $77.50 $72.10 $75.89 $82.46 $80.14
7) $101.01 $175.64 $152.17 $136.49 $143.00
8) $84.16 $102.36 $95.75 $97.19
9) $302.01 $335.75 $317.17 $328.99 $297.48
10) $62.10 $75.18 $67.90 $72.44 $77.67 $68.46 $64.33

PREPARING A BUDGET

available. The second step is to decide what kinds of *expenses* or costs you will have. It is helpful to list expenses in large categories.

Exercise A: List two kinds of expenses that can be included in each category.

1) Housing
2) Food
3) Clothing
4) Transportation
5) Insurance
6) Gifts
7) Entertainment
8) Savings
9) Health
10) Miscellaneous

Some consumer groups publish *budget guidelines*, or plans. One such plan is shown by the *circle graph* below. The family's income is divided into portions so that a certain amount of the money can be used for each expense. Dividing the circle into sections shows the relative size of each category.

Family Income After Taxes

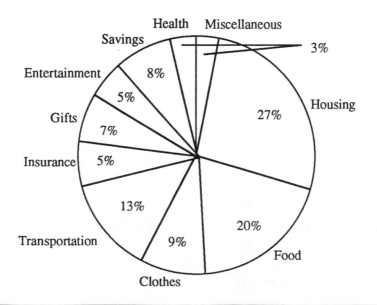

Example: Lotta Plans has an average monthly income of $645.10. She uses the budget plan shown on page 200. How much money does she budget for each expense?

Step 1: Multiply each percent by the amount available.

a) Housing	27%	x	$645.10	=	$174.18
b) Food	20%	x	$645.10	=	$129.02
c) Clothes	9%	x	$645.10	=	$58.06
d) Transportation	13%	x	$645.10	=	$83.86
e) Insurance	5%	x	$645.10	=	$32.26
f) Gifts	7%	x	$645.10	=	$45.16
g) Entertainment	5%	x	$645.10	=	$32.26
h) Savings	8%	x	$645.10	=	$51.61
i) Health	3%	x	$645.10	=	$19.35
j) Miscellaneous	3%	x	$645.10	=	+ $19.35
					$645.11

Step 2: Add the individual amounts to check for errors. The difference of 1¢ is due to rounding.

Exercise B: Use the budget plan shown on page 200 for each of these monthly incomes. Find the amount of money that is to be budgeted for each category. Check your work by adding. The total may vary slightly from original figures due to rounding.

1) $810.15
2) $455.07
3) $496.45
4) $476.19
5) $992.80
6) $857.13
7) $713.28
8) $337.21
9) $1,128.03
10) $505.08
11) $1,037.69
12) $622.49

ADJUSTING A BUDGET

Some people examine their spending patterns before they plan their budgets. They calculate the yearly totals and then compute the percent spent in each category. Study the following example.

Part of Ann U. All's Yearly Expenditures				
Month	Food	Housing	Clothes	Car
January	$140.00	$251.50	—	$152.77
February	$152.10	$251.50	—	$150.12
March	$97.38	$251.50	$25.90	$158
April	$102.76	$302.67	$146.56	
May	$95.59	$251.50	$10.50	
June	$111.21	$251.50	—	
July	$93.85	$287.10	—	
August	$108.72	$251.50		
September	$134.67	$251.50		
October	$166.44	$251.50		
November	$99.93	$251.50		
December	$110.84	$251.50		
Totals	$1413.49	$3104.7		

Example: Ann spent $1,413.49 last year on food. Approximately what percent of her $15,804.19 net income was this?

Step 1: Write the ratio. $\dfrac{\text{expenses}}{\text{income}}$ $\dfrac{1{,}413.49}{15{,}804.19}$

If you have a calculator, perform the division.
$1413.49 \div 15{,}804.19 = .0894376 \approx .09$ or 9%

Step 2: If not, round the numbers and approximate the answer.
$\dfrac{1400}{16000}$

Step 3: Simplify the ratio. $\dfrac{1400}{16000} = \dfrac{14}{160} = \dfrac{7}{80}$

Step 4: Divide to find the decimal.

$$\frac{.087}{80)\overline{7.000}} \approx .09$$

Step 5: Write answer as a percent. $.09 = 9\%$

Exercise A: Work the following problems given on pages 203 and 204.

1) What percent of the net income of $17,307.20 was spent on each category?
   a) Housing $5,538.30
   b) Food $4,153.73
   c) Clothes $1,730.72
   d) Transportation $2,596.08
   e) Insurance $865.36
   f) Gifts $692.29
   g) Entertainment $519.22
   h) Savings $173.07
   i) Health $1,038.43

2) What percent of the net income of $23,695.06 was spent on each category?
   a) Housing $6,160.72
   b) Food $4,975.96
   c) Clothes $2,132.56
   d) Transportation $3,317.31
   e) Insurance $1,421.70
   f) Gifts $1,895.61
   g) Entertainment $1,184.75
   h) Savings $1,658.65
   i) Health $947.80

3) Tina Bopper has a part-time job and earns a net income of $37.75. This is how she spends her money each week.
   Records and Tapes .....$3.00   Entertainment.............$6.75
   Savings ....$25.00   Hair and makeup........$3.00
   What percent of her income is spent in each category?

4) A small business has an average monthly gross income of $39,000.

   a) What percent is spent in each of these categories?

Rent	$4,265
Operations	$1,325
Materials	$5,756
Payroll	$20,950
Advertising	$1,450

   b) What percent remains as profit?

COMPUTER APPLICATION

Use the following computer program to figure the percent of net income spent in each category of a budget. See the directions in the back of this text for directions in using computer programs.

```
10    REM  ADJUSTING A BUDGET
20    REM  CHAPTER 9
30    PRINT " A D J U S T I N G   A   B U D G E T "
40    PRINT "WHAT IS THE NET INCOME";
50    INPUT N
60    PRINT "HOW MUCH IS SPENT ON ONE CATEGORY";
70    INPUT S
80    PRINT " PERCENT SPENT:  "; INT ( ( S / N + .005 ) * 100 ) ; "%"
90    PRINT "MORE PROBLEMS? ( Y = YES, N = NO )";
100   INPUT A$
110   IF A$ = "Y" THEN GOTO 60
120   END
RUN
```

USING CIRCLE GRAPHS

You can make a circle graph to show the relative sizes of budget categories.

Every circle contains 360°. To find out how large to make a *sector*, or section of the circle, multiply 360° by the percent of income. The result will tell you the number of degrees to include in that sector.

Example: Sir Kill's family spends 23% of their income for food.

$$360° \times .23 = ? \text{ degrees of the circle}$$

360	Number of degrees in a circle
x .23	Percent of income
1080	
720	
82.80 ≈ 83°	

The food sector represents 83°.

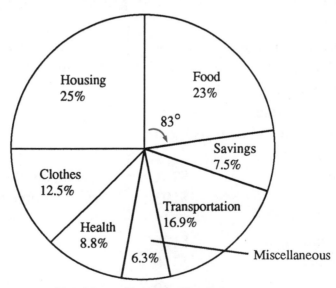

Sir Kill's Family Budget

Exercise A: Complete these problems. Use the graph on page 205.

1) Find the number of degrees for each of the sectors of the Kill family budget circle graph. Note that the total number of degrees may not be 360, due to rounding.
   a) Housing
   b) Clothes
   c) Savings
   d) Health
   e) Transportation
   f) Miscellaneous

2) List some possible reasons why food and transportation are such large expenditures for this family.

3) Draw a circle graph to display the following budget.

Food	24%
Housing	15%
Clothing	20%
Cars	10%
Health	10%
Miscellaneous	21%

4) A family has a monthly net income of $965.00. The average monthly expenses are listed below. Draw a circle graph to show the percent of income that is spent in each category.

Housing	$241
Food	$193
Clothes	$145
Transportation	$125
Investments	$116
Health	$48
Miscellaneous	$97

CONSUMER HUMOR

We always wanted to buy our own home but couldn't.

Why? Was your income too low?

No, our income was fine. It was our outgo that was too high.

BALANCING A BUDGET

Balancing a budget means determining the state of finances after a given budget period. A person can learn if there is money remaining or a debt. The amount allotted for a certain budget category may not be entirely spent during the month. Some money may be saved to spend the next month.

Exercise A: Copy and complete this budget record for July.

	Food	Rent	Clothes	Cars
June Balance +July Budget	$4.10 + 175.65	0 310.50	13.50 25.00	3.15 70.00
Funds Available - July Expenses	179.75 - 176.50	_____ 310.50	_____ 18.00	_____ 67.36
July Balance +August Budget	3.25 + 175.65	_____ _____	_____ _____	_____ _____
Funds Available	178.90	_____	_____	_____

	Gifts	Savings	Miscellaneous
June Balance +July Budget	$36.50 + 20.00	0 45.00	176.10 57.50
Funds Available - July Expenses	_____ - 10.99	_____ 45.00	_____ 65.60
July Balance +August Budget	_____ _____	_____ _____	_____ _____
Funds Available	_____	_____	_____

Exercise B: Answer these questions about the budget shown on page 207.
1) What was the total amount budgeted for July?
2) What was the total amount spent in July?
3) What percent of the income was actually spent in July?

Exercise C: Copy and complete this budget record for an income of $975.35.

	Food	Shelter	Clothes
	25%	30%	20%
January Balance +February Budget	$1.15 +_____	11.65 _____	0 _____
Funds Available - February Expenses	_____ - 236.36	_____ 303.50	_____ 86.58
February Balance	_____	_____	_____

	Cars	Savings	Miscellaneous
	18%	5%	2%
January Balance +February Budget	36.09 +_____	0 _____	82.74 _____
Funds Available - February Expenses	_____ - 111.06	_____ 48.77	_____ 97.36
February Balance	_____	_____	_____

Exercise D: Look at the completed budget record shown in Exercise C. Find the total amount spent in January.

Mr. I. Otto Savemore has an opportunity to buy some nice clothes at a January sale. His monthly clothes budget is $24.00, and he has $5.10 left from December. Otto decides to spend $36.00 at the sale. How should he record this?

Step 1: List the December balance.

$$\begin{array}{r} \$5.10 \\ +\ 24.00 \\ \hline \end{array}$$

Step 2: Add the January budget allotment for clothes.

$$\begin{array}{r} \$29.10 \\ -\ 36.00 \\ \hline ? \end{array}$$

Step 3: Subtract the expenses. $36.00 is too large to subtract from $29.10. To find how much greater Otto's expenses were, reverse the numbers and subtract.

$$\begin{array}{r} \$36.00 \\ -\ 29.10 \\ \hline \$6.90 \end{array}$$

Otto has overspent his budget by $6.90.

Step 4: There are two ways to record this overspending. One is to write the new balance as -$6.90. Another is to write the number $6.90 in red, to indicate a debt.

Step 5: In February, Otto will have to repay his debt to the clothes allotment.

January Balance	- $6.90
+February Budget	$24.00
Funds Available	$17.10

$$\begin{array}{r} \$24.00 \\ -\ \ 6.90 \\ \hline \$17.10 \end{array}$$

Exercise E: Answer these questions.

1)   When Otto wants to overspend his budget, where does he get the extra money?

2)   Anita Loan had a balance of $32.50 in May for gifts. Her allotment for the month was $17.60. She was invited to two bridal showers, two weddings, and a birthday party. The gifts she purchased amounted to $63.95. What was the balance for this category at the end of May?

3)   What was Anita's balance for gifts at the beginning of June?

4)   Chuck Roast planned a barbecue party for some friends. His entertainment budget was $25.86, and his food budget had an extra $10.57. How much money was available to spend on the party?

5)   Chuck spent $52.75. He split this expense debt evenly between food and entertainment. How much "in debt" were food and entertainment?

6)   Eileen Ona Friend borrowed $3.58 from her friend to purchase some shampoo last month. Her new allotment in miscellaneous was $30.00. How much did she have after repaying her friend?

7)   Manny Buckslater overspent his transportation allotment because he replaced his brake shoes. He spent $17.84 more than he budgeted. How much was available the next month if 17% of his $656.10 was for transportation?

Solve these problems given on pages 211 and 212.

1) Find the average monthly income for these weekly incomes: $157.10, $356.48, $216.90, and $257.03.

2) How much of a $376.80 monthly net income is allotted for food if 23% is budgeted?

3) What percent of $376.80 is budgeted for housing and repairs if $113.04 is allotted?

4) Draw a circle graph to represent this budget.

Housing	27%
Food	24%
Cars	19%
Clothes	15%
Health	8%
Savings	5%
Miscellaneous	2%

5) Read the information for the six categories listed on pages 211-212. Balance this budget for an income of $700.

	Housing	Food	Clothes
	28%	25%	10%
Old Balance + New Budget	$16.76 +_____	- $10.50 _____	- $3.94 _____
Funds Available - Expenses	_____ - 200.00	_____ 186.40	_____ 57.87
New Balance	_____	_____	_____

	Cars	Health	Savings and Miscellaneous
	15%	2%	20%
Old Balance +New Budget	$111.50 +_____	$36.88 _____	$47.89 _____
Funds Available - Expenses	_____ - 235.84	_____ 10.94	_____ 100.00
New Balance	_____	_____	_____

CHAPTER 10

BANKING AND INVESTING

When the scientific genius, Albert Einstein, was asked to name man's greatest invention, he surprised everyone by saying "Compound interest." The earning of interest is important in banking. Banks are businesses. In order to make a profit, banks lend money. Here's how it works.

Jane — money / interest — Banker — money / interest — Jack

1. Jane puts her money into a savings account in the bank.
2. The bank lends this money to Jack. Jack pays the bank for the use of this money. That payment is called *interest*.
3. The bank keeps some of the interest it earns from Jack; it also pays Jane for the use of her money. That payment is called *interest,* too.

People put their money into bank accounts for several reasons. One reason is to keep it safe. Another is to earn interest. What other reasons can you think of? This chapter will help you develop mathematical skills needed to understand banking and investing. You will learn to compute simple and compound interest, balance a checkbook, keep track of checks, and read a stock report.

SIMPLE INTEREST

The fees on some loans are computed by simple interest. *Simple interest* is a one-time payment or fee charged for the use of the money loaned.

Rule: I = PRT. Interest is equal to the *Principal* (amount loaned) times the *Rate* (percent of interest charged) times the *Time* (number of years the money is loaned).

Example: Rich Ladd lent $500 to his cousin, who paid him 7% simple interest each year. At the end of three years, the cousin paid back the loan. What was the total amount that Rich collected?

Step 1:	Find the interest.	$500	Principal
	I = PRT	x .07	Rate
	I = $500 x 7% x 3	$35.00	
	I = $500 x .07 x 3	x 3	Time in years
		$105.00	Interest
Step 2:	Add the interest to the principal to find the total amount.	$500	Principal
		+ 105	Interest
		$605	Total amount

Exercise A: Find the simple interest earned and the total amount in each case.

	Principal	Rate	Time	Interest	Total Amount
1)	$300	5%	2 years	_____	_____
2)	$150	6%	3 years	_____	_____
3)	$658	10%	1 year	_____	_____
4)	$22	5%	4 years	_____	_____
5)	$128	$6\frac{1}{2}\%$ (.065)	10 years	_____	_____
6)	$1,000	$5\frac{1}{4}\%$	5 years	_____	_____
7)	$10	$7\frac{3}{4}\%$	2 years	_____	_____
8)	$98	$8\frac{1}{2}\%$	1.5 years	_____	_____
9)	$1,527	$10\frac{1}{4}\%$	3.5 years	_____	_____
10)	$43	$12\frac{3}{4}\%$	6.25 years	_____	_____

Example: Manny Bucks lent money to his brother for 3 months. How much interest did he earn on $100 at $5\frac{3}{8}$ % simple interest?

Step 1: Change the rate to a decimal.

$5\frac{3}{8}$ % = $.05\frac{3}{8}$

$.05\frac{3}{8}$ = .05**375**

$$\frac{3}{8} = \quad \begin{array}{r} .375 \\ 8 \overline{)3.000} \end{array}$$

Step 2: Time must be expressed in years, not months. Change 3 months to a decimal part of a year. To convert months to years, divide by 12.

3 months = .25 year

$$\frac{3}{12} = \quad \begin{array}{r} .25 \\ 12 \overline{)3.00} \\ \underline{24} \\ 60 \\ \underline{60} \end{array}$$

Step 3: Multiply.

I = P x R x T

I = $100 x .05375 x .25

```
          .05375    Rate
      x    $100     Principal
        $5.37500
      x      .25    Time in years
      $1.3437500    Interest
```

Manny earned $1.34 interest.

Exercise B: Find the simple interest earned and the total amount in each case.

	Principal	Rate	Time	Interest	Total Amount
1)	$100	$5\frac{1}{2}$%	6 months	_____	_____
2)	$500	$6\frac{1}{8}$%	9 months	_____	_____
3)	$600	$7\frac{1}{2}$%	3 months	_____	_____
4)	$900	$4\frac{3}{4}$%	12 months	_____	_____
5)	$1,500	$8\frac{1}{2}$%	18 months	_____	_____
6)	$7,000	$7\frac{3}{8}$%	15 months	_____	_____
7)	$8,796	$6\frac{7}{8}$%	24 months	_____	_____
8)	$4,023	$5\frac{5}{8}$%	33 months	_____	_____
9)	$10,000	$6\frac{1}{4}$%	21 months	_____	_____
10)	$20,000	$7\frac{1}{4}$%	45 months	_____	_____

COMPOUND INTEREST

Many people deposit their money into *savings accounts* in the bank. These accounts earn interest for the depositor. Banks usually compute this amount as compound interest. When figuring compound interest on savings accounts, the *principal* is the amount deposited into the account. The *rate* is the percent of interest earned by the depositor. The *time* is the number of years that the money is kept in the account. A depositor earns *compound interest* on both the original principal and any interest added to the account.

Example: Willy Grow deposited $100 into an account that yielded 5% interest, compounded twice a year. Calculate the amount in the account after one year.

		$100	Principal
Step 1:	Compute the interest for the first 6 months.	x .05	Rate
		$5.00	
	$I = \$100 \times 5\% \times \frac{6}{12}$	x .5	Time in years
	$= \$100 \times .05 \times .5$	$2.50\not{0}$	Interest
Step 2:	Add the interest to the original deposit, or principal, to find the new principal.	$100.00	Principal
		+ 2.50	Interest
		$102.50	New principal
Step 3:	Compute the interest for the second 6 months.	$102.50	Step 2 principal
		X .05	Rate
	$I = \$102.50 \times 5\% \times \frac{6}{12}$	$5.1250	
	$= \$102.50 \times .05 \times .5$	x .5	Time in years
		$2.56250	≈ $2.56 Interest
Step 4:	Add interest to the principal to find the new principal.	$102.50	Step 2 principal
		+ 2.56	Interest
		$105.06	New principal

At the end of one year, Willy had $105.06 in his account.

Interest that is compounded twice a year is said to be compounded semi-annually.

At the right is a table showing the number of times per year interest is compounded.

Compounded	Times per Year
Annually	1
Semiannually	2
Quarterly	4
Monthly	12
Daily	360

Exercise A: Compute the new principal at the end of one year when the interest is compounded semiannually.

	Principal	Rate of Interest	New Principal
1)	$100	6%	_____
2)	$100	7%	_____
3)	$100	$5\frac{1}{2}\%$	_____
4)	$100	$6\frac{1}{4}\%$	_____
5)	$100	$7\frac{1}{2}\%$	_____

Exercise B: Compute the new principal at the end of one year when the interest is compounded quarterly.

	Principal	Rate of Interest	New Principal
1)	$100	$5\frac{1}{2}\%$	_____
2)	$200	$5\frac{1}{2}\%$	_____
3)	$300	$5\frac{1}{2}\%$	_____
4)	$400	$5\frac{1}{2}\%$	_____
5)	$500	$5\frac{1}{2}\%$	_____

Exercise C: Compute the new principal at the end of four months when the interest is compounded monthly. ($\frac{1}{12} = .083$)

	Principal	Rate of Interest	New Principal
1)	$1,000	6%	_____
2)	$5,000	$5\frac{3}{4}\%$	_____
3)	$1,500	8%	_____

Example: Woody Save wants to know how much his $3,000 investment will be worth in 20 years at 16% interest compounded yearly.

Step 1: Use the table on page 219, "Amounts for $1.00 Compounded Annually." Locate the amount of money that $1.00 will be worth after 20 years at 16%. In the "Years" column, find 20. Go across. Look down the column for 16%. Find 19.461.

Step 2: Multiply 19.461 by the value of the deposit.

$$\begin{array}{r} 19.461 \\ \times\quad \$3000 \\ \hline \$58383.00\cancel{0} \end{array}$$

An investment of $3,000 at 16% interest compounded annually will grow to $58,383.00 in 20 years.

Exercise D: Calculate the value at maturity for each investment with compound interest. Use the table on page 219.

	Initial Investment	Rate of Interest	Number of Years	Value at Maturity
1)	$2,500	17%	10	_____
2)	$2,500	17%	20	_____
3)	$2,500	17%	25	_____
4)	$7,000	15%	25	_____
5)	$7,000	18%	25	_____
6)	$6,850	16.5%	8	_____
7)	$3,940	15.5%	11	_____
8)	$20,000	16%	23	_____
9)	$46,800	17.5%	12	_____
10)	$54,960	18%	15	_____

Exercise E: Calculate the value at maturity for each investment with simple interest. Compare these values with those earned with compound interest.

Amounts for $1.00 Compounded Annually

Years	15%	15.5%	16%	16.5%	17%	17.5%	18%
1	1.150	1.155	1.160	1.165	1.170	1.175	1.180
2	1.323	1.334	1.346	1.357	1.369	1.381	1.392
3	1.521	1.541	1.561	1.581	1.602	1.622	1.643
4	1.749	1.780	1.811	1.842	1.874	1.906	1.939
5	2.011	2.055	2.100	2.146	2.192	2.240	2.288
6	2.313	2.374	2.436	2.500	2.565	2.632	2.700
7	2.660	2.742	2.826	2.913	3.001	3.092	3.185
8	3.059	3.167	3.278	3.393	3.511	3.633	3.759
9	3.518	3.658	3.803	3.953	4.108	4.269	4.435
10	4.046	4.225	4.411	4.605	4.807	5.016	5.234
11	4.652	4.880	5.117	5.365	5.624	5.894	6.176
12	5.350	5.636	5.936	6.250	6.580	6.926	7.288
13	6.153	6.510	6.886	7.282	7.699	8.138	8.599
14	7.067	7.519	7.987	8.483	9.007	9.562	10.147
15	8.137	8.684	9.265	9.883	10.539	11.235	11.974
16	9.358	10.030	10.748	11.514	12.330	13.201	14.129
17	10.761	11.585	12.468	13.413	14.426	15.511	16.672
18	12.375	13.381	14.462	15.627	16.879	18.226	19.673
19	14.232	15.455	16.776	18.205	19.748	21.415	23.214
20	16.367	17.850	19.461	21.209	23.106	25.163	27.393
21	18.822	20.617	22.574	24.708	27.033	29.566	32.324
22	21.645	23.812	26.186	28.785	31.629	34.740	38.142
23	24.891	27.503	30.376	33.535	37.006	40.820	45.008
24	28.625	31.766	35.236	39.068	43.297	47.963	53.109
25	32.919	36.690	40.874	45.514	50.658	56.357	62.669

DOUBLING YOUR MONEY

Investors double their money when the amount of simple interest earned equals the amount invested, or the principal. How long does it take?

$$I = PRT$$

Example #1:   P = $100 $100
                R = 5%   x .05
                T = 20 years $5.00
                I = $100 x .05 x 20 = $100.00   x   20
                                             $100.00

Example #2:   P = $300 $300
                R = 10%   x .10
                T = 10 years $30.00
                I = $300 x .10 x 10 = $300.00   x   10
                                             $300.00

Example #3:   P = $200 $200
                R = 4%   x .04
                T = 25 years $8.00
                I = $200 x .04 x 25 = $200.00   x   25
                                             $200.00

In each example shown above, the interest equals the principal. The investor has "doubled" his money.

Rule: To find the number of years it takes to double money at a given rate of simple interest, divide 100 by the rate of interest.

Example: How many years are necessary to double money at 20% simple interest?

$$\begin{array}{r} 5 \text{ years} \\ 20\overline{)\,100} \end{array}$$

It will take five years for the money to double.

Exercise A: Find the number of years necessary for an investment to double at each of these rates of simple interest.

1) 5%	2) 10%
3) 25%	4) 4%
5) 2%	6) 1%
7) 50%	8) 40%
9) 15%	10) 8%
11) 12%	12) 11%

Money doubles faster with compound interest than with simple interest. Instead of dividing into 100, you divide into 72.

Rule: To find the approximate number of years necessary to double money at a given rate of compound interest, divide 72 by the rate of interest.

Exercise B: Find the number of years necessary for an investment to double at each of these rates of compound interest.

1) 6%	2) 12%
3) 8%	4) 9%
5) 4%	6) 3%
7) 18%	8) 24%
9) 10%	10) 5%
11) 20%	12) 11%

CHECKING ACCOUNTS

A *checking account* allows depositors to draw checks against money deposited in the account. Checks are a convenient and safe means of payment. A *check* is a written order directing a bank to pay money as instructed. It may be cashed only by the person to whom it is written, unless that person signs the check over to a second party. It is safer to mail a check than to mail cash. After the check is returned to you, you have proof of payment.

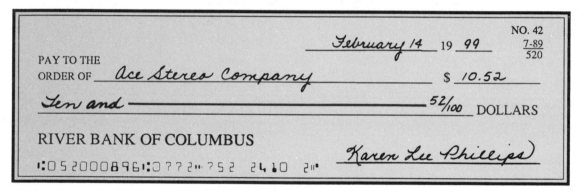

When you write a check, you must fill in five items. Notice the placement of each item on the checks shown on this page.

1. The date
2. The name of the person or company who is to receive payment (the payee)
3. The amount written in digits
4. The amount written in words
5. Your signature

It is important to write amounts in words correctly on checks. The words for numbers between 20 and 100 are hyphenated when the number has two words.

Examples: 85 is written as "Eighty-five."
24 is written as "Twenty-four."
99 is written as "Ninety-nine."

The word "and" is reserved for the decimal point.

The cents are written as a fraction of a dollar, since the word "Dollars" appears at the end of the line.

Examples: $444.44 is written: Four hundred forty-four and $^{44}/_{100}$.
$306.10 is written: Three hundred six and $^{10}/_{100}$.
$17.36 is written: Seventeen and $^{36}/_{100}$.

When there are no cents, the fraction is usually written with zeros.

Example: $97.00 is written: Ninety-seven and $^{00}/_{100}$

Some people write the word "No" or the letters "xx" instead of zeros.

Examples: Ninety-nine and $^{No}/_{100}$
Four and $^{xx}/_{100}$

Exercise A: Write each of these amounts in words as you would on a check.

1) $25.86	2) $37.16	3) $143.00
4) $905.15	5) $1,327.56	6) $48.18
7) $296.75	8) $449.37	9) $57.49
10) $18.18	11) $61.60	12) $70.61
13) $45.76	14) $87.72	15) $384.48

KEEPING THE ACCOUNT UP TO DATE

Checkbooks include forms so check writers can keep a record of money in the checking account. Some checks have a *stub*, a part of the checkbook that remains after the check has been removed.

On the stub you write the previous balance of the account, the amount of the check, and subtract to find the new balance remaining. If you make a deposit, you write the amount and add it to find the new balance.

Some checking accounts charge a fee for processing each check that is written. Such a fee is written on the check stub as a deduction. Subtract any deductions to find the new balance brought forward.

No. 42		
Feb. 14 , 19 99		
To Ace Stereo		
	Dollars	Cents
Bal. Fwd.	75	00
Deposits		
Total	75	00
This check	10	52
Balance	64	48
Deductions		15
Bal. Fwd.	64	33

Study the example of a check stub shown on the top of this page. Notice how the numbers on each line are computed.

CONSUMER HUMOR

The bank says that your checking account is overdrawn by $10.00.

Oh, dear! No problem. I'll just write the bank a check for $10.00.

Some checkbooks have a check *register* instead of stubs. Each *transaction* (deposit or withdrawal) is recorded on this form. A deposit is added to the previous balance. A payment (written check) is subtracted from the previous balance. The resulting answer is called the new balance.

Notice the example of a check register shown on the next page.

Example: Peggy Bank's checking account balance was $345.79 on January 15. During the rest of January, Peggy wrote six checks and made two deposits. Shown below is a copy of her check register. Notice how the figures on each line are computed.

CHECK=CK		DEPOSIT=D	HOME COMPUTER=HC			MACHINE=M		PHONE=PH	
Date	Trans No.	Type of Trans	Description	Amount of Trans (-)	Amount of Deposit (+)	Fee (-)	Tax Item	Bal. Fwd.	
								345	79
1-15	301	CK	A-1 Drug Store	7.27				- 7	27
								338	52
1-16	302	CK	Telephone Co.	15.38				- 15	38
								323	14
1-18		D	Paycheck		200.00			+ 200	00
								523	14
1-21	303	CK	River Bank, mortgage	159.25				- 159	25
								363	89
1-21	304	CK	LaHem Clothing Store	84.60				- 84	60
								279	29
1-25		D	Paycheck		200.00			+ 200	00
								479	29
1-28	305	CK	Food World	35.72				- 35	72
								443	57
1-30	306	CK	Plastic Money Card	257.00				- 257	00
								186	57

Exercise A: This account began with a balance of $297.15. Find the new balance after each transaction.

	Date	Description	Transaction	Amount
1)	10/15	Paycheck	Deposit	$155.10
2)	10/16	Food Farm	Check	$84.12
3)	10/18	City Power Co.	Check	$37.45
4)	10/21	Sally About	Check	$10.00
5)	10/22	Paycheck	Deposit	$155.10
6)	10/23	Big Oil Co.	Check	$97.39
7)	10/28	River Bank	Check	$150.79
8)	10/29	Paycheck	Deposit	$155.10
9)	11/1	Tell E. Phone Co.	Check	$28.98
10)	11/2	Cash	Check	$40.00
11)	11/3	Charge-A-Lot Card	Check	$210.89
12)	11/4	Paycheck	Deposit	$155.10
13)	11/5	Food Farm	Check	$96.78
14)	11/5	Sue's News	Check	$31.10
15)	11/6	Manny Dept. Store	Check	$12.56
16)	11/6	Birthday present	Deposit	$10.00
17)	11/8	Prime Plumbers	Check	$36.50
18)	11/11	Paycheck	Deposit	$155.10
19)	11/14	Ace Insurance	Check	$5.48
20)	11/14	Christmas Club	Check	$20.00

COMPUTER APPLICATION

The balance in a checking account will change after a check has been written or a deposit has been made into the account. Some people use a computer program to keep their checking accounts up to date.

Use the following computer program to find the new balance after each transaction. See the appendix in the back of this text for directions in using computer programs.

```
10      REM  KEEPING THE ACCOUNT UP TO DATE
20      REM  CHAPTER 10
30      PRINT " C H E C K B O O K   B A L A N C E "
40      PRINT "WHAT IS THE BALANCE IN THE CHECKBOOK";
50      INPUT B
60      PRINT "TRANSACTION TYPE?"
70      PRINT " ( D=DEPOSIT,  C=CHECK,  S=STOP )";
80      INPUT T$
90      IF T$ = "S"  THEN GOTO 190
100     PRINT "AMOUNT";
110     INPUT A
120     IF T$ = "D"  THEN GOTO 160
130     IF T$ = "C"  THEN GOTO 150
140     GOTO 60
150     LET A = A * -1
160     LET B = B + A
170     PRINT " NEW BALANCE:  $";B
180     GOTO 60
190     END
RUN
```

RECONCILING A CHECKING ACCOUNT

People with checking accounts receive *monthly statements* or summaries from their banks. Such statements show recent transactions plus the current balance of an account. Some banks also return the canceled checks. Information in the checkbook must be compared, or *reconciled,* with the bank statement to make sure that no mistakes were made.

The balance on the bank statement seldom equals the one in a person's checkbook. Here are some reasons why the bank balance and the checkbook balance may not agree:

- Some checks that were written may not have been returned by the bank yet.
- Some deposits may have been made, but they have not been *processed* yet or been through all the steps of being handled by the bank.
- The person or the bank made an error.

To reconcile a checking account, follow these four steps:

Step 1: Add all the amounts of unprocessed deposits.

Step 2: Add that sum to the bank balance.

Step 3: Add all the amounts of unreturned checks.

Step 4: Subtract that sum from the bank balance.

Once those steps have been done, the checkbook balance should match the adjusted bank balance. If it does not, someone has made an error.

Example: Follow the steps on the next page to reconcile this checking account.

Bank balance:	$476.15	
Unprocessed deposits:	$10.56	$15.00
Unreturned checks:	$65.00	$25.13
	$146.10	$210.59
Checkbook balance:	$54.89	

Step 1: Add the deposits.

    $10.56

  + 15.00

    $25.56   Deposits

Step 2: Add the total deposits to the bank balance.

  $476.15   Bank balance

  + 25.56   Deposits

  $501.71   Balance after Step 2

Step 3: Add unreturned checks.

    $65.00

     25.13

   146.10

  + 210.59

  $446.82   Checks

Step 4: Subtract the total of unreturned checks from the bank balance figured after Step 2.

  $501.71   Balance after Step 2

  - 446.82   Unreturned checks

    $54.89   Adjusted bank balance

The adjusted bank balance agrees with the checkbook balance of $54.89.

Exercise A: Reconcile each account listed on pages 229-230. Find out whether the adjusted bank balance agrees with the checkbook balance. List the differences, if any.

	Bank Balance	Unprocessed Deposits	Unreturned Checks		Checkbook Balance
1)	$1,253.09	None	$9.40	$158.23	$723.26
			$26.51	$71.23	
			$19.05	$98.92	
			$113.40	$32.99	
2)	$2,582.20	$143.00	$8.40	$73.93	$694.05
			$46.00	$33.32	
			$26.85	$27.75	
			$1,519.37	$19.75	
			$87.15	$189.13	
3)	$856.43	$400.00	$29.95	$95.35	$533.28
			$23.13	$49.60	
			$25.37	$72.79	
			$122.50	$300.00	

	Bank Balance	Unprocessed Deposits	Unreturned Checks		Checkbook Balance
4)	$3,065.96	$171.53	$77.36	$527.98	$1,850.05
			$29.23	$62.10	
			$117.51	$188.58	
			$166.56	$218.12	
5)	$3,747.50	None	$60.00	$22.99	$2,250.08
			$1,000.00	$72.85	
			$96.86	$27.09	
			$36.95	$99.54	
			$19.95	$63.18	
6)	$613.23	$60.00	$8.00	$5.00	$181.98
		$20.00	$5.00	$92.00	
			$400.00	$1.25	
7)	$2,291.63	$798.90	$73.00	$44.09	$2,387.74
			$29.61	$40.99	
			$238.00	$131.90	
			$47.20	$67.92	
			$30.00		
8)	$2,876.75	$16.56	$26.94	$1,008.00	$1,114.25
			$532.00	$16.98	
			$144.84	$33.74	
9)	$774.19	None	$44.00	$46.20	$617.56
			$52.86	$23.67	
10)	$2,201.39	$629.88	$29.94	$235.00	$1,101.72
			$1,005.00	$60.02	
			$370.00	$29.31	

STOCK MARKET MATHEMATICS

The capital or money a corporation raises comes from stocks and bonds. Bonds are loans to the corporation. *Stock* is divided into equal shares that are actually part of the corporation. A buyer of shares of stock becomes part owner of the corporation issuing the stock.

Stocks are priced in eighths of a dollar. When you see a stock price listed as $19^7/_8$, each *share* will cost $19.875. Many people purchase stock in *round lots*, multiples of 100 shares, so no one worries about needing a half of a cent.

Example: $19.875 x 100 = $1987.50

Table of Eighths	Value in Cents	Table of Eighths	Value in Cents
$^1/_8$	$12^1/_2$ ¢	$^5/_8$	$62^1/_2$ ¢
$^2/_8 = {}^1/_4$	25¢	$^6/_8 = {}^3/_4$	75¢
$^3/_8$	$37^1/_2$ ¢	$^7/_8$	$87^1/_2$ ¢
$^4/_8 = {}^2/_4 = {}^1/_2$	50¢	$^8/_8 = {}^4/_4 = {}^2/_2 = 1$	100¢

Example: Bullish Company stock closed at $24^1/_4$. The next day the stock went "up" $3^3/_8$. What was the new price?

Add the numbers. Use the eighths chart to find the common denominator.

$$24\,{}^1/_4 = 24\,{}^2/_8$$
$$+\quad 3\,{}^3/_8 = \quad 3\,{}^3/_8$$
$$\overline{\qquad\qquad 27\,{}^5/_8}$$

The new price of Bullish Company stock was $27^5/_8$, or $27.625.

CONSUMER HUMOR

I once wondered why so many people in the world were named Smith. Then I saw in the stock pages a company named Smith Manufacturing Company!

Example: Shares of India, Inc., were being sold for $48^7/_8$. Then the price went up $2^3/_8$. What was the new price?

Add the numbers.

$$\begin{array}{r} 48\,^7/_8 \\ +\ 2\,^3/_8 \\ \hline 50\,^{10}/_8 \end{array}$$

Simplify. $^{10}/_8 = 1^2/_8$ or $1^1/_4$

$50 + 1^1/_4 = 51^1/_4$.

The new price of India, Inc., was $51^1/_4$.

Exercise A: Find the new price of each stock after its increase.

	Stock	Price	Up	New Price
1)	Blue, Inc.	$91^3/_4$	$4^3/_8$	_____
2)	Diss Co.	$25^7/_8$	$2^1/_2$	_____
3)	Unn Ltd.	$7^3/_8$	$^3/_4$	_____
4)	Peace Corp.	$10^1/_2$	$1^1/_8$	_____
5)	Extra Firm	$18^5/_8$	$^3/_8$	_____
6)	Close Assn.	$39^1/_2$	$1^1/_4$	_____
7)	Never Works	$22^1/_2$	$^1/_8$	_____
8)	General Impressions	$18^3/_4$	$1^5/_8$	_____
9)	Over Supply	$93^1/_2$	$1^1/_4$	_____
10)	Low Co.	$25^7/_8$	$^5/_8$	_____
11)	Live Stock	$25^3/_8$	$1^7/_8$	_____

When the selling price of stock is more than the purchase price, the stockholder makes a *profit*. Where purchase price is more than the selling price, the stockholder has a *loss*.

Example: Speck U. Lator bought a stock at 14⁵/₈ and sold it for 18³/₄. What was his profit?

Subtract.	18 ³/₄ =	18 ⁶/₈
Find common denominators.	- 14 ⁵/₈ =	- 14 ⁵/₈
		4 ¹/₈

The profit per share was 4¹/₈.

Example: Ann Vestor bought a stock at 32¹/₄ and sold it for 25⁵/₈. What was her loss per share?

Subtract.	32 ¹/₄ =	32 ²/₈ =	31¹⁰/₈
Find common denominators.	- 25 ⁵/₈ =	25 ⁵/₈ =	- 25 ⁵/₈
			6 ⁵/₈

Ann's loss per share was 6⁵/₈.

Exercise B: Compute the profit per share.

	Bought	Sold	Profit
1)	59⁷/₈	65¹/₂	_____
2)	12⁷/₈	13⁵/₈	_____
3)	28³/₈	29⁵/₈	_____
4)	48³/₄	59⁵/₈	_____
5)	33⁵/₈	38¹/₈	_____
6)	14¹/₂	18³/₈	_____
7)	26⁷/₈	30¹/₂	_____
8)	35¹/₄	39³/₄	_____

Exercise C: Compute the loss per share.

	Bought	Sold	Loss
1)	$45^1/_2$	$39^7/_8$	____
2)	$22^7/_8$	$21^5/_8$	____
3)	$19^5/_8$	$18^3/_8$	____
4)	$16^1/_8$	$13^5/_8$	____
5)	$14^1/_2$	$12^3/_8$	____
6)	$40^1/_4$	$36^3/_8$	____
7)	28	$23^7/_8$	____
8)	$48^3/_8$	$44^1/_2$	____
9)	$39^1/_8$	$34^5/_8$	____
10)	$72^3/_8$	$68^3/_4$	____

Exercise D: Compute the profit or loss per share.

	Bought	Sold	Profit or Loss	
1)	$18^3/_8$	$16^1/_8$	____	Loss
2)	$39^1/_4$	$38^1/_4$	____	Loss
3)	$46^1/_8$	$45^5/_8$	____	Loss
4)	$35^3/_4$	37	____	Profit
5)	$82^3/_8$	83	____	Profit
6)	$51^1/_2$	$50^1/_4$	____	Loss
7)	$103^1/_2$	$65^1/_8$	____	Loss
8)	$19^3/_8$	$18^7/_8$	____	Loss
9)	$40^1/_2$	$29^5/_8$	____	Loss
10)	$5^3/_8$	$10^3/_4$	____	Profit

Example: Find the cost of 100 shares of stock priced at $20^5/_8$.

Step 1: Convert the fraction to a decimal.

$$\frac{5}{8} = \begin{array}{r} .625 \\ 8\overline{)5.000} \end{array}$$

Step 2: Add the decimal to the whole number. Write the number as dollars and cents.
$20.625

Step 3: Multiply the price by the number of shares.

$20.625	Price per share
x 100	Number of shares
$2,062.500	Cost

The cost of 100 shares of stock is $2,062.50

Exercise E: Find the cost of these shares of stock.

1) 100 shares at $12^3/_8$
2) 850 shares at $9^5/_8$
3) 200 shares at $52^1/_4$
4) 200 shares at $6^3/_4$
5) 150 shares at $28^1/_2$
6) 900 shares at $15^5/_8$
7) 100 shares at $16^7/_8$
8) 600 shares at $7^1/_8$
9) 300 shares at $7^3/_4$
10) 400 shares at 31
11) 200 shares at $37^1/_4$
12) 950 shares at $47^5/_8$
13) 700 shares at $56^7/_8$
14) 400 shares at $4^3/_8$
15) 900 shares at $36^5/_8$
16) 900 shares at $48^7/_8$
17) 800 shares at $32^1/_4$
18) 1,000 shares at 18
19) 500 shares at $29^1/_2$
20) 1,500 shares at $15^1/_2$

Example: Ima Broker has $1,000 to invest. She likes a stock selling for $52^1/_2$. How many shares could she purchase? Find the cost.

Step 1: Divide $1000 by the cost per share. Discard the remainder.

$$
52.5. \overline{)1000.0.} \quad \begin{array}{r} 19. \\ \hline \end{array}
$$

$$
\begin{array}{r}
19. \\
52.5.\,)\overline{1000.0.} \\
\underline{525} \\
4750 \\
\underline{4725} \\
25
\end{array}
$$

Step 2: Multiply the cost per share times the number of shares purchased.

$52.50	Cost per share
x 19	Number of shares
$997.50	Total cost

Exercise F: For each amount available, compute the number of shares that can be purchased. Then compute the total cost.

	Money Available	Cost per Share		Money Available	Cost per Share
1)	$500	$6^1/_2$	2)	$4,000	$26^1/_8$
3)	$1,000	$20^1/_4$	4)	$100	$4^1/_4$
5)	$1,500	$12^3/_4$	6)	$500	$^3/_8$
7)	$2,000	$15^3/_8$	8)	$75	$^5/_8$
9)	$800	$9^3/_4$	10)	$1,200	$20^1/_2$
11)	$600	$1^5/_8$	12)	$300	$4^5/_8$
13)	$2,500	$10^1/_2$	14)	$900	$4^1/_2$
15)	$3,000	$3^1/_4$	16)	$10,000	$87^1/_2$
17)	$1,800	$16^3/_4$	18)	$6,500	$20^3/_8$
19)	$6,000	$26^7/_8$	20)	$7,500	$16^1/_8$

EVALUATING PROFITS AND LOSSES

Investors are concerned about the "return on their money." They compute the percent of increase in a stock's price. The higher the percent of increase, the better.

Example: Cy Lent invested in a noise pollution company. He bought the stock at $11\frac{1}{4}$ and sold it at 17. Find the percent of increase.

Step 1: Subtract to find the increase, or profit.

$$
\begin{array}{rcll}
17 & = & 16\,^4/_4 & \text{Selling price} \\
-\;\;11\,^1/_4 & = & 11\,^1/_4 & \text{Purchase price} \\
\hline
& & 5\,^3/_4 & \text{Profit}
\end{array}
$$

Step 2: Write both the purchase price and the profit as decimals.
$11\frac{1}{4} = 11.25$ Purchase price
$5\frac{3}{4} = 5.75$ Profit

Step 3: Divide the profit by the purchase price. Round the answer to two decimal places.

$$
\begin{array}{r}
.511 \approx .51 \\
11.25.\overline{)5.75,000} \\
\underline{5625} \\
1250 \\
\underline{1125} \\
1250 \\
\underline{1125}
\end{array}
$$

Step 4: Write this decimal as a percent.
$.51 = 51\%$

The price of Cy's stock increased 51%.

Example: Miss Spent invested in a tube company. She bought the stock at $47^3/_8$ and sold it for $32^7/_8$. What was the percent of decrease?

Step 1: Subtract to find the decrease, or loss.

$$
\begin{array}{rcll}
47\,^3/_8 & = & 46\,^{11}/_8 & \text{Purchase price} \\
-\ 32\,^7/_8 & = & 32\,^7/_8 & \text{Selling price} \\
\hline
14\,^4/_8 & = & 14^1/_2 & \text{Loss}
\end{array}
$$

Step 2: Write both the purchase price and the loss as decimals.
$47^3/_8 = 47.375$ 　　　Purchase price
$14^1/_2 = 14.5$ 　　　Loss

Step 3: Divide the loss by the purchase price. Round the answer to two decimal places.

$$
\begin{array}{r}
.306 \approx .31 \\
47.375.\,)\overline{14.500.000} \\
142125 \\
\hline
287500 \\
284250 \\
\hline
3250
\end{array}
$$

Step 4: Write this decimal as a percent. $.31 = 31\%$
Miss Spent's stock decreased 31%.

Exercise A: State whether each investment below realized a profit or a loss. Compute the percent of increase or decrease.

	Purchase Price	Selling Price		Purchase Price	Selling Price
1)	12	$8^1/_4$	2)	$17^1/_2$	$28^1/_2$
3)	25	$17^3/_8$	4)	$19^3/_4$	$30^1/_4$
5)	21	$16^3/_4$	6)	$15^1/_2$	$23^1/_4$
7)	8	$9^3/_4$	8)	$70^1/_2$	$54^1/_4$
9)	20	27	10)	$7^5/_8$	$10^7/_8$
11)	$9^7/_8$	$3^5/_8$	12)	$11^5/_8$	$8^5/_8$
13)	9	$11^1/_4$	14)	30	$22^1/_8$
15)	7	$10^1/_4$	16)	$50^1/_4$	$57^1/_2$

EARNING DIVIDENDS

Corporations divide their profits among their *shareholders,* the people who own the stock. A *dividend* is the amount of profit that a shareholder earns for each share of stock. The term comes from **divid**ing profits at the **end** of an earning period. Stock that pays dividends is called *income stock.*

Example: Hy Yield bought 425 shares of an income stock. The company paid a dividend of $1.30 per share. What was Hy's total dividend?

Multiply the dividend by	425	Shares
the number of shares held.	x $1.30	Dividend per share
	127 50	
Hy Yield's dividend	425	
was $552.50.	$552.50	Total dividends

Exercise A: Compute the total dividend for each investment.

	Dividend per Share	Number of Shares		Dividend per Share	Number of Shares
1)	$.80	300	2)	$7.85	900
3)	$8.38	150	4)	$5.87	1,438
5)	$.72	273	6)	$1.60	768
7)	$2.48	50	8)	$2.67	958
9)	$5.24	335	10)	$7.68	1,392

Example B: Compute the number of shares that can be purchased in each case.
1) Ann Vest wanted to use her dividends to purchase more stock. She owned 1,376 shares. The dividend was $1.72 per share. How many shares of stock priced at $71 could she purchase?
2) Mark Ette owned 153 shares of stock selling for 14³/₄. How many more shares could he purchase after receiving a dividend of $.80 per share?
3) Val U received a dividend of $1.36 on each of her 398 shares. How many shares could she buy at 15⁷/₈?

Solve these problems.

1) Compute the simple interest on a $1,000 loan at $16^3/4\%$ for 5 years.

2) Calculate the amount of money in the savings account at the end of six months. The principal was $100, the rate was 10%, and the interest was compounded quarterly.

3) Estimate the length of time that it would take to double your money at 15.86% with compound interest.

4) Write this amount in words: $3,476.89.

5) Compute the new checkbook balance.
   Previous balance: $465.98
   Checks written: $10.00, $14.95, $6.07, and $109.10
   Deposits made: $30.00

6) Reconcile the following account. Does this checkbook balance agree with the adjusted bank balance?
   Bank balance: $304.79
   Checkbook balance: $206.19
   Unreturned checks: $110.17
   Unprocessed deposits: $12.58

7) Find the cost of 900 shares of stock selling for $57^5/8$.

8) Compute the percent of loss on shares of stock that were purchased at $27^5/8$ and sold at $15^3/8$.

CHAPTER 11

PAYING TAXES

Every tax that citizens pay has a purpose. State and federal agencies collect taxes and use the *revenues* for the common good. Fire and police protection, schools, roads, and street lights are just a few of the benefits that come from tax dollars.

In this chapter you will review the writing of large numbers both in words and in digits. You will learn about the federal budget. You will also learn the mathematics involved in figuring federal and property taxes.

THE KEY TO LARGE NUMBERS

Large numbers are difficult to read quickly. To help you read large numbers, writers often use words in place of extra digits. Study the examples of large numbers given on the next page.

Large numbers can be written both in digits and in words.

Example: You can write three million dollars in words as $3 million.
You can write three million dollars in digits as $3,000,000.

Recall:	1 thousand	=	1,000
	1 million	=	1,000,000
	1 billion	=	1,000,000,000
	1 trillion	=	1,000,000,000,000

Example: Write the following amount in digits: $1.25 million.

Step 1:	Locate the decimal point in the number.	$1.25 million ↑
Step 2:	Recall that a *million* has 6 zeros in the number.	1,000,000
Step 3:	Move the decimal point as many places as the number of zeros in the figure named by the word.	1 25⌣⌣⌣⌣⌣⌣.
Step 4:	Write a zero in each empty place.	1 250 000.⌣⌣⌣⌣⌣⌣
Step 5:	Begin at the decimal point. Put a comma after each group of 3 digits.	1,250,000.
Step 6:	If the number represents money, place the dollar sign in front of the number.	$1,250,000.

Exercise A: Write the following amounts in digits.
1) 1.6 million
2) 605.6 billion
3) 72.5 trillion
4) 250 thousand
5) $416 million
6) $260.408 billion

Exercise B: The following problems contain pairs of numbers. Write each number in digits. Decide which number is larger in each case.
1) 200 million or 1 trillion
2) 18.8 million or 10 billion
3) 64 billion or 6.4 million
4) 32 thousand or 32 million
5) 500 thousand or .5 million
6) 10 billion or 1 trillion

Exercise C: Look in a newspaper and find five amounts written in words. Write each number in digits.

THE FEDERAL BUDGET

Each January the president submits a budget to Congress. This budget shows where the tax money will come from and how these revenues will be spent.

Example: This circle graph shows the sources of federal money for a typical year. According to this graph, 43¢ of every dollar received comes from individual income taxes.

$$\frac{43¢}{\$1} = \frac{43¢}{100¢} = 43\%$$

That figure means that 43% of the total *receipts,* or money received, comes from individual income taxes.

Sources of Revenue

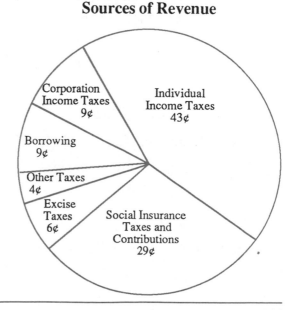

Corporation Income Taxes 9¢

Individual Income Taxes 43¢

Borrowing 9¢

Other Taxes 4¢

Excise Taxes 6¢

Social Insurance Taxes and Contributions 29¢

Example: In one year the federal income was $605.6 billion. How much of that came from individual income taxes?

43% of federal income came from individual income taxes.

To find 43% of $605.6, you multiply.

$$\begin{array}{r} \$605.6 \\ \times\ \ .43 \\ \hline 18168 \\ 24224 \\ \hline \$260.408 \end{array}$$

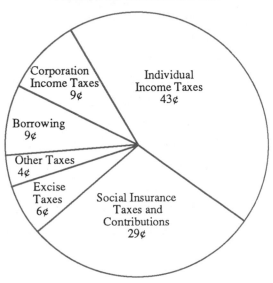

**The Government Dollar
Where It Comes From**

That year the federal government received $206.408 billion from individual income taxes.

Exercise A: Tell what percent of the receipts came from each source of federal revenue. Then calculate the amount in billions of dollars. Use information from the graph above to find your answers. The first answer has been completed for you as an example.

	Source	Percent	Amount in Billions
1)	Individual Income Taxes	*43%*	*$260.408*
2)	Social Insurance Taxes and Contributions	____	_____
3)	Excise Taxes	____	_____
4)	Other Taxes	____	_____
5)	Borrowing	____	_____
6)	Corporation Income Taxes	____	_____

Example: In the same year, the federal expenditures were $661.2 billion.

This circle graph shows how this money was spent during that year.

**The Government Dollar
Where It Goes**

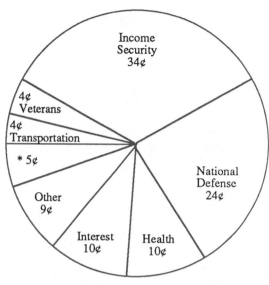

* Education, Training, and Social Services

Exercise B: Tell what percent of the expenditures went for each item. Then calculate the amount in billions of dollars. Use information from the graph above to find your answers.

Source	Percent	Amount in Billions
1) Income Security	_____	_____
2) National Defense	_____	_____
3) Health	_____	_____
4) Interest	_____	_____
5) Veterans	_____	_____
6) Transportation	_____	_____
7) Education, Training, and Social Services	_____	_____
8) Other	_____	_____

Exercise C: The sample federal budget shown on these two pages does not balance. How much more money was spent than was received?

PAYING TAXES

Federal taxes are determined by two facts: how much money you make and how many deductions and exemptions you have. The total money you make is called your *income*. *Deductions and exemptions* are amounts of money you may subtract from your income before you figure your taxes.

For example, you may subtract as an exemption an amount of money for each person who depends on you for support. Such a person is called a *dependent*.

Deductions can also be subtracted from total income. In some cases, deductions are allowed for:
*   interest you pay on your mortgage,
*   money you spend on medical bills,
*   losses not covered by insurance,
*   and many others.
There are a large number of such deductions. We will study some of them.

After you subtract all of the exemptions and deductions from your income, the remainder is called *taxable income*. This amount is used to figure how much federal income tax you owe.

Example: Dee Duckshun had exemptions of $3,000 for dependents. Her deductions included $345 for damage caused to her house by a lightning storm and $2,500 for child care expenses. What was her taxable income if she had an income of $62,500?

Step 1: Total exemptions and deductions.

$3,000	Exemptions for dependents
345	Uninsured losses
+ 2,500	Child care expenses
$5,845	Total exemptions and deductions

Step 2: Subtract the total exemptions and deductions from her total income.

$62,500   Total income
- 5,845   Total exemptions and deductions
$56,655   Taxable income

Her taxable income is $56,655.

Exercise A: The following four taxpayers have listed their allowable exemptions and deductions. Copy this chart onto your own paper. Calculate the total exemptions and deductions. Then find the taxable income in each case.

Item	Exemptions and Deductions	Total Exemptions and Deductions	Total Income	Taxable Income
1) Exemptions for dependents Allowable medical expenses	$4,100 1,600		$42,586	
2) Exemptions for dependents Interest paid Business travel costs	$6,150 856 939		$79,421	
3) Business loss State taxes Rentals loss	$14,987 1,234 658		$125,890	
4) Exemptions for dependents Child care costs Business costs	$4,100 875 358		$36,941	

READING THE TAX TABLE

Some taxpayers with taxable incomes of less than $50,000 must use a tax table to find the amount of tax that they should pay. This table comes with their federal income tax forms.

Example: Mr. and Mrs. Brown are filing a joint return. Their *taxable income* (the amount on which taxes are paid) is $23,270.

In the tax table, they find the $23,250-$23,300 income line. Next, they find the column for Married filing jointly and read down this column. The amount shown where the income line and filing status column meet is $3,491. This amount is their tax.

At least	But less than	Single	Married filing jointly	Married filing separately	Head of a household
				Your tax is—	
23,200	23,250	3,975	3,484	4,394	3,484
23,250	23,300	3,989	3,491	4,408	3,491
23,300	23,350	4,003	3,499	4,422	3,499

If line 37 (taxable income) is—		And you are—				If line 37 (taxable income) is—		And you are—			
At least	But less than	Single	Married filing jointly •	Married filing separately	Head of a household	At least	But less than	Single	Married filing jointly •	Married filing separately	Head of a household
			Your tax is—						Your tax is—		
19,000						**20,000**					
19,000	19,050	2,854	2,854	3,218	2,854	20,000	20,050	3,079	3,004	3,498	3,004
19,050	19,100	2,861	2,861	3,232	2,861	20,050	20,100	3,093	3,011	3,512	3,011
19,100	19,150	2,869	2,869	3,246	2,869	20,100	20,150	3,107	3,019	3,526	3,019
19,150	19,200	2,876	2,876	3,260	2,876	20,150	20,200	3,121	3,026	3,540	3,026
19,200	19,250	2,884	2,884	3,274	2,884	20,200	20,250	3,135	3,034	3,554	3,034
19,250	19,300	2,891	2,891	3,288	2,891	20,250	20,300	3,149	3,041	3,568	3,041
19,300	19,350	2,899	2,899	3,302	2,899	20,300	20,350	3,163	3,049	3,582	3,049
19,350	19,400	2,906	2,906	3,316	2,906	20,350	20,400	3,177	3,056	3,596	3,056
19,400	19,450	2,914	2,914	3,330	2,914	20,400	20,450	3,191	3,064	3,610	3,064
19,450	19,500	2,925	2,921	3,344	2,921	20,450	20,500	3,205	3,071	3,624	3,071
19,500	19,550	2,939	2,929	3,358	2,929	20,500	20,550	3,219	3,079	3,638	3,079
19,550	19,600	2,953	2,936	3,372	2,936	20,550	20,600	3,233	3,086	3,652	3,086
19,600	19,650	2,967	2,944	3,386	2,944	20,600	20,650	3,247	3,094	3,666	3,094
19,650	19,700	2,981	2,951	3,400	2,951	20,650	20,700	3,261	3,101	3,680	3,101
19,700	19,750	2,995	2,959	3,414	2,959	20,700	20,750	3,275	3,109	3,694	3,109
19,750	19,800	3,009	2,966	3,428	2,966	20,750	20,800	3,289	3,116	3,708	3,116
19,800	19,850	3,023	2,974	3,442	2,974	20,800	20,850	3,303	3,124	3,722	3,124
19,850	19,900	3,037	2,981	3,456	2,981	20,850	20,900	3,317	3,131	3,736	3,131
19,900	19,950	3,051	2,989	3,470	2,989	20,900	20,950	3,331	3,139	3,750	3,139
19,950	20,000	3,065	2,996	3,484	2,996	20,950	21,000	3,345	3,146	3,764	3,146

Exercise A: Use the tax table on page 248 to determine the tax due in each case.

	Filing Status	Taxable Income
1)	Single	$19,525
2)	Single	$20,400
3)	Married filing jointly	$20,975
4)	Single	$20,000
5)	Married filing separately	$20,702
6)	Head of household	$19,105
7)	Single	$20,708
8)	Married filing jointly	$19,000
9)	Head of household	$20,750
10)	Married filing separately	$19,212
11)	Single	$19,826
12)	Married filing separately	$20,425
13)	Married filing jointly	$19,999
14)	Head of household	$20,510
15)	Single	$19,600
16)	Married filing jointly	$20,140
17)	Head of household	$19,315
18)	Single	$20,543
19)	Married filing separately	$20,111
20)	Married filing jointly	$19,405

USING A TAX SCHEDULE

The instruction booklet that accompanies income tax forms contains several tax rate schedules.

Schedule Y is used by certain married persons. Those filing joint returns use Schedule Y-1 on the left. Those filing separate returns use Schedule Y-2 on the right.

Schedule Y-1—Use if your filing status is **Married filing jointly or Qualifying widow(er)**

If the amount on Form 1040, line 37, is: Over—	But not over—	Enter on Form 1040, line 38	of the amount over—
$0	$32,450	. . . . . . .15%	$0
32,450	78,400	**$4,867.50 + 28%**	**32,450**
78,400	162,770	**17,733.50 + 33%**	**78,400**
162,770	. . . .	Use **Worksheet** below to figure your tax.	

Schedule Y-2—Use if your filing status is **Married filing separately**

If the amount on Form 1040, line 37, is: Over—	But not over—	Enter on Form 1040, line 38	of the amount over—
$0	$16,225	. . . . . . .15%	$0
16,225	39,200	**$2,433.75 + 28%**	**16,225**
39,200	123,570	**8,866.75 + 33%**	**39,200**
123,570	. . . .	Use **Worksheet** below to figure your tax.	

Tax Rate Schedules

Use these tax rate schedules ONLY if your taxable income (Form 1040, line 37) is $50,000 or more. If your taxable income is less than $50,000, use the tax table.

Even though you cannot use the tax rate schedules shown above if your taxable income is less than $50,000, the schedules show all levels of taxable income so that taxpayers can see the tax rate that applies to each level.

Example: Anita and Jack Hammer have a taxable income of $58,655.37. Compute their tax by using Schedule Y-1 given on page 250. They are filing a joint return.

Step 1: Locate the tax bracket in Schedule Y-1.
$58,655.37 is:

Over—	But not over—	The tax is—	of the amount over—
$32,450	78,400	4,867.50 + 28%	32,450

Step 2: Subtract $32,450 from the taxable income.

$58,655.37
- 32,450.00
$26,205.37

Step 3: Multiply the amount over $32,450 by 28%.
28% = .28

$26,205.37
x   .28
$7,337.50

Step 4: Add this amount to $4,867.50.

$4,867.50
+ 7,337.50
$12,205.00

The Hammers' tax is $12,205.00

Exercise A: Compute the tax on each of these incomes. Use Schedules Y-1 and Y-2 given on page 250.

1) $54,000   joint
2) $67,200   separate
3) $72,123   separate
4) $61,462   separate
5) $53,200   joint
6) $75,150   joint
7) $162,000   joint
8) $85,243   joint
9) $65,762   separate
10) $74,754   separate

REFUND OR BALANCE DUE

Federal income tax is withheld from employees' wages each payday. By the end of the year, it is possible that too much money was withheld. If that happens, the employee will get a *refund* of the extra money. However, if not enough money was withheld, the person then has a *balance due* on his tax return and must pay additional taxes.

Example: Willie Pay, the head of a household, had a taxable income of $20,359.72. During the year $4,234.18 was withheld from his pay for federal income taxes. Did Willie Pay receive a refund, or did he pay additional taxes?

Step 1: Read the amount of tax due from the Tax Table given on page 248.

$3,056

Step 2: Compare the tax due with the amount withheld.
$3,056.00 is less than $4,234.18.
Too much money was withheld. Willie got a refund.

Step 3: Find the amount of the refund. Subtract the amount of tax due from the amount withheld.

$4,234.18	Withheld
- 3,056.00	Tax due
$1,178.18	Refund

Willie received a tax refund of $1,178.18.

Exercise A: Use your answers from page 249 concerning the tax due. Compute the amount to be refunded or the balance due in each case.

	Filing Status	Taxable Income	Amount of Tax Withheld
1)	Single	$19,525	$4,000
2)	Single	$20,400	$5,000
3)	Married filing jointly	$20,975	$3,500
4)	Single	$20,000	$4,000
5)	Married filing separately	$20,702	$4,700
6)	Head of household	$19,105	$3,230
7)	Single	$20,708	$3,100
8)	Married filing jointly	$19,000	$4,300
9)	Head of household	$20,750	$4,101
10)	Married filing separately	$19,212	$5,000
11)	Single	$19,826	$3,100
12)	Married filing separately	$20,425	$4,123
13)	Married filing jointly	$19,999	$3,468
14)	Head of household	$20,510	$3,004
15)	Single	$19,600	$4,020
16)	Married filing jointly	$20,140	$2,764
17)	Head of household	$19,315	$3,423
18)	Single	$20,543	$4,687
19)	Married filing separately	$20,111	$3,823
20)	Married filing jointly	$19,405	$3,599

THE KEY TO ORDERING DECIMALS

Example: Place these decimals in order from smallest to largest.

| 1.345 | 1.324 | 2.03 | 11.4 | 1.21 | 1.3 |

Step 1: Write the decimals in a list. Line up the decimal points.

1.345
1.324
2.03
11.4
1.21
1.3

Step 2: Ordering decimals is like alphabetizing. Scan each decimal from left to right. Begin with the whole numbers. Sort them. Put the smallest number first and the largest number last.

1 .345
1 .324
1 .21
1 .3
2 .03
11 .4

Step 3: If some decimals have equal whole numbers, look at their tenths place. Sort the numbers according to tenths.

1. 3 45
1. 3 24
1. 2 1
1. 3
2. 0 3
11. 4

1. 2 1
1. 3 45
1. 3 24
1. 3
2. 0 3
11. 4

Step 4: If any decimals have equal whole numbers and tenths, look at their hundredths place. Sort the numbers according to hundredths.

1.2 1
1.3 4 5
1.3 2 4
1.3
2.0 3
11.4

1.2 1
1.3
1.3 2 4
1.3 4 5
2.0 3
11.4

Step 5: Continue until all decimal places have been sorted.

Exercise A: Order each row of decimals from smallest to largest. Follow the five steps shown on pages 254-255.

1) 2.43   2.425   2.417   2.4   2.491

2) 7.003   7.216   7.03   7   7.19

3) 11.231   11.123   11.321   11.132   11.213

4) .78   .781   .779   .7799   .77999

5) 1.01   1.1   .9   1   1.001

Exercise B: Order each row of decimals from largest to smallest. Follow the five steps shown on pages 254-255.

1) 5.31   5.309   5.2   5.177   5.00009

2) 2.36   2.359   2.358   2.45   2.1788

3) 4.25   4.255   4.2555   4.249   4.24

4) 10.01   10.011   10.1   10   11

5) .1   .11   .111   .1111   .1101

CONSUMER HUMOR

Let's order some decimals.

Oh, waiter! We'll have 2 tenths, 4 hundredths, and a .007 on the side.

PROPERTY TAX

Local governments raise revenues for local projects by taxing owners of property. Property tax is based on the value of the property.

The *assessed value* of a property is a percent of its *market value,* or selling price on the open market. The assessment rate is determined by the local government and is used for tax purposes.

The *property tax* is a percent of the assessed value. This rate is also set by local governments.

Example: Ona Home would like to calculate her property tax. These are the facts:

    a) The market value of the property is $75,500.
    b) The assessment rate is 48%.
    c) The property tax rate is $47.30 per $1,000 of assessed value.

Step 1: Multiply the market value by the assessment rate to find the assessed value.

$$\begin{array}{ll} \$75,500 & \text{Market value} \\ \underline{\times \qquad .48} & \text{Assessment rate} \\ \$36,240.00 & \text{Assessed value} \end{array}$$

Step 2: Find the tax rate as a percent.

$47.30 per $1,000

Write the fraction. Divide.

$$\frac{47.30}{1000} \qquad 1000 \overline{)\, 47.3000}^{\,.0473} = 4.73\%$$

Step 3: Multiply the assessed value by the tax rate.

$$\begin{array}{ll} \$36,240 & \text{Assessed value} \\ \underline{\times \quad .0473} & \text{Tax rate} \\ \$1714.152 & \approx \$1,714.15 \end{array}$$

Ona's property tax was $1,714.15.

Exercise A: Compute the assessed value for each property.

	Market Value	Assessment Rate
1)	$60,000	45%
2)	$70,000	50%
3)	$75,000	40%
4)	$65,000	52%
5)	$67,250	47%
6)	$71,500	60%
7)	$80,240	42%
8)	$63,275	55%
9)	$60,005	43%
10)	$78,423	48%

Exercise B: Express each of these tax rates as a percent.

1) $3.67 per $100 of assessed value
2) $42.10 per $1,000 of assessed value
3) $3.52 per $100 of assessed value
4) $4.01 per $100 of assessed value
5) $37.51 per $1,000 of assessed value
6) $50.09 per $1,000 of assessed value
7) $4.50 per $100 of assessed value
8) $500 per $10,000 of assessed value
9) $3.99 per $100 of assessed value
10) $4.11 per $100 of assessed value

Exercise C: Calculate each of these property taxes.

	Assessed Value	Property Tax Rate
1)	$27,000	3.67%
2)	$35,000	4.21%
3)	$30,000	3.52%
4)	$33,800	4.01%
5)	$31,607	3.75%
6)	$42,900	5.01%
7)	$33,700	4.5%
8)	$34,801	5%
9)	$25,802	3.99%
10)	$37,643	4.11%

COMPUTER APPLICATION °

Use the following computer program to express property taxes rates as percents. See the appendix in the back of this text for directions in using computer programs.

```
10    REM PROPERTY TAX
20    REM CHAPTER 11
30    PRINT "P R O P E R T Y   T A X"
40    PRINT "EXPRESSING THE TAX RATE AS A PERCENT"
50    PRINT "WHAT IS THE DOLLAR RATE";
60    INPUT D
70    PRINT "WHAT IS THE BASE AMOUNT";
80    INPUT B
90    PRINT " TAX RATE = "; D / B * 100 ;"%"
100   END
RUN
```

EFFECTIVE TAX RATE

Both the assessment rate and the property tax rate affect the amount of taxes due. The *effective tax rate* is the product of the assessment rate and the property tax rate.

Example: For Rhoda Horse's ranch, the assessment rate is 46%. The property tax rate is $32.56 per $1,000. What is the effective tax rate?

Step 1: Write the property tax rate as a decimal.

$$\frac{32.56}{1000} = 1000 \overline{)32.56000} \quad .03256$$

Step 2: Write the assessment rate as a decimal.

$$46\% = .46$$

Step 3: Then multiply the property tax rate by the assessment rate.

$$\begin{array}{r} .03256 \\ \times \quad .46 \\ \hline 19536 \\ 13024 \\ \hline .0149776 \end{array}$$

.03256   Property tax rate
x .46   Assessment rate

.0149776   Effective tax rate

Step 4: Round this answer to three places.

$$.0149774 \approx .015$$

Rhoda's effective tax rate is .015 or 1.5%.

Exercise A: Rhoda's ranch has a market value of $450,000. Compute her property tax.

1) Assessment method: $450,000 x .46 x .03256 = ?

2) Effective rate method: $450,000 x .015 = ?

Exercise B: Follow the steps shown on page 259. Calculate the effective tax rate for each property. Then circle the lower effective rate in each pair.

		Assessment Rate	Property Tax Rate	Effective Tax Rate
1.	a)	35%	$36.70 per $1,000	_____
	b)	50%	$2.50 per $100	_____
2.	a)	40%	$3.04 per $100	_____
	b)	35%	$3.26 per $100	_____
3.	a)	25%	$47.23 per $1,000	_____
	b)	30%	$42.16 per $1,000	_____
4.	a)	42%	$3.70 per $100	_____
	b)	37%	$4.20 per $100	_____
5.	a)	33%	$425 per $10,000	_____
	b)	39%	$3.70 per $100	_____
6.	a)	42%	$1.60 per $100	_____
	b)	36%	$22 per $1,000	_____
7.	a)	28%	$3.75 per $100	_____
	b)	35%	$2.87 per $100	_____
8.	a)	41%	$5 per $100	_____
	b)	37%	$53 per $1,000	_____
9.	a)	36%	$4.10 per $100	_____
	b)	45%	$3.50 per $100	_____
10.	a)	40%	$1.72 per $100	_____
	b)	31%	$2.35 per $100	_____

Solve these problems on pages 261 and 262.

1) Calculate 38% of $209.7 billion.

2) What is the tax for a married person who is filing separately and whose taxable income is $19,576? Use the income tax table given on page 248.

3) What is the tax for a head of a household whose taxable income is $20,655? Use the income tax table given on page 248.

4) A married person filing a separate return has a taxable income of $20,327. During the year $3,243 was withheld from wages. Does this person owe more taxes, or does he get a refund? What amount will this person owe or be refunded?

5) Compute the income tax on a taxable income of $65,872 for a couple who is filing a joint return. Use Schedule Y-1 given on page 250.

6) A married couple filing separately has a taxable income of $68,210. What is their tax? Use Schedule Y-2 given on page 250.

7) Compute the property tax on an estate with a market value of $170,000.
   • The assessment rate is 46%.
   • The tax rate is $37.84 per $1,000 of assessed value.

8) Express $42.75 per $1,000.00 as a percent.

9) What is the difference between the market value of a property and its assessed value?

10) Find the effective tax rate for an assessment rate of 47% and a tax rate of $3.89 per $100 of assessed value.

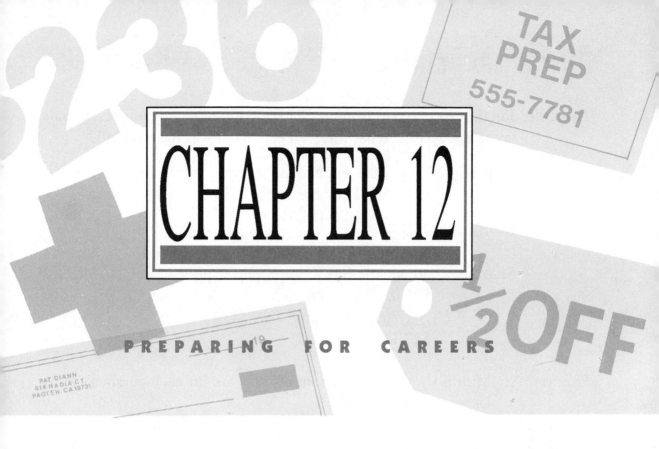

PREPARING FOR CAREERS

Practically every career requires some knowledge of mathematics. In this chapter you will practice mathematical skills that are used by some people in six career fields: salesclerks, electricians, auto mechanics, carpenters, drafters, and machine operators. Being able to compute mathematics will help you to prepare for your chosen career.

SALESCLERKS

Sales tax is computed on the sale of goods and services. It is figured as a percentage of the purchase price and is collected by the seller.

One job for a salesclerk is to find the correct amount of sales tax and then add it to customers' purchases. The rate of sales tax varies from state to state. A few states do not have a sales tax.

Example: Jon E. Kasch sold a customer $21.05 worth of merchandise. The sales tax rate was 5%. What was the tax? What was the total bill?

Step 1: Multiply the purchase price by the rate to find the sales tax.

$21.05   Purchase price

x   .05   Rate (5%)

$1.0525   ≈ $1.06   Sales tax   (Round to **next** cent.)

Step 2: Add the sales tax to the purchase price to find the total bill.

$21.05   Purchase price

+   1.06   Sales tax

$22.11   Total bill

Exercise A: Multiply to find the amount of sales tax for each purchase below. Use a sales tax rate of 5%.

1) $11.30   2) $24.85   3) $52.98
4) $9.95   5) $35.25   6) $168.42

A faster way to find the sales tax is to consult the chart that many stores post for their clerks.

Example: Shown below is part of a chart for state sales tax. Look in this chart for the sale bracket containing $21.05. Read the tax. Add the tax to the purchase price. $21.05 + $1.06 = $22.11.

5% State Sales Tax					
Amount of Sale	Tax	Amount of Sale	Tax	Amount of Sale	Tax
.01 - .20	.01	10.01 - 10.20	.51	20.01 - 20.20	1.01
.21 - .40	.02	10.21 - 10.40	.52	20.21 - 20.40	1.02
.41 - .60	.03	10.41 - 10.60	.53	20.41 - 20.60	1.03
.61 - .80	.04	10.61 - 10.80	.54	20.61 - 20.80	1.04
.81 - 1.00	.05	10.81 - 11.00	.55	20.81 - 21.00	1.05
1.01 - 1.20	.06	11.01 - 11.20	.56	21.01 - 21.20	1.06
1.21 - 1.40	.07	11.21 - 11.40	.57	21.21 - 21.40	1.07
1.41 - 1.60	.08	11.41 - 11.60	.58	21.41 - 21.60	1.08
1.61 - 1.80	.09	11.61 - 11.80	.59	21.61 - 21.80	1.09
1.81 - 2.00	.10	11.81 - 12.00	.60	21.81 - 22.00	1.10

Exercise B: Find the sales tax for each of these purchases. Then compute the total bill in each case. Use the 5% sales tax chart given on page 264.

	Purchase	Sales Tax	Total		Purchase	Sales Tax	Total
1)	$1.43	____	____	2)	$11.30	____	____
3)	$11.90	____	____	4)	$10.75	____	____
5)	$.85	____	____	6)	$21.50	____	____
7)	$10.90	____	____	8)	$10.45	____	____
9)	$1.20	____	____	10)	$21.00	____	____
11)	$20.90	____	____	12)	$11.00	____	____
13)	$21.35	____	____	14)	$10.17	____	____
15)	$20.39	____	____	16)	$.38	____	____
17)	$21.07	____	____	18)	$10.39	____	____
19)	$20.97	____	____	20)	$11.08	____	____

Many cash registers compute the amount of change due to a customer. Salesclerks are responsible for giving the correct change. Clerks are trained to give change with the smallest number of bills and coins. Study the following example.

Example: Pete Za must give a customer $16.47 in change. How should he make change with the smallest number of bills and coins?

Pete should use:

One ten-dollar bill	$10.00
One five-dollar bill	$5.00
One one-dollar bill	$1.00
One quarter, two dimes, and two pennies	+ .47
	$16.47

Exercise C: Copy and complete this chart. The first item has been done for you. It is the example problem shown on page 265.

Change Due	Bills				Coins			
	$20	$10	$5	$1	Quarters	Dimes	Nickels	Pennies
1) $16.47		*1*	*1*	*1*	*1*	2		2
2) 42¢								
3) 89¢								
4) $1.23								
5) $3.62								
6) $8.37								
7) $11.01								
8) $19.99								
9) $24.32								
10) $51.48								
11) $78.43								

COMPUTER APPLICATION

Use the following computer program on pages 266-267 to review your knowledge of sales tax. This game will keep score for you. Find out what happens when you answer all the problems correctly!

See the appendix in the back of this text for directions in using computer programs.

```
10    REM SALESCLERKS
20    REM CHAPTER 12
30    PRINT "FIND THE SALES TAX GAME"
40    PRINT "WHAT SALES TAX RATE DO YOU WANT TO USE";
50    INPUT R
60    PRINT " O. K.   LET'S SEE WHAT YOU CAN DO WITH " ;R;"%
      SALES TAX!"
```

```
70     LET S = 0
80     FOR P = 1 TO 10
90     PRINT "AMOUNT OF SALE  $";
100    READ A
110    PRINT A;"                SALES TAX";
120    INPUT T
130    LET X = INT ( A * R + .9 ) / 100
140    IF X = T THEN GOTO 170
150    PRINT "    OOPS — I THINK IT'S $";X
160    GOTO 190
170    PRINT "    THAT'S RIGHT!"
180    LET S = S + 1
190    NEXT P
200    PRINT "YOUR SCORE IS ";S;" OUT OF 10."
210    IF S = 10 THEN GOTO 240
220    PRINT "BETTER LUCK NEXT TIME!"
230    GOTO 250
240    GOSUB 300
250    END
260    DATA  1.43,11.29,11.89,10.75,.85,21.49,10.89,10.45,1.19,21
300    PRINT "                               $$$"
310    PRINT "                           $$    $$"
320    PRINT "        S A L E S          $$"
330    PRINT "                           $$"
340    PRINT "        T A X                $$$"
350    PRINT "                                $$"
360    PRINT "        W I Z A R D !          $$"
370    PRINT "                               $$"
380    PRINT "                           $$    $$"
390    PRINT "                             $$$"
400    RETURN
RUN
```

THE KEY TO SQUARE ROOT

The *square root* of a number is one of two equal factors of that number.

Examples: 4 x 4 = 16   4 is the square root of 16 because
$\sqrt{16} = 4$ 4 is one of two equal factors of 16.

2 x 8 = 16   2 is not the square root of 16.
The factors 2 and 8 are not equal.

Exercise A: Find the following square roots.

1) $\sqrt{4}$ 2) $\sqrt{25}$
3) $\sqrt{36}$ 4) $\sqrt{81}$
5) $\sqrt{100}$ 6) $\sqrt{1}$
7) $\sqrt{64}$ 8) $\sqrt{144}$
9) $\sqrt{49}$ 10) $\sqrt{9}$

Rule: To find the square root of a number when the factors are not known, you can divide and average.

Example: Find the square root of 56. $\sqrt{56} = ?$

Step 1:   Choose any number and divide it into 56. Let's try 7, since 7 x 7 is 49, and 49 is close to 56.

$$7\overline{)56} \quad \frac{8}{}$$

Step 2:   The square root is between 7 and 8. Average 7 and 8.

$$\begin{array}{r} 7 \\ +8 \\ \hline 15 \end{array} \qquad 2\overline{)15.0} \quad \frac{7.5}{}$$

Step 3: Divide 56 by the average. Round to the nearer tenth.

$$\sqrt{56} \approx 7.5$$

$$
\begin{array}{r}
7.46 \approx 7.5 \\
7.5.\overline{)56.0.00} \\
\underline{525} \\
350 \\
\underline{300} \\
500
\end{array}
$$

To check your work:
Test 7.5 by squaring it.

$$
\begin{array}{r}
7.5 \\
\times\, 7.5 \\
\hline
375 \\
\underline{525} \\
56.25 \approx 56
\end{array}
$$

7.5 is close to the square root. More decimal places may be found by averaging 7.5 and 7.46 and returning to step 3.

A calculator gives the square root of 56 as 7.483314.... This number rounded to the nearer tenth is 7.5.

Exercise B: Use the "divide and average" method to find the following square roots. Round your answers to the nearer tenth.

1) $\sqrt{300}$
2) $\sqrt{38}$
3) $\sqrt{654}$
4) $\sqrt{128}$
5) $\sqrt{256}$
6) $\sqrt{21}$
7) $\sqrt{409}$
8) $\sqrt{345}$
9) $\sqrt{717}$
10) $\sqrt{1024}$

CONSUMER HUMOR

Did you hear that Joan lost her job at the nursery?

Yes, all her trees grew square roots.

ELECTRICIANS

Electricians use formulas in their work. These formulas yield information about electrical current. A handy way to remember the formulas is to use the word WIRE.

W = power measured in *watts*
I = intensity measured in *amps*
R = resistance measured in *ohms*
E = electromotive force measured in *volts*

Formulas for finding watts:

1) $W = EI$

2) $W = I^2R$

3) $W = \dfrac{E^2}{R}$

Formulas for finding amps:

4) $I = \dfrac{E}{R}$

5) $I = \sqrt{\dfrac{W}{R}}$

6) $I = \dfrac{W}{E}$

Formulas for finding ohms:

7) $R = \dfrac{E}{I}$

8) $R = \dfrac{W}{I^2}$

9) $R = \dfrac{E^2}{W}$

Formulas for finding volts:

10) $E = IR$

11) $E = \dfrac{W}{I}$

12) $E = \sqrt{WR}$

Example #1: Find the intensity of a current that supplies 250 watts of power and has 2.5 ohms of resistance.

Step 1: Choose the formula for intensity (I) that uses watts (W) and ohms (R). This is formula #5 on page 270.

$$I = \sqrt{\frac{W}{R}}$$

Step 2: Replace the letters with their values.

$$I = \sqrt{\frac{250}{2.5}}$$

Step 3: Simplify.

$$I = \sqrt{100}$$

Step 4: Find the square root.

$$\sqrt{100} = 10$$

The intensity is 10 amps.

Example #2: Find the power in a circuit with 12 amps and 1.5 ohms.

Step 1: Choose the formula for power (W) that uses amps (I) and ohms (R). That formula would be #2 on page 270.

$$W = I^2 R$$

Step 2: Replace the letters with their values.

$$W = 12^2 \times 1.5$$

Step 3: 12^2 means 12 x 12.

$$W = 12 \times 12 \times 1.5$$

Step 4: Multiply the product of 12 x 12 by 1.5.

$$12 \times 12 = 144$$

$$
\begin{array}{r}
144 \\
\times\ 1.5 \\
\hline
720 \\
144 \\
\hline
216.0 \\
\end{array}
$$

The power in the circuit is 216 watts.

Example #3: Find the force (E) in an electric circuit that has 250 watts (W) and 4.9 ohms (R).

Step 1: Choose the formula for E that uses W and R. That is formula #12 on page 270.

$$E = \sqrt{WR}$$

$$E = \sqrt{250 \times 4.9}$$

Step 2: Multiply W x R.

$$
\begin{array}{r}
250 \\
\times\ \ 4.9 \\
\hline
2250 \\
1000 \\
\hline
1225.0
\end{array}
$$

$$E = \sqrt{1225}$$

Step 3: Find the square root.

a) Guess 30.
$$30^2 = 30 \times 30 = 900$$

$$\begin{array}{r} 40.8 \approx 41 \\ 30\ \overline{)1225.0} \end{array}$$

b) Average 41 and 30.

$$
\begin{array}{r}
30 \\
+\ 41 \\
\hline
71
\end{array}
$$

$$\begin{array}{r} 35.5 \\ 2\ \overline{)71.0} \end{array}$$

c) Divide by 35.5.

$$\begin{array}{r} 34.5 \\ 35.5,\ \overline{)1225.0,0} \end{array}$$

d) Average 34.5 and 35.5.

$$
\begin{array}{r}
34.5 \\
+\ 35.5 \\
\hline
70.0
\end{array}
$$

$$\begin{array}{r} 35 \\ 2\ \overline{)70} \end{array}$$

e) Divide by 35.

$$\begin{array}{r} 35 \\ 35\ \overline{)1225} \end{array}$$

The force in the circuit is 35 volts.

$$E = \sqrt{1225} \qquad E = 35$$

Exercise A: Complete this chart by calculating the missing quantities. Use the formulas on page 270. Round answers to the nearer hundredth.

	W (in watts)	I (in amps)	R (in ohms)	E (in volts)
1)	128 W	_____	2 ohms	_____
2)	100 W	5 amps	_____	_____
3)	_____	7 amps	_____	120 volts
4)	7280 W	_____	_____	1000 volts
5)	_____	10 amps	16 ohms	_____
6)	_____	_____	2 ohms	240 volts

Exercise B: Solve the following problems. Use the formulas on page 270.

1) A toaster uses 1200 watts. It is plugged into a 120-volt outlet. How many amps will the toaster draw?

2) A waffle iron uses 1300 watts. It is also plugged into a 120-volt outlet. How many amps will the waffle iron draw?

3) Find the total number of amps drawn by both appliances in problems #1 and #2.

4) Most household wiring supplies 15 amps to an outlet. Should you run both the waffle iron and the toaster at the same time from the same outlet?

5) What might be the result of overloading an electrical outlet?

CONSUMER HUMOR

Did you hear that Joe, the electrician, opened a car lot?

Yes, he's selling mobile ohms and voltswagens.

AUTO MECHANICS

Mechanics' tools come in standard sizes. There are metric tools that use decimal measurements, and there are customary tools that use fractional inch measurements.

Example: Pat Answer was tightening a fitting. She found that the $\frac{3}{8}$'' wrench was too loose. She asked her helper, Andy Didhelp, to give her the next size smaller wrench. These 15 wrenches were in the tool box.

$$\frac{1}{16}\text{''} \qquad \frac{3}{16}\text{''} \qquad \frac{5}{16}\text{''} \qquad \frac{7}{16}\text{''} \qquad \frac{9}{16}\text{''} \qquad \frac{11}{16}\text{''} \qquad \frac{13}{16}\text{''}$$

$$\frac{15}{16}\text{''} \qquad \frac{1}{8}\text{''} \qquad \frac{5}{8}\text{''} \qquad \frac{7}{8}\text{''} \qquad \frac{1}{4}\text{''} \qquad \frac{3}{4}\text{''} \qquad \frac{1}{2}\text{''} \qquad 1\text{''}$$

Which one should Andy select? He must put the wrenches in order to select the next smaller wrench.

Pat's wrench →

Step 1: To compare fractions, use a common denominator. Use 16 since all of the denominators are factors of 16.

$$\frac{1}{8} = \frac{?}{16}$$

Divide.

$$8\overline{)16}^{\,2}$$

Multiply the numerator 1 by 2.

1 x 2 = 2

$$\frac{1}{8} = \frac{2}{16}$$

$\frac{1}{8}$	=	$\frac{2}{16}$
$\frac{3}{8}$	=	$\frac{6}{16}$
$\frac{5}{8}$	=	$\frac{10}{16}$
$\frac{7}{8}$	=	$\frac{14}{16}$
$\frac{1}{4}$	=	$\frac{4}{16}$
$\frac{3}{4}$	=	$\frac{12}{16}$
$\frac{1}{2}$	=	$\frac{8}{16}$
1	=	$\frac{16}{16}$

Step 2: Arrange the sizes from the smallest to the largest. Look at the numerators.

$\frac{1"}{16}$ Smallest wrench $\frac{9"}{16}$

$\frac{2"}{16} = \frac{1"}{8}$ $\frac{10"}{16} = \frac{5"}{8}$

$\frac{3"}{16}$ $\frac{11"}{16}$

$\frac{4"}{16} = \frac{1"}{4}$ $\frac{12"}{16} = \frac{3"}{4}$

$\boxed{\frac{5"}{16}}$ $\frac{13"}{16}$

$\frac{6"}{16} = \frac{3"}{8}$ ←Pat has $\frac{14"}{16} = \frac{7"}{8}$
this wrench.

$\frac{7"}{16}$ $\frac{15"}{16}$

$\frac{8"}{16} = \frac{1"}{2}$ $\frac{16"}{16} = 1"$ Largest wrench

The $\frac{5}{16}"$ wrench is the one that Andy should get.

Exercise A: Arrange each set of tool sizes from the smallest to the largest.

1) $\frac{3}{8}$ $\frac{5}{8}$ $\frac{7}{16}$ $\frac{1}{2}$ $\frac{5}{16}$

2) $1\frac{1}{2}$ $1\frac{1}{8}$ $1\frac{3}{16}$ $1\frac{5}{8}$ $1\frac{7}{16}$

3) $2\frac{5}{8}$ $2\frac{3}{4}$ $2\frac{9}{16}$ $2\frac{7}{8}$ $2\frac{11}{16}$

4) $\frac{11}{16}$ $\frac{5}{8}$ $\frac{13}{16}$ $\frac{3}{4}$ $\frac{9}{16}$

5) $1\frac{1}{16}$ $1\frac{1}{32}$ $1\frac{1}{8}$ 1 $1\frac{1}{4}$

CARPENTERS

Carpenters must make precise measurements. The building industry continues to use the customary system of measurement. Carpenters need to develop the skill of making exact customary measurements.

Example: Measure these *line segments*.

1) To the nearer inch: 4"

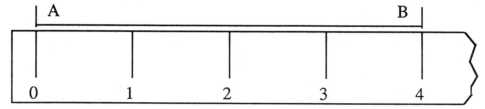

2) To the nearer half of an inch: $3\frac{1}{2}$"

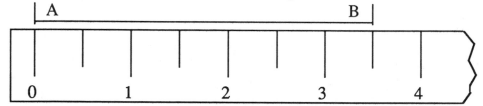

3) To the nearer quarter of an inch: $3\frac{3}{4}$"

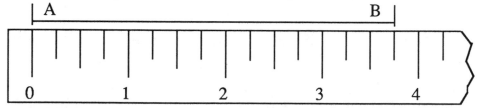

4) To the nearer eighth of an inch: $3\frac{6}{8}$" = $3\frac{3}{4}$"

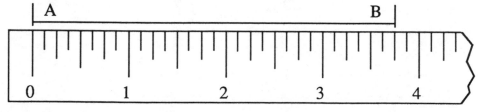

5) To the nearer sixteenth of an inch: $3\frac{12}{16}$ " $= 3\frac{3}{4}$ "

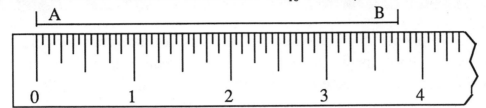

Exercise A: Measure each line segment to the nearer quarter of an inch.

1) ──────────
2) ──────────────────────
3) ─────────────
4) ────────────────────────────
5) ───────────
6) ────────────────────
7) ──────────────────────────────────

Exercise B: Measure each line segment to the nearer eighth of an inch.

1) ───────────
2) ────────────────────────
3) ────────────────────────────────
4) ──────────────────
5) ───────────────────────────
6) ──────────────────
7) ───────────────────────

Exercise C: Measure each line segment to the nearer sixteenth of an inch.

1) ─────
2) ──────────────────────
3) ────────────────────────────
4) ───────────────────────
5) ────────────────────────────────
6) ──────────────────────────────────
7) ──────────────────────────────

DRAFTERS

Drafters are people who draw *blueprints*, plans, and sketches for construction and manufacturing projects. They must make scale drawings of finished products that are being planned. Most drawings are smaller than the actual product. A *scale* gives the ratio of the size on a drawing, map, or model to the original size.

For example, a $\frac{1}{12}$ *scale drawing* means that a line one inch long on the drawing represents a 12-inch line on the finished product.

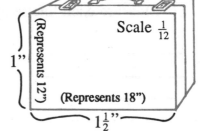

Scale $\frac{1}{12}$

(Represents 12")

1"

(Represents 18")

$1\frac{1}{2}$"

Example: Penn Sill made a $\frac{2}{15}$ scale drawing. She showed a measurement of 30 inches. How long was her line on the drawing?

Step 1: Multiply the scale by the actual measurement.

$$\frac{2}{15} \times 30"$$

Step 2: Write both factors as fractions.

$$\frac{2}{15} \times \frac{30}{1}$$

Step 3: Look for common factors in the numerators and denominators. 15 and 30 have a common factor, 15. Divide 15 and 30 by 15.

$$\frac{2}{\cancel{15}_1} \times \frac{\cancel{30}^2}{1}$$

Step 4: Multiply the numerators. Multiply the denominators.

$$\frac{2}{1} \times \frac{2}{1} = \frac{4}{1} = 4$$

The line on the drawing was four inches long.

Exercise A: Compute the scale length for each drawing.

	Scale	Actual Length	Scale Length			Scale	Actual Length	Scale Length
1)	$\frac{1}{8}$	32"	_____		2)	$\frac{3}{16}$	64"	_____
3)	$\frac{1}{4}$	48"	_____		4)	$\frac{3}{16}$	32"	_____
5)	$\frac{3}{8}$	24"	_____		6)	$\frac{7}{8}$	56"	_____
7)	$\frac{1}{4}$	20"	_____		8)	$\frac{3}{8}$	40"	_____
9)	$\frac{3}{32}$	96"	_____		10)	$\frac{5}{8}$	64"	_____

The actual measurement may be expressed as a mixed number.

Example: Rita Blueprint must compute the length of a $\frac{1}{2}$ scale line for a $3\frac{3}{8}$" measurement.

Step 1: Multiply the scale by the measurement. $\frac{1}{2}$ x $3\frac{3}{8}$"

Step 2: Write the mixed number as a fraction. $3\frac{3}{8} = \frac{24}{8} + \frac{3}{8} = \frac{27}{8}$

Step 3: Multiply. $\frac{1}{2}$ x $\frac{27}{8} = \frac{27}{16}$

Step 4: Simplify. $\frac{27}{16} = 1\frac{11}{16}$"

Exercise B: Compute the scale length for each drawing.

	Scale	Actual Length	Scale Length			Scale	Actual Length	Scale Length
1)	$\frac{1}{7}$	$3\frac{1}{16}$"	_____		2)	$\frac{1}{5}$	$4\frac{3}{8}$"	_____
3)	$\frac{1}{8}$	$5\frac{1}{8}$"	_____		4)	$\frac{1}{3}$	$11\frac{1}{4}$"	_____
5)	$\frac{3}{7}$	$5\frac{3}{8}$"	_____		6)	$\frac{4}{11}$	$5\frac{1}{2}$"	_____
7)	$\frac{7}{8}$	$6\frac{3}{8}$"	_____		8)	$\frac{4}{5}$	$7\frac{1}{2}$"	_____
9)	$\frac{5}{9}$	$12\frac{3}{4}$"	_____		10)	$\frac{6}{7}$	$12\frac{1}{4}$"	_____

MACHINE OPERATORS

Many machines are driven by belts and gears. Operators change gears to speed up or to slow down an operation.

A *gear* is a wheel with teeth around the rim. It is used to drive machines and change speeds of operations. By interlocking its teeth with a second gear, a *driver gear* transfers motion to a second gear. The second gear is called the *driven gear*. *RPM* is the *revolutions per minute* of the driver gear, and *rpm* is the *revolutions per minute* of the driven gear.

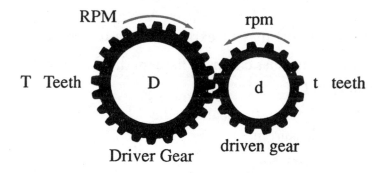

Rule: For any two gears, a driver gear (D) and a driven gear (d), with speeds RPM and rpm, and numbers of teeth T and t, the following proportion is true:

$$\frac{RPM}{rpm} = \frac{t}{T}$$

Example: Hy Geer needs to change a driver gear to increase the speed of the driven gear.

The speed of the driver gear (D) was 240 RPM.

The desired speed of the driven gear (d) was 360 rpm.

The number of teeth (t) in the driven gear was 40.

How many teeth (T) must be on the driver gear to achieve this speed?

Step 1: Write the proportion.

$$\frac{\text{RPM}}{\text{rpm}} = \frac{t}{T} \qquad\qquad \frac{240}{360} = \frac{40}{T}$$

Step 2: Solve the proportion.

    a) Simplify the fraction by dividing by 10 and then by 12.

$$\frac{\overset{2}{\cancel{240}}}{\underset{3}{\cancel{360}}} = \frac{40}{T}$$

    b) Multiply across the equal sign.

$$\frac{\boxed{2}}{\boxed{3}} = \frac{\boxed{40}}{T} \qquad\qquad 3 \times 40 = 120$$

    c) Divide the product by the third number. (In this case, divide 120 by 2)

$$2\overline{)120} \;\; \overset{60}{} \qquad\qquad T = 60$$

Hy Geer needs a gear with 60 teeth.

Exercise A: Complete the chart by finding the missing items.

	Teeth	RPM	teeth	rpm
1)	4	50	___	20
2)	40	___	30	8
3)	___	60	28	15
4)	56	42	28	___
5)	___	250	25	100
6)	75	12	___	100
7)	70	___	56	100
8)	10	35	___	70
9)	___	20	12	50
10)	12	40	36	___

CHAPTER REVIEW **12**

Solve these problems.

1) Find the 5% sales tax and compute the total bill for a purchase of $10.95. Use the tax chart given on page 264.

2) A customer's change was $7.68. List the bills and coins a sales-clerk would have given as change.

3) Calculate the square root of 361.

4) Compute the power produced by 110 volts over resistance of 36 ohms. Use a formula given on page 270.

5) Compute the resistance of a current that produces 2400 watts on a 20-amp line. Use a formula given on page 270.

6) Sort these sizes from the smallest to the largest.
$10\frac{1}{8}$ $\qquad$ $10\frac{3}{4}$ $\qquad$ $10\frac{1}{16}$ $\qquad$ $10\frac{3}{16}$ $\qquad$ $10\frac{3}{8}$ $\qquad$ $10\frac{1}{4}$

7) Measure this line segment to the nearer quarter of an inch.

8) Measure this line segment to the nearer eighth of an inch.

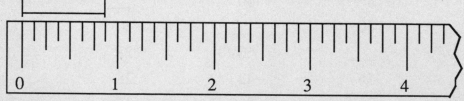

9) Find the length of a line segment that represents $3\frac{3}{4}$" on a $\frac{2}{5}$ scale drawing.

10) How fast does a driver gear turn if it has 80 teeth (T) and drives a 35-tooth gear (t) at 400 rpm?

APPENDIX: COMPUTER PROGRAMS

The objectives for the use of these computer programs are twofold.

1. The students will discover that the computer uses the same algorithms that they use to solve the problems.
2. The students will understand that the computer does only what they tell it to do and that it shows no creative powers to decide how to solve the problems. Also, the students will find that the computer is far better at computation than humans are.

Each computer program is designed as an enrichment activity. Generally, the programs occur where the computations are cumbersome or in some way difficult to compute by hand. The programs do not teach any new mathematics and may be ignored without loss of mathematical content. However, their use is encouraged so that students will investigate how the computer program accomplishes the same task as they do with their mathematical computation. Additionally, it should be noted that student interest is often increased by the use of computers.

The computer programs included in the text are written in BASIC (Beginners All-purpose Symbolic Instruction Code), and most BASICs act as interpreters of the programs you write. This is true of most Apple and IBM-compatible BASICs. It is intended that the programs in this textbook can be run using any BASIC interpreter. We have tried to use instructions that all BASIC interpreters will accept.

However, if you encounter an error message from your interpreter, first check your typing to be sure that you have entered the correct code. If the error persists, consult the BASIC manual for your computer for an alternate command to accomplish the same results. Because of the small opportunity for incompatibility, teachers should plan to run each program before they wish to use it in the classroom.

After starting the BASIC program on your computer, type in each line with its line number. Pay careful attention to the punctuation. To check your typing, use the LIST command and verify each line with the computer program in the textbook. If they match, you should RUN the program.

Type RUN at the BASIC prompt and press the ENTER or RETURN key. When you are finished, type SYSTEM and press the ENTER key to exit the interpreter.

Certain operations will result in extra decimal places in the answer. The rounding algorithm uses the integer function (INT) and adds a rounding factor (0.005). Reference program on textbook page 36, line 80.

Note to Instructor: Depending on the experience of your students, you may wish to key in the instructions (code) yourself. Use your BASIC manual to find out how to SAVE and re-LOAD the programs when you want to use them.

GLOSSARY

A

a.m.—an abbreviation for *ante meridian;* the hours before noon

Amp—a measure of the intensity of electrical current

Annual—yearly; relating to a period of 12 months

Annual wages—the amount of money earned during a full year

Area—the number of squares of a given size that cover a surface; the surface included within a set of lines

Assessed value—a figure based on a percent of the market value of property; the rate is determined by the local government and is used for tax purposes

At (@)—a term and symbol used to indicate unit price; for example, 3 pairs of socks @ $2.59 per pair or 6 cans of oil @ $1.95 per can

Average—the arithmetic mean; the average is found by dividing the total of a set of figures by the number of items

B

Balance due—a payment owed by the taxpayer when too little taxes have been withheld by the end of the year

Balancing a budget—determining the state of finances after a given budget period, whether there is money remaining or a debt

Banker's Rule—a person may borrow up to 2.5 times his or her annual income

Base price—the first amount listed on the sticker price of a car; the price includes standard equipment but not options or transportation and handling charges

Basic processes—activities necessary for maintaining life; for example, heartbeat, breathing, and digestion

Bimonthly—every two months, or 6 times a year

Biweekly—every two weeks; or 26 times a year

Blueprints—maps, mechanical drawings, or architectural plans

Brand name—goods identified by name as the product of a single firm or manufacturer; a characteristic or distinctive kind

Budget—a plan for managing income and expenses, usually for a set period of time (month, year, etc.)

Budget guidelines—an outline of suggested budget policies or plans

C

Calorie—a measurement of heat energy; the amount of energy needed to raise the temperature of one gram of water one degree Celsius

Catalog—a listing of items arranged in an organized way; descriptions are often included

Celsius—relating to a temperature scale on which 0° represents the freezing point of water and 100° represents the boiling point of water

Charge account—a person's account with a store or company to which the purchase of goods is charged and paid for at a later date

Check—a written order directing a bank to pay money as instructed

Checking account—a bank account against which a depositor can draw checks

Circle graph—a circular chart divided into sections to show relative sizes or amounts; also called pie chart

Coach—a railroad passenger car intended primarily for day travel

Commission—payment based on a percentage of total sales; salespeople generally earn commissions

Compound interest—interest paid on both the original principal plus any interest added to date; compound interest is usually computed on deposits placed into savings accounts

Consumed—used

Contractors—people that agree to erect buildings, to perform work, or to provide supplies on a large scale

Coverage—the area of wall that a can of paint is supposed to cover, usually measured in square feet; for example, 100 square feet per quart

Coverage rate—the percent paid for homeowners insurance protection

Cross product—the answer obtained by multiplying the denominator of one fraction with the numerator of another

Cubic feet—units used to measure volume; on a water meter, one unit of water equals 100 cubic feet

D

Deductions—money withheld from gross pay; for example, federal income taxes, social security payments, union dues, or health insurance

Deductions and exemptions—amounts of money you may subtract from your income before you figure your taxes

Deferred price—the total amount paid in down payment plus monthly payments

Denominator—the part of a fraction that is below the line and that tells the number of parts in the whole; in the fraction $1/2$, the denominator 2 shows that something has been divided into two halves

Dependent—a person who depends on another person for support

Depreciate—to lose value

Dials—the part of a meter that shows how many units of the product have been consumed since the meter was installed

Discount—an amount subtracted from the regular price, often given for cash or prompt payment or to reduce prices for a sale

Dividend—the amount of profit that a shareholder earns for each share of stock; the term comes from the idea of *divid*ing profits at the *end* of an earning period

Double—a hotel room designed for occupancy by two people

Double roll—an amount of wallpaper that covers twice the wall area as a single roll

Double time—payment of two times the regular hourly rate; often used to compute pay for work done on Sundays or holidays

Down payment—part of the full price paid at the time of purchase with the balance to be paid later

doz.—an abbreviation for dozen, a group of 12

Dozen (doz.)—a group of 12

Drafters—people who draw blueprints, plans, and sketches for construction and manufacturing projects

Driven gear—a gear to which motion is transferred from a driver gear

Driver gear—a gear that transfers motion to a second gear, called a driven gear

E

Effective tax rate—the product of the assessment rate and the property tax rate

EPA rating—Environmental Protection Agency estimate of how far a car can travel on one gallon or liter of gas; figures are given for both city and highway driving in terms of miles per gallon or kilometers per liter

Established lawn—ground covered with grass

Estimate—to judge approximately the value or worth of something; to determine roughly

Exchange rate—the ratio at which the principal unit of money of two countries may be exchanged; such ratios change frequently and up-to-date tables must be used

Excursion rate—a reduced fare allowed when a trip is not taken at peak times

Expenses—financial outlays, or money spent to pay for specific costs; typical expenses include housing, clothing, transportation, insurance payments, etc.

Expiration date—the point at which something comes to an end; for example, the time after which a cents-off store coupon can no longer be used

Expire—to come to an end

Extension—an extra telephone connected to the principal line

F

Factor—the number being multiplied

Financed—borrowed; provided funds on credit under specified terms

Fixed-rate mortgage—a financed loan on property in which the interest rate and the monthly payments on principal and interest remain the same until the loan is paid off

Flat rate—the basic amount charged for monthly telephone service

Full-serve pump—a service station at which attendants pump gas and provide other services for customers

G

gal.—an abbreviation for gallon, a unit of capacity equal to four quarts

Gallon (gal.)—a unit of capacity equal to four quarts

Gear—a wheel with teeth around the rim; used to drive machines and change speeds of operations

Gears—mechanisms that turn the pointer on the dial of a utility meter

Greatest common factor—the largest factor of two numbers

Gross pay—the amount of full earnings before deductions

H

Homeowners insurance—a policy covering both the home and its contents for damage or loss caused by fire, smoke, theft, severe weather, or collision by a vehicle; some policies cover injuries incurred by people on the property

Hour (hr.)—a measure of time equal to 60 minutes

Hourly rate—the amount of money paid for each hour of work

hr.—an abbreviation for hour, a measure of time equal to 60 minutes

I

Income—the total money you earn

Income stock—stock that pays dividends

Insulation—materials used to prevent transfer of electricity, heat, or sound

Interest—a fee charged on the unpaid balance of a charge account; a payment or fee charged to the borrower for the use of money loaned; also the amount paid to a depositor for money kept in a savings account

International units (I.U.)—the amount of a nutrient or vitamin that produces a particular biological effect agreed upon as an international standard

K

Key digit—the digit to which a number is to be rounded

Kilometers per hour (km/h)—a metric measurement of speed

Kilowatt—a unit of electricity equal to 1000 watts

Kilowatt hour (kwh)—a unit of electricity equal to the energy used by one kilowatt in one hour

L

Landlord—the owner of property leased or rented to another

Layaway—a plan under which customers can buy clothes, pay part of the price as a deposit, and receive the items when the remainder of the price is paid

lb.—an abbreviation for pound, a unit of capacity equal to 16 ounces

Lease—a contract to rent property for a particular amount of money and for a specified period of time

Legend—a list that explains the symbols used on a map

Liability—insurance that protects the owner against claims resulting from an accident that is his or her fault; it covers personal injuries and property damage

Liable—legally responsible for damage done

Line segment—a part of a line

Loss—a decrease in value; the amount by which

the purchase price of an item is more than the selling price

M

m²—an abbreviation for square meters, a unit used for measuring area

Market value—the selling price of the property on the open market

Materials—supplies needed for making or doing something

Meter—a device used to measure the amount of gas, electricity, or water used by a customer

Mileage—the total number of miles traveled in a day, year, etc.; the average number of miles a car will travel on a gallon or liter of gas

Mileage diagram—a map or drawing that gives the driving distance in miles between major cities

Miles per hour (mph)—a customary measurement of speed

min.—an abbreviation for minute, a measure of time equal to 60 seconds

Minimum payment—the smallest amount that can be paid on a charge account

Minute (min.)—a measure of time equal to 60 seconds

Molding—a decorative strip used to finish a room; for example, at the base of the walls or around windows

Monthly payment—the amount of money paid every month in repayment of a loan

Monthly statement—a summary sent out by the bank and showing recent transactions plus the current balance of an account

Mortgage—a financed loan on property

Mortgage insurance—a policy purchased by the owners of mortgaged property; if an insured owner dies, the insurance company pays the balance owed on the house to the beneficiary

N

Net pay—the amount a worker receives after deductions are subtracted from gross pay; also known as take-home pay

Ninety Days Same As Cash—a plan by which the purchase price must be paid in full within 90 days after the date of purchase; no interest is charged for the use of this plan

Notions—small items needed to complete a sewing project; for example, thread, snaps, or zippers

Numerator—the part of a fraction that is above the line and that tells how many parts are used; in the fraction $1/2$, the numerator 1 indicates one of two parts

Nutrient—a substance or ingredient that furnishes nourishment

Nutritionists—specialists in the study of nutrition or the process of nourishment

O

Odometer—a device that counts the miles a car has traveled; located on a car's dashboard

Ohm—a measure of electrical resistance

Options—extra items added to a car; for example, AM/FM stereo radio or air conditioning

Ounce (oz.)—a unit of capacity equal to one-sixteenth of a pound

Overtime—working time beyond a standard day or week; the wage paid for overtime

oz.—an abbreviation for ounce, a unit of capacity equal to one-sixteenth of a pound

P

Package plans—low-priced trips planned for groups of people; these plans may include hotel rooms, transportation, some meals, tourist and side trips, and other special services

Parlor car—an extra-fare railroad passenger car intended for day travel and equipped with individual seats

Parts and labor—a billing system at auto repair shops whereby customers pay for new or rebuilt items plus an amount per hour for work done by mechanics

Pattern—a form or model used for making things; a dressmaker's pattern pieces and directions for making clothes

Peak season—the time of year when business is at its best; for instance, at the beach in summer or in the mountains during ski season

Per—for each or for one; for example, miles per gallon, miles per hour, or cost per gallon

Percent (%)—part per one hundred

Percentage—an amount, not a percent; the amount is calculated by multiplying a percent times a number

Perimeter—the distance around a figure

Piecework—work done by the unit and paid according to the number of units completed

Pkg.—an abbreviation for package

p.m.—an abbreviation for *post meridian;* the hours after noon

Pound (lb.)—a unit of capacity equal to 16 ounces

Premium—the cost of an insurance policy

Principal—the amount of money loaned to a creditor; also the amount of money deposited into a savings account and earning interest

Processed—a term used to describe a check or a deposit that has completed the steps of being handled by the bank

Profit—a gain or increase in value; the amount by which the selling price of an item is more than the purchase price

Property tax—a figure based on a percent of the assessed value; the rate is set by local governments

Proportion—two equal ratios; for example, $^2/_4 = ^1/_2$

Q

Quart (qt.)—a unit of capacity equal to two pints or to one-fourth of a gallon

Quarterly—four times a year, or once every three months

R

Range—how far a car can travel on a given number of gallons or liters of gas; the range is found by multiplying the EPA rating times the tank capacity

Rate—the percent of interest charged as a fee on a loan; also the percent of interest earned on a savings account

Rate of commission—the percent used to compute commissions; for example, 25% or 3%

Ratio—a comparison of two quantities; for example, $^1/_4$

RDA (Recommended Daily Allowance)—the nutrient levels required to maintain energy and growth

Rebate—a return of part of a payment offered as a special deal to buyers

Rebuilt—describing items that have been reconstructed or extensively repaired

Receipts—money received

Reconcile—to compare and check the accuracy of information recorded in the checkbook against bank statements

Refund—a payment returned to the taxpayer when too much taxes have been withheld by the end of the year

Register—a form on which bank account transactions and resulting new balances are recorded

Regular price—the ordinary price of an item; the regular price minus the sale price will indicate the amount saved

Renaming hours—to express time in a form that is equal to the original; for example, 1 hour = 60 minutes

Renter's Rule—a person should spend no more than one week's income for a month's rent

Revenues—the income (such as from taxes) that federal or state agencies collect and use for the common good

Revolutions per minute—the rotations or turns per minute of a driver gear (RPM) or a driven gear (rpm)

Round lots—multiples of 100 shares of stock

RPM—the revolutions per minute of a driver gear

rpm—the revolutions per minute of a driven gear

S

Salaried people—professional and supervisory people who are paid a fixed amount of money at regular intervals

Salary—payment of a fixed amount of money at regular intervals (weekly, biweekly, etc.)

Sales tax—a tax computed on the sale of goods and services; it is figured as a percentage of the purchase price and is collected by the seller

Savings account—bank account in which a depositor can earn interest on money deposited

Scale—a ratio of the size on a drawing, map, or model to the original size (½ scale); an indication of the relationship between the distances on a map and the corresponding actual distances (1 inch = 6 miles)

Scale drawing—a picture that shows the relative sizes of actual objects

Sector—a wedge-shaped section of a circle graph; the size is found by multiplying 360° times a percent or a fraction

Self-serve pump—a service station at which customers may pump their own gas

Semiannually—every six months, or 2 times a year

Semimonthly—twice a month; or 24 times a year

Shareholders—the people who own the stock of a corporation

Shares—the equal parts into which the entire capital stock of a corporation is divided

Simple interest—a one-time payment or fee charged for the use of money loaned; simple interest = principal x rate x time

Single—a hotel room designed for occupancy by one person

Single roll—an amount of wallpaper that covers 72 square feet

Square—the product of a number multiplied by itself; for example, 25 is the square of 5

Square meters (m²)—a unit used for measuring area

Square root—one of two equal factors of a number; for example, 5 is the square root of 25 because 5 x 5 = 25

Statement—a monthly record sent to charge account customers; it indicates all payments and charges to date

Stock—the element in a corporation that is divided into shares; a buyer of shares of stock becomes part owner of the corporation issuing the stock

Straightline distance—a distance measured along a straight line; the shortest distance between two points on a map

Stub—the part of a checkbook that remains after the check has been removed; it serves as a record for the information written on the check, for deposits made, and for resulting new balances

Suite—a group of hotel rooms occupied as a unit

T

Take-home pay—the amount a worker receives after deductions are subtracted from gross pay; also known as net pay

Taxable income—the total income (minus deductions and exemptions) on which taxes are paid

Time—the period of time for which money is loaned; also the period of time for which money is deposited into a savings account (time is usually measured in years or parts of years)

Time and a half—payment of one and one-half, or 1.5, times the regular hourly rate; often used to compute overtime pay on regular workdays, Monday through Saturday

Time zone—a geographical region within which the same standard time is used; the world is divided into 24 different time zones

Tip—extra money given in appreciation of good service

Total interest—a total fee for borrowing money found by subtracting the amount borrowed (the principal) from the amount paid to the bank over the life of the loan

Tourist season—a period of the year when many people visit a given area; the highest rates are in effect during this peak season

Trace (T)—a very small and often barely detectable amount

Train schedule—a chart or table indicating arrival and departure times of trains at all the stops on a given route

Transaction—the act of depositing to or withdrawing from a bank account

Transportation/handling—a fee charged to the buyer of a car

U

Unit—a single quantity; for example, a cubic foot of water or a kilowatt hour of electricity

Unit price—the cost of one unit of something; for example, the cost per pound or per gallon

Utilities—services for the home, such as gas, electricity, water, and telephone

V

Variable-rate mortgage—a financed loan on property in which the interest rate and the monthly payments may change periodically

Volt—a measure of electromotive force

W

Wages—the money received on payday; the amount is found by multiplying the number of hours worked by the hourly rate

Wall area—the perimeter of the floor times the height of the room

Watt—a unit of electrical power; named after James Watt, a Scottish inventor

Y

Yard (yd.)—a measure of length equal to three feet

Yield—the amount of servings provided by a given recipe

INDEX